THE FLETCHER JONES FOUNDATION
HUMANITIES IMPRINT

The Fletcher Jones Foundation has endowed this imprint to foster innovative and enduring scholarship in the humanities.

The publisher gratefully acknowledges the generous support of the Fletcher Jones Foundation Humanities Endowment Fund of the University of California Press Foundation.

Grateful acknowledgment is also made to the John Daverio Endowment of the American Musicological Society, funded in part by the National Endowment for the Humanities and the Andrew W. Mellon Foundation.

Reclaiming Late-Romantic Music

The Ernest Bloch Professorship
of Music and the Ernest Bloch Lectures
were established at the University of California
in 1962 in order to bring distinguished figures
in music to the Berkeley campus from time to time.
Made possible by the Jacob and Rosa Stern
Musical Fund, the professorship was founded
in memory of Ernest Bloch (1880–1959),
the first beneficiary of the Stern Fund and
Professor of Music at Berkeley
from 1940 to 1952.

THE ERNEST BLOCH PROFESSORS

1964	Ralph Kirkpatrick	1993	Susan McClary
1965–66	Winton Dean	1994–95	Wye J. Allanbrook
1966–67	Roger Sessions	1995	Jonathan Harvey
1968–69	Gerald Abraham	1997	Lydia Goehr
1970–71	Leonard B. Meyer	1998	Izaly Zemtsovsky
1972	Edward T. Cone	1999	David Huron
1975–76	Donald Jay Grout	2002	Roger Parker
1977	Charles Rosen	2003	Steven Stucky
1979–80	William Malm	2005	William Bolcom
1980–81	Alan Tyson	2007	Martha Feldman
1980–81	Andrew Porter	2008	Steve Mackey
1983	Ton De Leeuw	2009	Steven Feld
1983	James Haar	2010	Pedro Memelsdorff
1985	Richard Crawford	2010	Peter Franklin
1986	John Blacking	2011	Fred Lerdahl
1987	Gunther Schuller	2013	George E. Lewis
1989	George Perle	2013	Martin Stokes
1989	László Somfai	2014	Georgina Born

Reclaiming Late-Romantic Music

Singing Devils and Distant Sounds

Peter Franklin

UNIVERSITY OF CALIFORNIA PRESS
Berkeley · Los Angeles · London

University of California Press, one of the most
distinguished university presses in the United States,
enriches lives around the world by advancing scholarship
in the humanities, social sciences, and natural sciences. Its
activities are supported by the UC Press Foundation and
by philanthropic contributions from individuals and
institutions. For more information, visit www.ucpress.edu.

University of California Press
Berkeley and Los Angeles, California

University of California Press, Ltd.
London, England

© 2014 by The Regents of the University of California

Library of Congress Cataloging-in-Publication Data

Franklin, Peter, author.
    Reclaiming late-romantic music : singing devils and
distant sounds / Peter Franklin.
       pages   cm.—(Ernest Bloch lectures)
    Includes bibliographical references and index.
    ISBN 978-0-520-28039-7 (cloth : alk. paper)
    1. Music—19th century—History and criticism.
2. Music—Philosophy and aesthetics.   I. Title.
    ML196.F73   2014
    780.9′034—dc23   2013031179

Manufactured in the United States of America

22 21 20 19 18 17 16 15 14
10 9 8 7 6 5 4 3 2 1

In keeping with a commitment to support
environmentally responsible and sustainable printing
practices, UC Press has printed this book on Natures
Natural, a fiber that contains 30% post-consumer waste
and meets the minimum requirements of ANSI/NISO
Z39.48–1992 (R 1997) (*Permanence of Paper*).

This book is dedicated to my maternal grandmother, Lily Salmons (née Phillips, 1878–1944), whom I never met, but who brought up six children, survived the London Blitz before evacuating to Chesterfield (where she died of cancer), and was, in her youth, a much-loved maidservant.

Contents

List of Illustrations	ix
Introduction	xi
1. Setting the Scene: Grandiose Symphonics and the Trouble with Art	1
2. Pessimism, Ecstasy, and Distant Voices: Listening to Late-Romanticism	23
3. Sunsets, Sunrises, and Decadent Oceanics	53
4. Making the World Weep (Problems with Opera)	82
5. Late-Romanticism Meets Classical Music at the Movies	110
6. The Bitter Truth of Modernism: A Late-Romantic Story	140
Notes	171
Index	191

Illustrations

1. Caspar David Friedrich, *The Wanderer above the Mists*/Liszt conducting the premiere of his *Legende von der heiligen Elisabeth*. / 3
2. Akseli Gallen-Kallela, *Symposion*. / 77
3. Adolf Weissman, *Der klingende Garten: Impressionen über das Erotische in der Musik*. / 98
4. Bette Davis and Paul Henreid. / 116
5. Manuscript pages from Steiner's score for *Now, Voyager*. / 118
6. Bette Davis in *The Private Lives of Elizabeth and Essex*. / 125
7. Schreker, *Der ferne Klang*. / 149
8. Photograph of rehearsal for *Der Schmied von Gent*. / 153
9. From *Der Schmied von Gent*. / 158
10. From *Der singende Teufel*. / 164

Introduction

"Each member of the audience sits alone, listening to the work of the great, dead composer."
—Christopher Small, *Musicking*

Imagine, then, the hushed throng in a large European concert hall, waiting upon the conductor's signal to an orchestra ranked in glittering array before him, in the nineteenth-century fashion. Perhaps, like Christopher Small, we should be suspicious of this curious social ritual, apparently celebrating power and heroic mastery before a docile mass of habituated admirers.[1] The silence is broken by a music whose solemn processional only gradually begins to be interrupted by rhetorical outbursts of more urgent emotion. These seem to initiate greater animation, as if in preparation for catastrophe, before calming once more. A more sensuous unfolding now quietly takes over; it will shortly embrace us with an impressive new theme that seems to aspire to higher things and grows in self-confidence. It carries our spirits forward, higher and higher, until a dizzying outburst of grandeur confirms the arrival of our heart's desire—perhaps we visualize a sunburst glory out of the mists of a mountain landscape. Slowly, however, the moment passes and the music quietens with the realization of loss, becomes a nostalgic lament for what was, what might have been. At last we begin to relax our sympathetic involvement as the conclusion approaches and we prepare to join in the expected ritual of applause. We signal our thanks to the conductor and his performers for what they have invoked in us, for the music we may shortly affect to mock as "late romanticism," as "a bit much," however well played. Private engagement is replaced by public disavowal (we prefer not to gush). We may nevertheless cherish for later recall this music more complex and multifaceted than our social disclaimers appear to allow.

The title of this book itself engages such things with enigmatic phrases that deliberately inspire further questions. What *is* "late-romantic music"? How romantic, and how late? And what, exactly, might we seek to reclaim it *from*? The still more or less current umbrella term *late-romantic* is familiar enough, in a colloquial sense, yet has been contested by specialist scholars (the German musicologist Carl Dahlhaus denounced it as a "terminological blunder of the first order"[2]). For many it will nonetheless evoke a particular sound and style of large-scale European orchestral and operatic music from the late nineteenth and early twentieth centuries, the kind of music that would sing its last long song in classical Hollywood film scores. Perhaps its lateness comes from its origins in the "late" nineteenth century, not least in the Germanic musical style and type of listening experience that was developed in the music dramas of Wagner and subsequently carried forward by his successor Richard Strauss. But there is more to say, and other composers and repertoires to refer to: Russian, Italian, French, and Eastern European, for example—also English and American.

In the end we might have to accept that it is difficult to define the term in any more concrete, style-orientated musicological way, for all that it received disciplinary validation from the excellent 1991 "Man and Music" volume, edited by Jim Samson and simply called *The Late Romantic Era: From the mid-19th Century to World War I*.[3] We could try to embark upon a list of characteristics. They might include the length of works, the comparatively large instrumental forces involved, tonality (however "expanded" or expressively stressed in post-Wagnerian fashion). Then might come a certain register of earnestness or "seriousness" adopted by the late-romantic, its tendency toward luxuriance and excess, associated with bourgeois experience, and also with decadence. More negative qualities could include the fact that it came to represent what Modernism "was not" after the First World War. But already the descriptive has become evaluative, as it must, as we grasp that the phrase includes both objective and subjective elements that are the product of cultural and historical custom and attitudes. To define late-romanticism in music can perhaps only be to negotiate, with critical intent, the many implications of the phrase on the basis of a clearly established aim of either celebrating it or engaging in its more negative diagnostic evaluation. Dispassionate definition is hardly possible. To celebrate the late romantic must certainly be to question and challenge the very terms in which existing definitions have been couched.

For example, in art history *late* often denotes the period in an individual artist's, or even a culture's, development that just precedes its end—perhaps in some sort of "Indian summer" like that in which Verdi produced *Otello* and *Falstaff* around the turn of the century. It may be late in the sense that it reflects the glories of earlier achievements or times. Which gives rise to the secondary association of lateness with decline, with decadence (albeit not in Verdi's case). One of the most recent authors to have attempted to confront the wider field of musical production and reception with which I am concerned here, and with ostensibly similar reclamational intent, is Stephen Downes, who opted precisely for the negatively charged term *decadence* in his book *Music and Decadence in European Modernism*.[4] Where Dahlhaus wanted simply to replace "late romanticism" *with* "modernism," Downes seems to problematize the mythic narrative that is implied in his title, where the latter term has a more positive, or at least more neutral charge in comparison with *decadence* to which it is often contrasted as if in a sort of developmental binary (out of the declining glories of decadence Modernism was born, we are told).

A problem with Downes's decadence is that precisely by wanting to reinsert it *into* a more broadly defined modernism, he is forced to work with and through the negative associations of the term that are somehow "given" in the modernist narrative. He adopts it as a musical-stylistic label that he must first establish as a meaningful designation for music marked by post-*Tristan* chromaticism and often tainted, philosophically and spiritually, by pessimism and a degree of perversity (down this road lay Strauss's *Salome,* of course). This he must then intellectually reconstrue in terms of Nietzsche's criticism of Wagner and the philosopher's notion of a kind of recuperative *necessity* to decadence as the only route to a specifically "dionysian" form of pessimism that holds the seeds of cultural and spiritual regeneration. It is an interesting approach, but as a musical analyst—albeit one of distinction and originality—Downes becomes prematurely locked into his categories and strategies for describing and appreciating specific musical works, just as he relies on rich comparisons with contemporary literary texts, while ignoring both the performative aspect of "decadence" and the material nature of the kind of musical-cultural experiences with which he is dealing. Above all he ignores the audiences for such music and how they used and valued the powerful experiences it offered them.

Were they all inevitably "decadent"? Would this not be to reinscribe the very construction of late romantic music as both "late" and "romantic" in colloquial ways that echo historical criticism of it as variously "bourgeois" (from the perspective of interwar modernists of bohemian sympathies) and also self-indulgent, feminine, and—yes—"decadent" from the perspective of bourgeois conservatives themselves?

The cultural character and politics of such awkwardly circular arguments are too complex to be resolved by adding further layers of definitional constraint. Which is why I shall retain the umbrella term *late romanticism* without any prejudgmental qualification, and why my task of reclamation will involve a critique of the way the term has been understood: not least as a critical category, rather like decadence itself. As such, *late romanticism* carries connotations of hyperexpressivity, quasi-commodified emotional experiences (perhaps of a nostalgically utopian hue), and of "programmaticism"—all things linked to popular ways of understanding music as narrative, as allegory, as inwardly visualized scenarios and dramas or outwardly dramatized musical plots in the opera house (and opera itself, of course, was once regarded as a dubious object of serious musical scholarship). Here I shall take late-romanticism to suggest a music marked by implicitly communicated meaning, mediated as private subjective experience prompted in public among the "unmusical." The music responsible is seen to be complicit in ways that render it (as we have seen), a normatively dubious, decadent, feminized, and thus *minor* status in the sense nevertheless boldly challenged by Lawrence Kramer, with the assistance of Deleuze and Guattari: "Separated from the mainstream ('deterritorialized'), it is explicitly political, and it speaks in a voice more collective than individual. But it is exemplary just for those reasons. 'We might as well say,' write Deleuze and Guattari, 'that minor no longer designates specific literatures but the revolutionary conditions for every literature within the heart of what is called great.'"[5]

The politics of late romantic musical passion will nevertheless be approached cautiously and in piecemeal fashion in the following chapters. To invoke politics at all, other than purely negatively, might sound unlikely as applied to a musical style positioned as the lamentable relic of their forebears by the modernist and avant-garde composers who defined themselves *against* it. They contested late romanticism's claims to any of the "greatness" of truly Great Music by virtue of its character as a prototypical form of mass entertainment. Such things were to be rejected on grounds that are metaphorically alluded to in the paired phrases of the second section of my title. The opposition of distant sounds and singing devils could simply figure late romantic music as on the one hand something past, partly forgotten and historically distanced: the residue of an old, late-nineteenth-century bourgeois world. Its distance might be a way of figuring and protecting ourselves from that pastness, as something superseded, just as the image of "singing devils" links it with the diabolical, with the manipulative voice of dubious power and authority of Small's "great, dead composers," and reinvokes the trope of decadence—what Modernism, the Weimar period, the "roaring twenties" were believed to have "overcome" (even in spite of the Great Depression and all the subsequent woes of the 1930s).

The actual source of these phrases is two operas by a sporadically remembered composer of that era, Franz Schreker (1878–1934): *The Distant Sound* (*Der ferne Klang*, 1912) and *The Singing Devil* (*Der singende Teufel*, 1928)—the one about the ramifications of a deluded composer's search for genial inspiration out there in the *au delà*, the other an opera about the confrontation between a colonizing church and a pagan tribe. Set in the partly mythical "dark ages," Schreker's *Der singende Teufel* imagined an ancient folk whose Dionysian, nature-worshipping ways come into conflict with the terrifying voice and devilishly gaping keyboard "mouth" of the mighty organ of an early Christian monastery that has been built in their forest, with whatever saintly intent. Romantic delusion confronts the violent exercise of power.

Acknowledging, like those operas (to which I will return), while also seeking to reinterpret and revalue the supposed failings of musical late-romanticism might be another way of defining my project of reclamation here—one that has close affiliations not only with Downes's study of decadence, but also, among other recent work, with Laurence Dreyfus's *Wagner and the Erotic Impulse* and even the cavils of his demanding critic J.P.E. Harper-Scott. The latter's catty review of Dreyfus's book in *The Wagner Journal* in its turn proposed an alternative way of reevaluating Wagner's works as presenting us with something still more challenging than the directness and eloquence (if once shocking) of Wagner's music of erotic desire that is variously "expressed," rewarded, or more frequently *frustrated* in Dreyfus's own account.[6] Perhaps Wagner remains a presiding source of the late-romantic manner as I will characterize it: counter-intuitively possessed of a critical, even a precisely *self*-critical awareness of its own character. Adorno's and Nietzsche's later criticism notwithstanding, such art might be interpreted as both celebrated and dramatized within the developing and implicitly "programmatic" narrative matrix in which Wagner, as Romantic Artist, symbolically divided his subjective self-image between fantasy "redeeming" heroes like Siegfried, Tristan, and Parsifal and more worldly, fallen and fated older men like Wotan, King Mark, Hans Sachs, and Amfortas. The last of these ostensibly allegorized the agony of the late artist's perilous facility for self-benediction and visionary utopianism—agonizing because of what we know about the dangerous psychological power and rational falseness of those aesthetic balms and balsams.

The relevant issues and implied musical field, in terms of both style and repertoire, are broad and complex: much more so than any single term perhaps encompasses; such a term would also have to reflect the social character of the kind of concert experience that I evoked at the outset—one which some have regarded as little more than the anachronistic prop of an outmoded bourgeois culture—perhaps to be scorned as a form of kitsch. My aim here will be to probe and challenge that estimation of the music I shall be concerned with. In order to do justice to it with some degree of honesty, I will periodically adopt an active, autobiographical, and participatory mode, like that of an ethnographer for whom understanding and participating are not easily separated. I do not speak of the participation of a musical performer here, but precisely that of a participating member of the outwardly passive, yet emotionally active, mass of the compliant audience and subject to all the critical questions that might be asked of it. They are, I believe, worth asking in like measure as the music in question is worth listening to and experiencing as something richly and problematically meaningful in both conceptual and bodily ways. Its meaning is translatable in linguistic and visual terms that are as culturally and historically determined, perhaps, as its apparently immediate (unmediated?) bodiliness and physicality that can feel intimately, even shockingly pleasurable and private. In this respect, what follows is perhaps as much a personal journey of exploration as it is a critical history of cultural practice.

. . .

My audience for the six lectures out of which this book grew was a generously welcoming one at the University of California in Berkeley, where I was Visiting Bloch Professor in the fall of 2010. My thanks are due to many colleagues in the music department there: to its then chairman Ben Brinner and to Bonnie Wade and Davitt Moroney, to Mary Ann Smart and her family (who showed me some of the great sights of the Bay Area), and to my kind self-appointed mentors and guides Nick

Mathew and James Davies. I am grateful, too, to the other staff members who eased me through the mysteries of both domestic and scholarly acclimatization to life in California and the local ways of the university. Here I must mention John Shepard and Cheryl Griffith-Peel in the wonderful Hargrove Music Library, Babs Winbigler and Nanette Hara in the upstairs department office, whose administrator Roia Ferrazares and her husband, David, also became valued friends. Sound technician Jay Cloidt and operations manager Jim Coates provided endless support, as did Kathleen Karn, communications manager at Herz Hall in Berkeley, who created the double image used in figure 1. No less valued were the students with whom I had regular dealings, including Nel Cloutier, Sean Curran, Jonathan Rhodes Lee, Tiffany Ng, and Mark Rogers. Will Coleman also played a part. Presiding over it all, of course, was the inspiring figure of Richard Taruskin, whose supportive comments and sometimes irreverent suggestions were as welcome and memorable as his kindly attempt to explain baseball to me.

Other friends and colleagues have assisted in various, often quite specific ways. Charlotte Purkis found some of my quotations; Christopher Hailey generously assisted with images for chapter 6; Emanuele Senici offered invaluable advice on chapter 4; Philip White has been a long-standing guide to Bayreuth and gatekeeper of my Wagnerian experiences there. James D'Arc, curator of the Brigham Young University Film Music Archive, generously assisted me in obtaining images from its collection of Max Steiner manuscripts and Jamie Keates in Oxford was once again indispensable for his technical way with digital images. I am also grateful to the Music Faculty at Oxford for generously supporting my leave in the fall of 2012 to complete this book, and to Mary Francis, Kim Hogeland, and my editors Mary Ray Worley and Jessica Moll at the University of California Press for their forbearance, for their support, and for making this book happen.

A final acknowledgment must take the form of an apology to Alex Rehding, whose 2009 book, *Music and Monumentality: Commemoration and Wonderment in Nineteenth-Century Germany*, sadly reached my desk too late for me to engage fruitfully with its arguments here. I am sorry to repay his acknowledgment of my own "background" presence there by citing that book in a similar way; it might relevantly have played a more foregrounded role here.

CHAPTER 1

Setting the Scene

*Grandiose Symphonics and the
Trouble with Art*

Within the period 1890–1914, and especially in the German-speaking lands, modernism chiefly manifested itself . . . as a radical intensification of means toward accepted or traditional ends (or at least toward ends that could be so described). That is why modernism of this early vintage is perhaps best characterized as *maximalism*. The cultural phase . . . was called the fin de siècle not only because it happened to coincide with the end of a century, but also because it reflected apocalyptic presentiments. . . . The acceleration of stylistic innovation, so marked as to seem not just a matter of degree but one of actual kind, requiring a new "periodization," looks now, from the vantage-point of the next fin de siècle, to have been perhaps more a matter of inflated rhetoric than of having new things to say.

—Richard Taruskin, *The Oxford History of Western Music*

Having invoked the autobiographical mode as a tool in my introduction, I should confess at once that this book is one in which I intend to indulge my passion for this period of Western musical history that I love and which, I suspect, many secretly cherish even as they avow that they probably shouldn't. As we have seen, it has accordingly been labelled transitional, decadent, over-inflated, and characterized by a desire always to be satisfying what Richard Taruskin has described as its apparently obsessive drive toward "maximalism."[1] In putting it this way—by confessing a more than modestly scholarly interest in a period so weighted with the concrete boots of critical put-downs—I inevitably invoke the politics of my subject even as I nervously prepare my apologetics for an era that is additionally awkward in that it fits no neat chronological box. Too many "periods" overlap here, across stretches of two adjacent centuries.

When these thoughts were originally presented as a series of public lectures, I perhaps eccentrically, but deliberately, described the era from which my examples were drawn as "the age of Leverkühn." The reference is to the fictional composer Adrian Leverkühn, whom Thomas Mann offered up in his 1946 novel *Doktor Faustus* as a sacrificial victim to the inexorable rise of high musical modernism of the "difficult," Schoenbergian kind. Since it is also a difficult novel that is as much admired as read, I should explain that Leverkühn was born in 1885 and died in 1940. The "difficulty" of the high modernist works that crown his tragic career, and which were meticulously imagined by Thomas Mann, was closely related to that of music by real-life composers like Schoenberg and Stravinsky; indeed, Leverkühn develops a synthetic compositional technique so like Schoenberg's technique of "composition with twelve tones" that the novel's publication led to rancorous exchanges between Mann and Schoenberg which resulted in the former eventually agreeing to include at the back of all subsequent copies an explicit acknowledgment that the technique apparently alluded to was "in truth the intellectual property" of Schoenberg.[2]

The difficulty of such music stemmed directly from its avoidance of the more conventional harmonic and melodic manners employed in late-romantic works that were being positioned by Theodor Adorno, the Frankfurt School Marxist philosopher and critic who was Mann's adviser on *Doctor Faustus,* as exemplifying the troublingly manipulative and ideologically compromised excesses of Wagnerian and post-Wagnerian symphonic and operatic music. Modernist and left-wing critics like Adorno considered such music to be commodified false consciousness, designed for easy consumption; what was being consumed they associated directly with the problems and ideology of an imperial, culturally bourgeois Europe rolling toward and through the revelatory disaster of the First World War. We "know where it all led," as commentators have been prone to put it, with darkly knowing emphasis. Late-romantic musical manners, as I shall call them, were thus critically consigned to guilty historical irrelevancy, and perhaps worse things still in the decades of fascism. Interwar modernists and avant-garde artists seemed advisedly to be seeking a different direction and different goals. They too nevertheless owed much to Romanticism, whose contradictory character I invoked in the double image that appeared on posters

FIGURE 1. Caspar David Friedrich, *The Wanderer above the Mists*, c. 1818 (Kunsthalle, Hamburg), overlaid with an artist's impression, from the *London Illustrated News*, 9 September 1865, of "Franz Liszt conducting the performance of his new oratorio in Pesth." (It was the premiere of his *Legende von der heiligen Elisabeth*.) Composite image created by Kathleen Karn.

advertising my lectures in Berkeley in 2010: Liszt conducting the first performance of his *Legend of St. Elisabeth* (*Die heilige Elisabeth*) in Budapest in 1864, overlaid with Caspar David Friedrich's famous 1818 painting of *The Wanderer above the Mists* on a lonely rocky outcrop in the mountains. This composite image is reproduced here as figure 1: the private moment of brooding or ecstatic reflection set against a public show of musical force in Liszt's grand urban concert-entertainment—the latter looks and was probably intended to be somehow religious and communally "improving" in the standard manner of Great Music in the West—"classical music." How were these two modes of aesthetic experience and cultural practice, public and private, actually linked? What aesthetic, subjective, and intellectual work accompanied that linkage?

The problem I shall be confronting here is really the problem of art and its audience in the age of modernism. Can bourgeois art survive its own self-criticism in public works that seem to fill the same spaces as the artworks of old, albeit "maximalized" in some way, while also advertising their desire to be liberatedly "something else"? This leads me back to Richard Taruskin and the thought-provoking introduction to his *Oxford History of Western Music*. As philosophers once used to write footnotes to Plato, so musicologists are bound to be writing footnotes to Taruskin for some time to come. What he does in his introduction, subtitled "The History of What?" is to frame one particular subspecies of a broader problem: namely the problem of talking and writing about art historically. He sets out an ideological distinction between the historian and the critic, indicating that where the latter may be permitted partiality and bias in favor of this or that, the former (the historian) will not take sides. Turning away from what he rightly regards as futile, self-renewing theoretical debates about whether and what music "means" to what it demonstrably *has meant,* he seeks to balance the more familiar history of production with a judicious history of *reception* that can only broaden the range of what is considered and the way it has been considered. Distancing himself from "new musicology" (which he mocks as aging "with stunning rapidity"[3]) and what he believes to be the baleful influence of Adorno on its authoritarian practice of "hermeneutics," he addresses the alternative Cold War dominance of "internalist," notes-on-the-page approaches whose ideological character was perhaps informed by a desire to avoid the suspected tendency toward totalitarian co-option of all more socially or contextually orientated historical approaches to music. Here Taruskin cites as a victim of that suspicion the East German Communist Party member Georg Knepler, Carl Dahlhaus's "equally magisterial East German counterpart," whose music-historical work is consequently much less widely known than that of his almost tiresomely over-translated West German counterpart. Taruskin has few words of praise for Dahlhaus, whose prestige he finds "otherwise inexplicable," his work given obsessively to "empty binarisms."[4]

A set of curious coincidences and connections led, as it happened, to Knepler being the external examiner for my own doctoral thesis on Mahler, long ago. I well recall the viva voce examination in his home in what was then, decisively and memorably, East Berlin—as I recall his startling opening comment ("Of course I have not read *all* of this"); and then there was the hassle of getting in and out of the GDR via the Friedrichstrasse border crossing. I was enormously impressed by Knepler and his clearly and directly expressed political idealism, but would have to say, albeit with admiration, that both he and Dahlhaus were equally creatures of their own time and place: objects as much as subjects of legitimate political-historical study—as we all are. But let us beware falling into the trap of appearing to permit those who have become "historical" no greater intellectual stature than what we can see "over," than what we can "survey," as other historical textbooks put it. That, of course, is too crude a manifestation of the discourse of modernism.

Provoked and inspired by Taruskin's magisterial history, I am moved to revisit one of his own objects of cautionary historical comment—Mahler's Second Symphony—for my initial example of the grandiose symphonics signaled in my chapter title. Given the association of "grandiose" with both grandiloquence and even maximalism, that very phrase, of course, flirts with allegiance to the historical superiority that I actually want to problematize in revisiting critical and historical anomalies that hedge both scholarly and popular discourse about so-called late-romantic music. The reasons for doing so are at once personal and historical: properly historical, in Taruskin's sense of wanting to avoid authoritarian pronouncements and pursue evidence of experienced musical meaning beyond abstrusely transcendent aesthetic theorizing. This may, of course, lead us back to Bourdieu on music's role in the "consumption of cultural goods" as "one of the primary means of social classification" and, almost inevitably, of social division.[5]

SONORIC SURVEILLANCE AND THE MASSES

Two writers not so far mentioned, two specific books, will help to further locate the aims and intellectual terrain of this project as involving at least three overlapping disciplines: art history, musicology, and the literary and philosophical history of modernism. The first two of these came together in Richard Leppert's remarkable, and too little celebrated, 1993 book, *The Sight of Sound: Music, Representation, and the History of the Body*.[6] While avowedly associated with the aims and methods of New Musicology in the 1980s, Leppert sought here to move somewhat beyond the pioneering work "on *particular* musical texts" by his colleagues Susan McClary, Lawrence Kramer, and Rose Subotnik ("necessary" as he accepted it to have been).[7] What he offered as "even more than this" took the form of a virtuosic interpretation of music's cultural-historical development and meaning as, and in, social discourse—specifically as represented in paintings of musical activity, roughly from the sixteenth century to the early twentieth.[8] In a sense he ends in and overlaps with the period that will occupy me here.

Leppert was concerned with what Kramer subsequently called "music as a cultural trope."[9] Where Kramer may turn to the hermeneutic elucidation of specific works, Leppert turns to paintings: representations of music-making in the center or at the periphery of some social or mythological scene. Early in the book he chooses Antwerp painter Abel Grimmer's *Spring* of 1607, in which foregrounded peasants work in a formal garden while in the background, across a winding river, a group of leisured aristocrats enjoys a performance by some musicians: "To the extent that this music is listened to, it is a passive engagement; but because passivity functions here as a sign of social division, it is a means of valorizing social difference. Not accidentally, it recapitulates the ancient Boethian precedence of the critic/auditor over the producer."[10]

In this way, Leppert extends the more usual iconographic and historical interest that musicologists might have in paintings. Sociocultural criticism here leads him, via Gramsci, to propose that this passively consumed music, as a sign of social difference and privilege, is also a form of activity "whose valorization is organized by rendering the body static": "Music in this guise acts as a sonoric surveillance on the body, holding it captive to contemplation with the social prescription of physical reaction. Not accidentally, whether the auditor actually contemplates is perfectly irrelevant to the demand."[11]

Leppert's subsequent course leads through a pictured series of binaries that he sees as constructing the history of Western music: high-status "culture" *versus* peasant passion and vitality, the assertion of order over the threat of lower-class music and anarchy. As he moves into the eighteenth and nineteenth centuries, he turns increasingly to the gendered opposition of musical contemplation (masculine) and the permitted domestic *practice* of it by women. Male reason (fueling Romantic idealism) is opposed to musical pleasure, as something problematically feminine and "embodied." Leppert's fascinating history ends a little bleakly. The possibility arises of musical activity in the Victorian parlor violating "what it intended to inscribe" as music comes increasingly to be confronted critically "in its divides across cultural lines, gender lines, and the lines separating high art from popular and mass culture."[12] But the final painting discussed, Fernand Khnopff's *Listening to Schumann* of 1883, inspires a disconcerting reading of the painter's mother, seated in her parlor, her hand raised to hide her face from our view as she listens to a pianist, whose right hand alone is visible as he plays Schumann to her. Leppert's interpretation is harsh: "The averted eyes of the painting's listener register the horror of the body, and a plea for something that cannot—ought not [to]—be: Schumann without loving, Schumann *qua* thought."[13]

As I move into the territory of the nineteenth-century concert hall and opera house, where the listener is not only feminized but reduced to becoming a member of an audience, a "mass," my tendency will be to want to disagree with this reading and add a rather different perspective on what might really have been happening. Khnopff's mother, in Leppert's reading, may internalize the patriarchal requirements of domestic and social order—but is her hand shielding her eyes from the pianist or from *us,* and the painter? Might they have revealed a different and more passionate reaction? Here I turn to a second source of inspiration and guidance: John Carey's wonderful, and still rather shocking, 1992 study *The Intellectuals and the Masses: Pride and Prejudice among the Literary Intelligentsia, 1880–1939.* Not only did Carey move further into what is precisely my period of interest here; he, like Leppert, confronts high art and the masses in a rather unusual way.

The primary subject of Carey's book was late-nineteenth and early-twentieth-century British intellectual culture and its fear, often amounting to detestation, of "the masses," whose pleasure it feminized in the standard fashion alluded to by Leppert, one of whose persistent topics was the patriarchal association of reason with male intellectuals, as opposed to embodied pleasure and performance, familiarly associated with women. A passage in which Carey describes an attack by Holbrook Jackson on the early-twentieth-century invention of tabloid newspapers, with their reliance upon pictures, conveniently links some of Leppert's preoccupations with the kind of music history I shall be concerned with here: "Holbrook Jackson held female readers responsible for the new evil of pictorial journalism. Women habitually think in pictures, he explains, whereas men naturally aspire to abstract concepts. 'When men think pictorially, they unsex themselves.'"[14]

Carey's intellectuals are many and various, their number including writers associated with Bloomsbury (Virginia Woolf, E.M. Forster) as much as F.R. Leavis and his hero D.H. Lawrence. And then come T.S. Eliot, Ortega y Gasset, George Gissing, Thomas Hardy, H.G. Wells, and Wyndham Lewis—to name but some of the more prominent figures whose preoccupations, prognostications, and anxieties Carey finally, and devastatingly, compares with those of Adolf Hitler. Their anxieties were directed at suburbia and the middle-class masses (and the hated clerks) that populate its ever-extending sprawl, covering the woods and fields of Merrie England and infecting its cultural values. A secondary theme of Carey's is artistic Modernism and the lengths to which the intellectuals went to make "modern" art incomprehensible and inaccessible to those same masses: "The principles around which modernist literature and culture fashioned themselves was the exclusion of the masses, the defeat of their power, the removal of their literacy, the denial of their humanity."[15]

We might think that he goes too far here, but the cumulative power of his examples (based on wide reading of the novels and other, sometimes "scientific," writing of the period) is as startling as his larger strategy of attempting to reclaim and understand mass cultural practices. This leads him, for example, to offer two chapters on H.G. Wells: "H.G. Wells Getting Rid of People" (the famous writer harbored clearly expressed thoughts about the need to control population by exterminating the fecund masses) and then "H.G. Wells Against H.G. Wells," in which the writer is seen to argue against himself, appearing anxious, in much of his later fiction, "to put forward ideas but not to be held accountable for them."[16] Carey suggests that he "makes it hard to guess his standpoint by putting what seem to be his views about the individual and the masses in the mouths of decidedly sinister characters."[17]

Carey's underlying critical project is not all negative, however. The novelist Arnold Bennett was mocked by Bloomsbury for his accent and manner as much as for the down-to-earth subject matter of his novels; he came, Carey points out, "from the provincial shopkeeping class": "The Bennett home, though beneath contempt from the viewpoint of metropolitan culture, seems to have been lively and artistic. The family enjoyed papers like *Tit-Bits* and *Pearson's Weekly*. Bennett later recalled his 'principal instrument of culture' was *The Girl's Own Paper,* which advised on aesthetic matters. He also devoured best-sellers."[18]

Carey hails Bennett as the hero of his book, alongside other writers, outside the circle of high-culture elitists, like Conan Doyle, whose famous detective, Sherlock Holmes—"a comforting version of the intellectual for mass-consumption"—is able "to disperse the fears of overwhelming anonymity that the urban mass brought": "Holmes's redemptive genius as a detective lies in rescuing individuals from the mass. . . . The appeal of the Holmesian magic and the reassurance it brings to the reader are, I would suggest, residually religious, akin to the singling out of the individual soul, redeemed from the mass, that Christianity promises."[19] Armed with Leppert's and Carey's mapping of the terrain upon which art, patriarchal power, and anxiety about the masses confronted opposing, gendered ways of accessing and utilizing the products of aesthetic culture, we might now return to German music and a German document of the Romanticism whose "late" manifestations concern me here.

BERGLINGER'S EXPERIENCE

I have already alluded to the problems that hedge the very term *late romanticism* as we apply it to the music I shall be talking about and have noted that Dahlhaus believed it to be a "terminological blunder." It has probably been in use too long to abandon on the grounds of academic pedantry. In fact, its problems are relevantly linked to those of "romanticism" itself, and particularly German Romanticism, whose character as dreamy, self indulgent, and nostalgic is often taken as read. Those three features translate easily into the more specific attributes of Romanticism listed by Taruskin in volume 2 of his *Oxford History:* as idealism and a belief that art seeks to articulate the ineffable—as Rousseauesque devotion to idiosyncrasy and (implicitly egoistic) uniqueness, and as the melancholy that inevitably attends its attempts to articulate the potentially terrifying "sublime."[20] Taruskin relevantly foregrounds E. T. A. Hoffmann's celebrated Romantic, chronological mapping of the "Viennese classics" (Haydn, Mozart, and Beethoven) as representing ever more demanding levels of the quest for the autonomous and ineffable, inspiring the ritualizing and "sacralization" of the concert experience that Taruskin attributes to the "iron rule of romanticism."[21]

Taruskin's account of musical Romanticism indeed betrays a mounting skepticism that is in a way perhaps more truly "romantic" than the cultural practice he thus mockingly construes. As a result, he perhaps misses an opportunity to spot how the quest for the Romantic ineffable in music generated a public discourse of autonomy and how the quasi-spiritual invocation of the redeeming transcendent was often mobilized to perform strategic cultural work of the kind explored by Richard Leppert and John Carey. This was apparently less to reveal than to mask the true character of what we might call "high" or "late" romantic music, as its structural conceits acquire the inner eyes, ears, and nervous expressive sensibilities of Wagner's "art of subtlest and most gradual transition," while being fueled in part by the very skepticism and ironic detachment whose contrariness it embraced.[22] In doing so, it arguably became the quintessential bourgeois art of private expression in public; an art that dare not speak its name, save in deliberately mocked "programs" and elucidations, and supposedly "silly" opera libretti (such things might well have inspired Holbrook Jackson's strictures about "thinking pictorially"). It was, nevertheless, an art that kept faith with German Romanticism's mixture of the enthusiastic spiritual-emotional quest and a skeptical ironizing of its lament at the impossibility of achieving the goal of that quest. Its secret nature was understood to be finely nuanced expressive revelation that maintained a close affinity with the nostalgic awareness of its own limitations (even as it achieves its rapturous flights of perhaps self-deluding "expression"). The critics of Romanticism, variously late and early, tend to take at face value the public discourse of Romanticism, which was certainly only ever one side of the coin of Romantic practice where music was concerned.

Literary scholars and philosophers have always known rather more about Romanticism than have musicologists. Even Dahlhaus, who knew a good deal, accepted that the definitional battle was as good as lost, and that the concept of "romantic music" was linked to a stereotype, "which, misleading as it may be, we cannot simply ignore, since it is so deeply ingrained as to be virtually ineradicable"[23] One need, however, only glance at some of the more recent titles in just one university press's list of books devoted to the history and criticism of German Romanticism to see how those outside musicology have nuanced stereotypical notions about "romanticism," variously early and late. Just after our own century's turn, Richard Eldridge published his book *The Persistence of Romanticism: Essays in Philosophy and Literature,* described on Cambridge University Press's website as arguing "that Romantic thought . . . remains a central and exemplary form of both artistic work and philosophical understanding."[24] More recently there came Andrew Franta's *Romanticism and the Rise of the Mass Public,* followed in 2010 by

Edward Larrissy's edited collection *Romanticism and Postmodernism*. In 2009 another multiauthored volume had appeared, edited by Nicholas Saul: *The Cambridge Companion to German Romanticism*. This closes with an essay by Margarete Kohlenbach, "Transformations of German Romanticism, 1830–2000," in which she proposes that polarizing developments in nineteenth-century German politics were accompanied by "interpretations of Romanticism that ignored, misunderstood or reinterpreted the apolitical, philosophical, non-traditionalist and aesthetically innovative concerns of early Romanticism," adding, "The resulting image of Romanticism as an anti-modern and conservative movement remained dominant until the 1960s."[25]

As Julian Johnson demonstrates in his recent book *Mahler's Voices*, Mahler's generation of the 1860s would have had a decidedly more nuanced sense of what Romanticism was. Mahler would have got it from his reading, not least of E.T.A. Hoffmann and Jean Paul Richter (a remarkable writer who had adopted Bayreuth over half a century before Wagner).[26] In spite of the relative inaccessibility of Jean Paul, of whose novels there exist only forgotten nineteenth-century translations, and the confusing association of Hoffmann with Offenbach, English-speaking music students have long had access, in all versions of Strunk's *Source Readings in Music History,* to at least one revealing key text of early German Romanticism: the closing section of Wackenroder's and Tieck's *Herzensergiessungen eines Kunstliebenden Klosterbruders* (literally "outpourings from the heart of an art-loving monk").[27] Do they read it? Had *I* read it sufficiently carefully before teaching the early nineteenth century and feeling obliged to do so? It can still come as quite a surprise. The source volume, written in 1797 by the twenty-three-year-old W.H. Wackenroder in collaboration with his friend Ludwig Tieck, was a deliberately haphazard-seeming multi-text: an assemblage of essays and poems, mostly on medieval and Renaissance art and with a Catholic bent imparted by Tieck. It concludes with Wackenroder's fictional life of a composer which reads like a blueprint for Mann's *Doctor Faustus* a century and a half before its time; it too is narrated by a friend of the composer (the art-loving monk, presented as the fictional author of the whole volume). "The Remarkable Musical Life of the Musician Joseph Berglinger," as this closing story is called, is remarkable not least for its ambivalence about the very thing it concerns: Art.

Berglinger is presented as one of the six children (the only son) of an impecunious doctor, a single parent "living in straightened circumstances."[28] Here, then, we encounter an untimely member of a *declining* middle class. His son Joseph not surprisingly aspires to higher things whose character is best revealed to him in the music he hears in churches—"sacred oratorios, canticles and chorales."[29] I cannot help suspecting that he was probably ready for Mahler:

> Expectantly, he would await the first sound of the instruments—and when it came bursting forth, mighty and sustained, shattering the dull silence like a storm from Heaven, and when the sounds swept over his head in all their grandeur—then it was that his soul spread great wings, as if he were rising up from a desolate heath, as if the curtain of dark cloud were dissolving before his mortal gaze, and he were soaring up to the radiant Heavens. Then he would hold his whole body still and motionless, fixing his eyes unmoving on the floor. The present receded, and his very being was purged of all that earthly ballast which is the very dust upon the polished mirror which is the soul.... Finally, at certain moments in the music, it seemed as if his soul were illuminated by a divine radiance. He would suddenly feel much wiser, as if he were looking down upon the earth and its teeming millions with a visionary's eyes and with a certain noble and serene sadness.[30]

Such passages are usually taken either as risible examples of romantic "purple prose" or simply as evidence of romantic idealism—believing that music really *was* linked to divine radiance and transcendent truth. But there's more here, more in Wackenroder's "Romanticism"—and in his narrator's account of Joseph's experience, which I confess I can recognize as closely related to the one I initially had of Mahler's Second Symphony. We note that Joseph's experience is "escapist" in an intense, bodily sense—but that the escape is also nuanced in sociopolitical terms: Joseph soars *upward, above* his fellow listeners, who merge into the "teeming millions" down upon whom he imaginatively gazes like some privileged ruler who sees and knows more than the huddled masses over whom he rules. The narrator goes further and tells us that Joseph subsequently felt "purer and nobler" and alienated from the now "repulsive" passersby through whom he makes his way home, convinced of the need to prolong his "sublime poetic ecstasy."[31]

The second half of the story tells us how he tried to do this, to marry the "mass" and "intellectual" identities within himself: by becoming a composer. Adorno would accuse Wagner, the upstart bourgeois music enthusiast, of following precisely Berglinger's path, first becoming a Kapellmeister who beats time, then a composer (playing upon the German word *schlagen*, meaning to beat, just as in English) who literally beats his listeners into submission with his mighty musical visions.[32] We are pitched into the domain of the singing devil. As was Joseph Berglinger, the closing phase of whose fate must, however, be carefully noted.

He is disillusioned by the strictures of the musical technique that he has to master, longing, like some precocious Debussy, to access more immediately the mysterious realms of musical affect. In the end he succeeds most fully by expressing his disillusionment musically in an Easter oratorio filled with the sounds of suffering. Embracing textbook literary Romantic nostalgia of the pre-1960s variety implicitly mocked by Margarete Kohlenbach in 2009, he had subsequently written to his father about how, now that he had found success, he wanted to reject the "culture" of his uncomprehending socialite admirers and "flee to the simple Swiss herdsman in his mountain, and join him in his Alpine songs for which he feels homesick."[33] His summatory complaint takes the following form: "In my youth I thought that through music I might escape all earthly woe, only to find myself now the more firmly bogged down in the mire. Alas! There can be no doubt that, stretch our spiritual wings as we may, we cannot escape the earth, for it pulls us back with brutal force and we fall again amongst the most vulgar of vulgar people."[34] The art-loving monk closes his account of Joseph's artistic odyssey by posing the startling question: whether his friend might not have been born "to enjoy art rather than to practise it."[35]

THE POLITICS OF MAHLER'S ROMANTICISM

I must now accept that my own first response to Mahler's Second Symphony was probably not quite what it seemed: a shatteringly direct and unmediated experience of a rehearsal run-through under Georg Solti. It took place on a Saturday morning in London's Royal Festival Hall, otherwise largely empty apart from thirty or forty secondary school students on prearranged trips. What I clearly recall experiencing was not a piece of "art," of cultural capital or decadent maximalism, but something liberating and revelatory, something physical as much as intellectual. It grabbed me by the throat, expanded my world, exploded it, and then overwhelmed me with a choral and orchestral festival of, indeed, grandiosely joyous celebration that left me blown away for days and weeks (did I ever recover?).

With the benefit of hindsight, I could say more to some imagined ethnographic interviewer from another culture: Whatever it felt like (and I was hearing the work for the first time), I can of course now see how the experience was mediated. I am pretty sure I had prepared myself to the extent of reading a little and finding the "program" reproduced by Alma Mahler in her *Memories and Letters of Gustav Mahler* (in Basil Creighton's unsatisfactory translation of the German original first published in 1940). Written for a Dresden performance of December 1901, Mahler had sent it to his sister Justine, whom he knew Alma would be visiting when the letter arrived; he wrote to Alma too, but without copying the program out again, in spite of assuring her that it was "actually intended" for her. It opens, like the symphony, in arresting style:

> We are standing beside the coffin of a man beloved. For the last time his life, his battles, his sufferings and his purpose pass before the mind's eye. And now, at this solemn and deeply stirring moment, when we are released from the paltry distractions of daily life, our hearts are gripped by a voice of awe-inspiring solemnity, which we seldom or never hear above the deafening traffic of mundane affairs. What next? It says. What is life—and what is death?
> Have we any continuing existence?
> Is it all an empty dream, or has this life of ours, and our death, a meaning?
> If we are to go on living we must answer this question.[36]

There was plenty to whet the appetite there, but the description of the Finale was tantalizingly specific, beginning as follows:

> FIFTH MOVEMENT
> We are confronted once more by terrifying questions.
>   A voice is heard crying aloud: The end of all living beings is come—the Last Judgement is at hand and the horror of the day of days has come.
>   The earth quakes, the graves burst open, the dead arise and stream on in endless procession. The great and little ones of the earth—kings and beggars, righteous and godless. . . . The wailing rises higher—our senses desert us, consciousness dies at the approach of the eternal spirit. The
>   "Last Trump"
> is heard—the trumpets of the Apocalypse ring out; in the eerie silence that follows we can just catch the distant, barely audible song of a nightingale. A last tremulous echo of earthly life![37]

I was thus prepared for a musical apocalypse that promised an epic, protocinematic scenario of terrifying cosmic splendor. I was also studying Mahler's First Symphony as an "Advanced-Level" set work, albeit with little more than the relevant half of Redlich's *Bruckner and Mahler* to go on (I should explain that A-levels were and are the final high school examinations in Britain, where one generally specializes in only thee or four subjects). My teacher's evident unease about how to deal with the Mahler, of which (I suspect) he had no more than skeptical distant knowledge, was of course guaranteed to encourage me to believe that *I* had special and direct access to it. As a product of the suburban middle classes, I would also, I guess, have to explain to that notional ethnographer of European music, who might have read Carey, something about social class and aspiration—not, perhaps, without relevance to Mahler's own class-conscious program about the leveling of "kings and beggars, righteous and godless" in the great procession of the risen dead.

As if to reinforce any reading of his creative project as authentically *late Romantic,* some of Mahler's later letters from New York to Bruno Walter echo the Wackenroder/Berglinger complex in an almost knowingly intensified form. As in Wackenroder, the *experience* of art, specifically music, remains numinous, revelatory, and idealized, while its practice is materialized and problematized. Here in 1909: "When I hear music—even when I am conducting—I hear quite specific answers to my questions—I am completely clear and certain."[38] Later that year Mahler wrote in a similar vein after conducting his First Symphony: "That is—what it is like *while I am conducting!* Afterwards it is all instantly blotted out (otherwise one just could not go on living). This strange reality of visions, which instantly dissolve into the mist like the things that happen in dreams, is the deepest cause of the life of conflict an artist leads."[39]

One might put it that it was part of Mahler's birthright as a bourgeois intellectual artist—whose aspiration to "soar" had been heightened, "maximalized" even, by his status as a Jew in Catholic Habsburg Vienna—to take art way too seriously: at least by the lights of those still powerful and ostensibly "philistine" aristocrats he would have encountered in the corridors of power as Director of the Imperial and Royal Court Opera. Their philistinism arguably masked an instinctive suspicion that art might in reality be a route to communication with the masses and thus an alternative practice of power. We encounter the humorous reflection of such figures in Robert Musil's great Vienna novel *The Man without Qualities* (1930–32), where we meet Count Leinsdorf, for whom "literature" was "bound up with Jews, newspapers, sensation-seeking booksellers, and the liberalistic spirit of the impotently wordy, commercially-minded third estate."[40]

We also encounter there Ermelinde Tuzzi, whose salon celebrated "striving towards the ideal," just so long (Musil put it) as there was "nothing concrete about this idealism":

> for concreteness suggests craftsmanship and getting down to craftsmanship meant dirtying one's hands; on the contrary, it was reminiscent of the flower paintings done by archduchesses, for whom models other than flowers are not suitable on grounds of propriety. And what was especially characteristic

of her idealism was the concept of "culture": it felt itself to be cultured through and through. It could also, however, be called harmonious, because it detested all that was uneven and unbalanced, and saw it as the function of education to bring into harmony with each other all the crude antagonisms that unfortunately exist in the world.[41]

Music, of course, could always be passed off as being all about "harmony"—unless its modern tendency to emphasize disharmony was signaled not only in the dramatic range of noises being made, but also in verbal programs that specified what these noises might signify. Such things distanced music from archduchesses and flower painting and brought it into the tiresome and sometimes threatening realm of those others, the Jews, newspapers, and sensation-seeking booksellers.

I realize that I am in danger here of reinscribing the myth of Modernism and the role in it of early twentieth-century maximalization that Richard Taruskin has analyzed and criticized so persuasively. In this respect it is of some considerable interest to note how Mahler fell out of that mythic narrative, when the post–Second World War avant-garde either dispensed with him as a mere "late-romantic" or damned him with faint praise as a "bridge" to the Second Vienna School and a "precursor" of Expressionism. He thus became surveyably historical and fell away from the focus of the narrative in a way that was somehow reinforced and underlined by his return in the 1960s as a *popular* symphonist who spoke to the masses and the impressionable young, like my own earlier self. This was the sort of thing that high-modernists bitterly disapproved of, even after Pierre Boulez started conducting Mahler and Wagner (and some of them were uneasy about that). Let us not forget the old animosity between High Modernists—whether or not knowingly Adornian—and mass culture. But let us also remember how powerful was the fear of Mahler's mass appeal even in some of his early critics. The stern Robert Hirschfeld in Vienna was quite ready to analyze the inherent meaning of Mahler's music, even as evinced in his notation. Each individual note seemed to him to acquire a quasi-democratic, or indeed anarchic nuance and intent of its own while dispensing "dionysian" excitement to Viennese burghers of a kind that might well put them off their sedate professional lives:

> The Musikvereinsaal ... once again became the setting for one of those dionysian festivals which the Mahler bacchantes and maenads of Vienna go in for with frenzied enthusiasm. ... a Mahler symphony is now used by a post-Hellenistic society to release the explosive forces which have been pent up in quiet bourgeois duties and professions. Deranged by such explosions,

the mind thoroughly upset by the tumult, it is impossible to engage in the least objective discussion.[42]

Hirschfeld was deadly serious in that time and place where music still mattered, was talked about and consumed like Apple's latest device or 3D movies. Mahler himself proved peculiarly aware of this in his way when, in a fascinating letter, he rationalized his own maximalism to the nine-year-old Gisela Tolney-Witt, who had no doubt been prompted to write to him by a conservative parent or teacher. Why, she appears to have asked, did he need such a large instrument as the extended Wagnerian symphony orchestra? This is an extract from his letter of 1893:

> With Beethoven the *new era* of music began: from now on the *fundamentals* are no longer mood—that is to say, mere sadness, etc.—but also the transition from one to the other—conflicts—physical nature and its effects on us—humour and poetic ideas—all these become objects of musical imitation.
>
> . . . I would now mention only one thing more, the physical necessity to enlarge the musical apparatus: music was becoming more and more common property—the listeners and the players becoming ever more numerous . . . We moderns need such a great apparatus in order to express *our* ideas, whether they be great or small. First—because we are compelled, in order to protect ourselves from false interpretation, to distribute the various colours of the rainbow over various palettes; secondly, because our eye is learning to distinguish more and more colours in the rainbow, and ever more delicate and subtle modulations; thirdly, because in order to be heard by many in our over-large concert halls and opera-houses we also have to make a loud noise.[43]

Material culture and cultural practice evidently and pragmatically played their part in Mahler's sense of his own "maximalism"—it was also, we gather, a medium for the communication of something precise and yet complex. Here we must be more specific, returning to the Second Symphony in order to reengage with the direct experience of the kind of music I am talking about. Thanks to the still growing corpus of recorded performances of all of Mahler's symphonies, that experience is widely accessible, although to hear the Second Symphony live in an "over-large" concert hall such as Mahler described, and in the company of a mass of willing listeners, is to find the experience provocative of many additional layers of response. In returning to a work that so defines what and why the music of this period means and matters to me, why I both love *and* worry about it, I therefore feel obliged to complete this particular footnote to Taruskin on maximalism by explaining why I modestly but earnestly want to add a "Yes, *but*. . . ."

SOUNDS HORRIBLE AND DISTANT

That the Second Symphony was *heard* as modern maximalism is reinforced by an anecdote about one of the very passages carefully analyzed by Taruskin—the maximally dissonant, shattering "retransition" of the first movement around cue 20. A chaotic-sounding climax, already apocalyptic in tone, masses warlike tropes of marching, of fanfares and dire portent that lead us toward a terrifying aural precipice. A *molto pesante* buildup of an ever more dissonant chord is achieved by rhythmically insistent reiteration of its components in the heavy brass and timpani, joined soon by horns, strings, and woodwind. Taruskin identifies the dissonant seven-note agglomeration as "a 'dominant thirteenth' chord, here making what amounts to its symphonic debut": "Connoisseurs of musical horror will recognize this cluster as the very chord that Beethoven had used in the finale of the ninth for the intensified repetition of the *Schrekensfanfaren*, the 'horror fanfares' (as Wagner called them) that precede the Ode to Joy."[44]

Taruskin describes it, taking his cue from Guido Adler, as exemplifying Mahler's maximalization of the way in which post-Beethovenian "great music" had "long been sacrificing ingratiating pleasure on the altar of edifying pain."[45] The whole climax certainly seems to herald a barbaric spectacle, like a public execution. But is this really just edifying pain, or rather, perhaps, unedifyingly pleasurable spectacle? A crescendoing roll on suspended cymbal, with sponge-tipped sticks, adds a thrilling visceral rushing sound like an approaching tsunami as the chord finally collapses in tumbling chromatic scales into a surprise recapitulation of the movement's opening. The anecdote to which I referred above was told by Wilhelm Kienzl, who recalled sitting between the thirty-one-year-old Richard Strauss and the thirty-six-year-old conductor Carl Muck at an 1895 rehearsal by Mahler for a performance of the first three movements of the still unpublished Second Symphony in Berlin. At the moment in question in the first movement: "Strauss, sitting on my left, turns to me with enthusiasm in his eyes, 'Believe me, there are no limits to musical expression!' At the same time, to my right, Muck's face is distorted with unmistakable revulsion and the single word, 'Horrible!' comes from between his teeth."[46]

What neither of those responses really does justice to, however, is just how "shattering," and *why* shattering, that movement is: precisely, I would argue, because it deliberately dramatizes a tension between expression and form, where the experience of each is heightened by the other—something the movement has prepared with self-destructively meticulous care. The contrast between first and second "subjects" is heightened gesturally and affectively by the contrast between the aggressively, eruptively questioning and threatening character of the first subject and the songlike, fragilely aspiring quality of the second in a fantasy land of E major (against the opening key of C minor). So far "out of it" is that second subject that it seems to become a marginal, ever more distant voice *commenting on* a foregrounded symphonic "argument" that is really a monologue. The massive structural return to the point where the movement had started asserts a voice of fatefully denying masculine power—as it does more stealthily after the final second-subject episode here—and I would note for any surviving New Musicologists (and I welcome them) that this second subject is "feminine" with a will and identifies itself as such with pride, notated portamenti and all. It cares little for "organic unity." Small wonder that Adorno would later write wonderfully about Mahler's music as an example of art whose goal and subject matter are its own theoretical impossibility: "Mahler's primary experience, inimical to art, needs art in order to manifest itself, and indeed must heighten art from its own inner necessity.... The enemy of all illusion, Mahler's music stresses its inauthenticity, underlines the fiction inherent in it, in order to be cured of the actual falsehood that art is starting to be."[47]

We might put it that Mahler keeps faith with the Romantic dream that, as we have seen, embraced the disillusionment and denial that were always a part of it, that represented the rational or waking side of Romanticism. He therefore gives us, in the Finale—what? Resurrection? The solace of "faith"? Taruskin proposes that the Finale be seen "either as an ecstatic renewal of faith in spite of everything, or as a desperate effort to drown out doubt."[48] That would certainly push the symphony firmly back into the dark domain of the Singing Devil, noisily embracing affirmation for doctrinal, or simply manipulative ends, or both at once (which would perhaps be worse). It is precisely this reading that inspires my "Yes, *but* . . ."—or perhaps more of a "Yes, *and*. . . ." It also leads me to some distant sounds, as signaling what levels of complexity and subtlety could be achieved *within* the maximal style, both by internal and "external" means. Let me be clear that when talking about symphonic programs and the like I will not compound the romantic legacy problem by speaking of the "extra-musical."[49] My interest here is rather in the hierarchical and territorial significance of music that is audibly placed outside the primary frame of the symphony, extending its domain into potentially limitless space. This might be to invoke Adorno's notion of *Durchbruch* or "breakthrough";[50] at its most extreme it involves music literally played from somewhere beyond the concert platform: behind the scenes or in some farther-removed location.

I have already quoted from the most famous version of the program—the one I read before my initial encounter with the symphony, the one reproduced by Alma Mahler.[51] As we know, he had sent it to her and his sister Justine in 1901, evidently rather pleased with it, although he affected to disparage it. Publication of Mahler's fascinating correspondence with his sister and other family members has brought into the public domain the full text of the letter he deliberately sent to *her,* with the program (that was also for Alma) that he said he had produced "for someone naïve."[52] The letter to Alma had included a veiled reference to royalty when he tells her (speaking of the program) that he really intended it for her eyes, and otherwise "would not have drawn it up for the king himself."[53] We learn from the letter to Justine that the King of Saxony was in fact its intended recipient; the King, via the conductor Ernst von Schuch, had requested that for his better enjoyment of the performance Mahler might provide a program (not long after the composer had publicly vowed, in 1900, to abandon such things).[54] The "politics" of Mahler's programs, in all senses of that word, are worthy of a study in their own right. Like many nineteenth-century composers, he was ever mindful of whom his explanatory glosses and titles were for and what messages they should send, negotiating inventively between what he *might* say and what he felt it judiciously *appropriate* to say. In this case, as in other versions of the Second's program, we have seen that he emphasized the socially leveling nature of the apocalypse his music was presenting. Mahler's social politics were ultimately not those of Joseph Berglinger. After the opening of the graves and the beginning of the "endless procession" of "the great and the little ones of the earth—kings and beggars, righteous and godless," the program had gone on to position us, the audience, as spectators of the great march of the dead: "all press on—the cry for mercy and forgiveness strikes forcefully on our ears. The wailing rises higher—our senses desert us, consciousness dies at the approach of the eternal spirit."[55]

The music maximally engulfs and involves us, manipulates us into imagining ourselves transformed from spectators into participants—something startlingly reinforced when (from cue 22) we begin to hear apocalyptic trumpets sounding now from *outside* the concert auditorium. But it is what happens next that endlessly fascinates. The climax of communal terror erupts into a mighty full orchestral fanfare which heralds ... what is, by comparison, a great—but not empty—silence. The songlike theme sometimes referred to as a "resurrection" motif, climbs now in transfigured calm among the epic spaces defined by descending fifths in horns and harps that majestically outline D flat major. Then, astonished and confused, we hear two distant sounds: the one a stereophonic performance by offstage apocalyptic brass and timpani on both sides of the playing area, and disappearing into precisely requested *ever greater distance,* the other an "onstage" solo flute and piccolo miming the effusively unknowing "distant, barely audible song of a nightingale, a last tremulous echo of earthly life!"[56] Numinous power fades against a small, improvisatory "sound of nature." It all dies away on a bare fifth—the nightingale holding to C sharp while the distant trumpets fade on D flat. Only now, surprisingly—if they are kept seated at this point (as Mahler sometimes preferred)—does the chorus, *ppp,* slowly and *"Misterioso,"* start to sing the first two stanzas of Klopstock's resurrection chorale that Mahler had heard at Hans von Bülow's memorial service (*"Todtenfeier"*) in Hamburg in 1894, and to which he added some significant text of his own.

Generations of commentators have resolutely failed to "read" the odd implications of that disappearing apocalypse, which Mahler himself emphasized by telling Natalie Bauer-Lechner: "There now follows nothing of what had been expected: no Last Judgement, no souls saved and none damned."[57] The 1901 program for the King of Saxony had gone further: "There is no punishment and no reward. An overwhelming love lightens our being. We know and are." While Mahler's added sung text flirts with the doctrinal imagery of Catholic resurrection and redemption, the great line *"What thou hast fought for* (or *overcome*—*"Was du geschlagen"*) *shall lead thee to God"* in fact proclaims a relativistic, and potentially political, message of the transvaluation of values as much as it bows the knee to a deity who seems rather to merit scare quotes here:

With wings that I won for myself	*Mit Flügen die ich mir errungen*
In the ardent striving of love,	*in heissem Liebesstreben,*
I shall fly away	*werd' ich entschweben*
To light glimpsed by no other eye!	*Zum Licht, zu dem kein Aug'*
	gedrungen!
I shall die in order to live!	*Sterben werd' ich, im zu leben!*
You shall rise again,	*Auferstehn' wirst du,*
My heart, in an instant!	*mein Herz, in einem Nu!*

| What you have overcome | *Was du geschlagen* |
| Will lead you to god! | *Zu Gott wird es dich tragen!* |

Mahler manipulates us, the listening masses, to the ends of including us, even representing us, in a musical experience that is also somehow *for us,* and him (more than the King of Saxony, perhaps). It is also a work that questions and even replaces itself before our very eyes and ears. In the chapters that follow I will explore other examples of late-romantic, "maximal" music by which I am still moved, which I love, while accepting how problematic it all was and remains. They echo a kind of musical cultural practice which dealt, I will suggest, in voices, passions, and perceptions that are not only those of power or delusion: voices variously sensual, fearful, critical, and lamenting. We may be swayed by the tumult and the grandeur of it, but we must also listen for and to the distant sounds within this disappearing music to arm ourselves against its singing devils, to understand how such music was itself urgently aware of their threat and their ironic laughter, in which it sometimes shared, yet whose denying Mephistophelean mockery it also feared and lamented.

CHAPTER 2

Pessimism, Ecstasy, and Distant Voices

Listening to Late-Romanticism

I looked at those Beethoven lovers, sitting there goggle-eyed and exclaiming: "That's by our Beethoven. It's a German work. There's a double fugue in the last movement." . . . Others were graphic: "The symphony represented the story of the origins of man—first chaos, then the divine 'Let there be light!' And the sun rose upon the first human, who was delighted with such magnificence—in short the whole first chapter of the Pentateuch!"

I grew angrier—and quieter. And how they all eagerly scanned their texts and finally applauded! I seized Eusebius by the arm and dragged him down the steps past the smiling faces.

—Robert Schumann, "Florestan's Shrovetide Oration Delivered after a Performance of Beethoven's Ninth Symphony," 1835[1]

One way to challenge oppressive historical narratives is to propose alternatives, albeit in the spirit of dialectical debate rather than of crude iconoclasm. Instead of seeking "modernist" impulses in the music of late-Romanticism (prejudged otherwise to be a manifestation of 'decadence' or 'maximalism'), we might, for example, propose that official European Modernism was itself entirely a late manifestation *of* Romanticism: from the perspective of the audience it was perhaps even a late, decadent phase of Romanticism. The modernists may have worn the patched jacket of the suburban intellectual rather than the silk dressing gown of the metropolitan aesthete, but the well-rehearsed oppositional binary between modernists and romantics could be culturally clarified as one in which each side constructed the other as irrelevant, on grounds which included social affiliation, class, and political sympathies. Adorno's New Music of the early twentieth century might similarly be recognized as no more nor less a function of the dialectic of Enlightenment than had been Romanticism itself. W. H. Wackenroder and E. T. A. Hoffmann had by 1800 already established a conceptual and potentially ironic distance between art as idea, even art as experienced, and art as a form of cultural practice and productive force. *This* binary already rested less upon an oppositional tension between styles than on a creative one between art and the audience on which it depended, out of whose ranks it would now be renewed without the sanction of external authority. The critical force of the ironic conceptual binary between art as idea and art as practice, often linked exclusively to "modernism," remained active within Romanticism even as it advanced into its late phase, acquiring in varying proportions characteristics of both "decadence" and populism. The forms in which its decline was represented, lamented, or even mocked still spoke to and relied upon a comparatively popular or mass audience.

Thomas Mann's Gustav von Aschenbach and Adrian Leverkühn—characters selected from either end of Mann's career, and of our period that spans the twentieth-century's two great wars, share the knowledge that already burdened Wackenroder's Joseph Berglinger as he laboriously traversed the boundary between the receivers and the practitioners of music. Both were, or became, "artists," seekers after artistic perfection, who, as a result, became disabled in some way as participants in normal social life and thus grew aware of the folly of aesthetic idealism or (in Leverkühn's case) its ancient proximity to the Devil's business. What Aschenbach (in *Death in Venice* in 1911) and Leverkühn (in *Doctor Faustus* in 1946) tended to lose, however, in their more abstracted and dysfunctional devotion to forms of aesthetic idealism within a narrative framework of decline, was Berglinger's lively memory of overwhelming, socially situated aesthetic *experience* as the site on which that idealism was forged, as was their affinity with "the decadent," who might appear to be its emblematic guardian. Sometimes the line between the decadent and the artist was blurred, each a performative function of the other. A curious story of covered tracks and self-hatred emerges here. We should not forget that it was, ironically, as an impoverished and socially aspiring Romantic art-escapist that Berglinger learned his haughty disdain for the "masses," for his fellow music enthusiasts. Similarly, it was as members of the audience at a performance of Beethoven's Ninth Symphony in 1835 that Schumann's "Band of David" would learn to scorn and distance themselves from their fellow listeners, seen as so many Philistines, so many ignorant burghers, social climbers, and readers of early versions of "How-to-bluff-your-way-in-art" guides. They alone, the members of the *Davidsbund* (as Schumann's alter ego Florestan would put it in "Florestan's Shrovetide Oration"), understood Beethoven and the Ninth as having reached a type and quality of expressive communication in music whose true nature could not apparently be grasped by the embarrassing formulations of those to whom it manifestly catered. And yet it relied upon that audience, which was far more populous and socially mixed even than the many onstage players, soloists, and choral singers who were needed to perform this decidedly public and rabble-rousing music. Whether as part of a group of music professionals, or as members of an esoteric community of self-appointed aesthetic cognoscenti, Schumann and his friends nevertheless affected to grow tired of crude, quotidian similes and metaphors and of the descriptive literary programs and narratives that were generated by the rapidly expanding industry of musical production and consumption in the nineteenth century, about which more needs to be said.

Long before Eduard Hanslick's subsequently celebrated 1854 prognostication *On the Musically Beautiful* (*Vom Musikalisch-Schönen*), the Romantic experience of music was as much mediated by popular hermeneutics as it was riven by anxieties and tensions about musical meaning as something graspable by the philistine masses—an anxiety which, for example, deeply scarred public discourse about the Lisztian "symphonic poem" (I will return to this in chapter 3). That particular new musical medium was arguably invented precisely for the developing mass audience for romantic "symphonic" experience in increasingly commoditized forms.[2] In practice, what would come to be regarded as the "New German school" style of modern music was modern in large part precisely because of its investment in explicit modes of musical communication, however complex or nuanced. These catered to a mixed lay public of concert- and operagoers; even the modernist Richard Strauss and members of the nascent Second Viennese School still, in the decade preceding the First World War, relied upon that public in preference to the over-powerful and often regressively conservative critics who sought to police its taste.[3] Mahler himself was persuaded to act as president of a short-lived Viennese musical secession, led by Schoenberg, Zemlinsky, and Alban Berg, which in 1904–5 still sought precisely to educate the *audience* in what, to them, was the "new music" of what we are still bound, for reasons discussed in the previous chapter, to call late romanticism.[4] Only afterward did the cultural politics of high modernism, in the interwar period, push Schoenberg fully into the Schumannesque position of rejecting outright the bourgeois audience, of which he had been a member, in favor of a Berglinger-like position of hauteur toward it and toward the kind of music consumer he himself had been. He thus ceased to write for the community of romantic listeners, adopting a radical experimental style, which sounded as inaccessible to the bourgeois concertgoer as Schumann claimed Beethoven "really" to have been. Others of his contemporaries would alternatively assume an inverted snobbery of the kind that insisted upon their spiritual and even family connection with the urban proletariat, the "working class," for whom they would write in what they believed to be a more suitable and comprehensible style even than that of the waltzes and marches of the less ethereal, middle-brow musical burghers.

As the "bourgeois artist" became an ever more problematic and critically interrogated category, those who still practiced bourgeois art were oddly placed. This was particularly true when what they produced was being consumed by a still economically powerful bourgeois audience that duly rejected music composed to alienate or shock it (which such music readily did, for all Schoenberg's later protestation that it was just a matter of development, of progress, and that he really wanted to be considered a "better sort of Tchaikovsky").[5] Those practitioners who did not wholeheartedly embrace an effectively downward-tending stylistic mobility that might aim to speak to or for a newer, less well-educated mass audience (whose manipulation by the developing mass media they feared), were condemned to the status of so-called decadents. Their ability nevertheless to communicate with listening concertgoers was often directly linked to their sense of disconnection from both the new mass audience of the urban proletariat *and* from that of the bourgeoisie they had always criticized or mocked. This led to them assuming, or perhaps having thrust upon them, a mantle of saddened superiority. At times they were forced to play the deracinated aristocrat, shunning the inherited national and cultural affiliations of their contemporaries. They might even assume the stage manners of aestheticized disdain toward the public realm whose "new" politics and "new" agendas they could treat with occasionally justified scorn, yet whose enthusiasm for what they produced and whose readiness to buy tickets and musical scores provided them with income. It is to the "late romantic" productions and the fate of two such composers that I turn here.

THE CULTURAL POLITICS OF THE "NEW MUSICAL LYRIC"

Let me begin with two decidedly superior, if not haughty expostulations. The first is by a critic writing about Rachmaninov in 1925 and lamenting the eclipse of his friend's fame; the second is by Frederick Delius in 1920:

> What magic power has spellbound the musical world and made fine and great musicians deaf to beauties in music and at the same time turned into great and profound connoisseurs some former agents of electrical societies, who could not distinguish one note from another?[6]

> The time has come when every musician of serious aims should declare, in the interests of the public, what is his attitude towards the current attempts on the part of Russian impresarios, Parisian decadents and the press-agents, to degrade his art to the level of a side-show at a fair.[7]

On the face of it, these two exasperated outbursts evoke the rhetoric and sentiments of conservative habitués of newspaper letters to the editor. Such things would have been common in the 1920s and evoke the regressive nostalgia of those attempting to shut the stable door long after the young stallions of modernism had bolted into the blue. In this very period the prominent German composer Hans Pfitzner—by no means as consistently conservative in musical style as he sounded in prose—would regularly issue polemical diatribes on what he regarded as the inanities of "modernist" aestheticians like Ferruccio Busoni or modernist-sympathizing critics like Paul Bekker. The latter's decidedly reader-friendly book on Beethoven had presented the Master as a composer whose music embodied and expressed a "poetic idea" which was the basis of its inspiration and which could be critically grasped and even expressed in language related to the programs of New German School symphonic poems.[8] Pfitzner's two most celebrated extended essays, excoriating Busoni and Bekker respectively, were the pamphlet "Danger of the Futurists" (*Futuristengefahr*) of 1917 and *The New Aesthetic of Musical Impotence* of 1920. They sound very much like what they were: injudicious pleas for the world to stop changing. Their language, in retrospect, occasionally anticipates the style and sentiments of later Nazi ideologues like Hans Severus Ziegler, the in-house critic for the Düsseldorf *Entartete Musik* exhibition of 1938, which sought to replicate something of the infamous Munich *Entartete Kunst* show of 1937.[9] Small wonder that Pfitzner's opponents, like Schoenberg's pupil Alban Berg, found that he had offered them the moral high ground, or that they took it with relish.[10]

There are certainly things to be treasured as much as mocked in Pfitzner's own music: for example, parts of his nationalistic Eichendorff Cantata *Von deutscher Seele* and of the 1917 opera *Palestrina*, about which Thomas Mann incidentally wrote admiringly and at some considerable length in his own historically compromised *Reflections of a Nonpolitical Man (Betrachtungen eines Unpolitischen)* of 1918.[11] Nevertheless, the cobwebbed remains of conservative critical polemics on its behalf hang unappetizingly in the way of any attempt to resituate "late romantic" music as a historical form of cultural practice, putting to one side the avant-garde's derogatory stereotyping with which it became freighted. Of course, the stereotypes stick and late romanticism "is" in large measure what it became: a locus of dismissive tropes like "self-indulgent," "overblown," "decadent," "maximal"—but all such tropes were generated from a perspective of which I am suggesting we might grow more wary.

In the previous chapter I accordingly outlined an approach with methodological implications that led me to address key parameters, relevant to the generation of meaning in Mahler's Second Symphony, which lie outside the normal bounds of pitch-based analysis, specifically highlighting programmaticism and positional and timbral aspects of his use of the orchestra. Other such parameters would include the deployment of effects of *"Steigerung"* (intensification) and climactic "flight," along with the more famous categories, like "breakthrough" and "suspension" that were proposed and employed by Adorno in his 1960 study of Mahler. These aspects of the composer's music, I suggested, seem to rely upon a mode of reception that itself had a history: one that takes us back to those early Romantics and W.H. Wackenroder's projection of the experience to which his character Joseph Berglinger had been so dangerously susceptible as a youthful music enthusiast. That listening history is very much bound up with the material and institutional history of the symphony concert.

What Christopher Small has examined critically as an outmoded ritual of bourgeois culture, marked at every level by the celebration of power and necessarily attended by repressions and taboos, might itself be revisited historically with greater ethnographic cool. William Weber, in his first book, *Music and the Middle Class,* had long ago begun to nuance our understanding of the nineteenth-century European symphony concert as a ritual marked by confrontations and interactions between classes and genders; these he believed to have been more dynamic and fluid than those relating to comparable confrontations and interactions in the opera house.[12] This is not to say that all was sweetness and light. I have already referred to Schumann's famous little 1835 piece about the performance of Beethoven's Ninth Symphony in which he typically adopted the masks of various complementary "selves" (like the emphatically political Romantic Florestan and the more poetically dreamy Eusebius). Out of his plea to reidealize Beethoven's music, and thus save it from its uncomprehending would-be admirers, came Romantically idealistic analysis in the manner implicitly proposed by Hanslick in *On the Musically Beautiful* (as "tonally moving forms," music to be regarded as "about" music rather than anything "extra-musical"—as the later catchphrase would have it—and its beauty therefore capturable only in specifically musical terms).[13] Yet there are indications that the Beethoven "experience" Schumann and his friends had had was difficult to put into words not because it was in some literal way "ineffable," but because it was in a rather particular way more than just intellectual, because, I venture, it was already approaching what Simon Frith, in his 1996 book *Performing Rites: The Value of Popular Music,* would hold up as an experience peculiar to "popular music" in the twentieth century: "What we mean by 'feeling' in popular music . . . is a physical as much as a mental experience. . . . As John Blacking argued persuasively, if grasping music means feeling it, then musical understanding is a bodily as well as a mental process."[14]

The music of "late romanticism" was in some measure just that: an experimental re-creation and intensification, in musical terms, of the Romantic *experience* of music, not least of what the early Romantics called "classical music." It was something that they themselves often either failed to realize or retreated from realizing until Wagner let all the cats out of the bag and produced what Adorno (another "late romantic" if ever there was) would describe as a kind of manipulative popular music for the bourgeoisie—film music *avant la lettre.*[15] But if I am suggesting that the history of the symphony concert should be brought back into alignment with the history of developing mass culture in the nineteenth century, we have clearly to confront the often over-determined significance of social difference and class which the late-romantics (or "romantic modernists"?) accepted when asserting their own identity. Nowhere was this more elaborately invoked than by those so-called (and often indeed self-styled) decadents—those contemporaries and heirs of Schumann's *Davidsbund* whose detestation of the bourgeoisie *and* the *Lumpenproletariat* might lead to an almost "aristocratic" disdain for the lower orders and, indeed, their bourgeois manipulators—the bosses and bankers who were now funding it all. Earlier models for such artists in literary Romanticism might have included the quasi-autobiographical figure of the aspiring painter Traugott in E. T. A. Hoffmann's story "The Artushof" (1815, published in 1816 and included in 1819 in volume 1 of the *Serapions-Brüder*). An acquaintance mocks his idealism and assures him that art is in truth only a "refreshment after serious business is done."[16] Traugott privately mocks such philistinism and emphasizes the critical perceptions underlying his Romantic desire to escape from the merchant's office in which he works:

> What is all the cogitation and all the scribbling intended to achieve? Only the acquisition of more and more money for the cashbox, only the greater splendour of Fafner's baleful hoard! But how an artist such as I longs to leave the city and with head held high breathe in all the reviving odours of spring so that his imagination is ignited and the liveliest pictures come into being within him?[17]

Later manifestations of Traugott would almost turn themselves into living embodiments of an internally conflicted and contradictory aesthetic critique of the economic system upon which they relied. Here I am thinking of J.-K. Huysmans's character Des Esseintes in his 1884 novel *À Rebours,* whose detestation of the bourgeois world of money and power leads him to escape entirely into a fantasy land of aesthetic artifice.[18] One might similarly think of Oscar Wilde insisting as follows, in the preface to *The Picture of Dorian Gray* (a novel in which *À Rebours* plays a small but significant role): "We can forgive a man for making a useful thing as long as he does not admire it. The only excuse for making a useless thing is that one admires it intensely. All art is quite useless."[19]

Note the seriousness and complexity of the threat to bourgeois rationality and economic good sense in all of this. The paradox of its authentically Romantic-modernist heritage is revealed nowhere more forcefully than in the fact that by the end of the century, the most passionately argued critique of decadence in music, meaning of Wagner's above all, was that of Friedrich Nietzsche, who dared to diagnose Wagner's incomparable art of musical "expression" (and Nietzsche agreed that it was that) as a symptom of a possibly French pathological disorder of psychosocial origin.[20] But Nietzsche, himself unshaken in his detestation of the bourgeoisie and the "rabble," would become the philosopher of choice for most of the 1890s Wagnerian decadents, not a few of them those same socialists and anarchists that Max Graf would later recall as having at the time been mocked as merely "fin de siècle" or "degenerate," from the bourgeois perspective most articulately focused by Max Nordau in his 1891 book *Entartung (Degeneration)*.[21] That perspective is in essence the one elaborated extensively by Stephen Downes in his *Music and Decadence in European Modernism*, discussed in my introduction.

The apparently unlikely task before us is to bring this new and apparently haughtily "decadent" late-romantic music of the 1890s and the first decades of the twentieth century into alignment with a historical understanding of the concert experience as somehow linked to the development of mass culture, as much, indeed, as it was a form of modernism. But as inheritors of the modernist critique of that same mass culture, questioningly or not, we are obliged to interrogate this music precisely in the act of reclaiming it. Was it able to "speak" in some way *other* than manipulatively to a mass audience? Might we "read" its complexity and the often directly expressed elitism of its producers as in some way both manifesting and *confronting* that complexity? It will prove helpful to consider for a moment just one theorist of the period, a devoted Nietzschean and Wagnerian who corresponded and was on friendly terms with both Mahler and Richard Strauss—both of whom happen to have written music in 1896 inspired by Nietzsche's anti-Christian projection of the *Übermensch* and the doctrine of Eternal Recurrence in *Also sprach Zarathustra*.

The theorist and critic in question was Arthur Seidl (1863–1928). In 1912 he republished four lectures he had given in Munich between 1898 and 1900 under the title *Moderner Geist in der deutschen Tonkunst. Gedanken eines Kulturpsychologen zur Wende des Jahrhunderts* (The modern spirit in German composition: Thoughts of a cultural psychologist at the turn of the century). The volume was dedicated to Richard Strauss and the lectures titled "Was ist Modern?" "Moderne Geist in der dramatischen u. instrumentalen Tonkunst," "Also sang Zarathustra," and "Moderner musikalische Lyrik." It is a fascinating little book, in which Seidl *distinguishes* what he called "authentically" modern music from that more recently and negatively branded as "decadent," "erotic," "hysterical," or "neuropathological."[22] Marginalizing the latter almost as a passing fashion, or presentational fad, Seidl wanted to emphasize an alternatively optimistic spirit for the new century, hailing Nietzsche as the clearest manifestation *of* the "modern spirit": the critic of Wagner and combater of decadence.[23]

The picture becomes more complicated with the subsequent proposition that two post-Wagnerian paths may be discerned: what he called left- and right-wing Wagnerism. The political implications seem intended, in that the conservative Humperdinck is presented as an exemplary "right-wing" Wagnerian, worshipfully wedded to the Master as a model (rather as Beethoven had been for the early Romantics), while Seidl's preferred left-wing Wagnerians use the Master as a starting point for new departures and are led by Strauss—this group including Mahler, Max von Schillings, Gustav Brecher, and others. If Seidl had a problem with Mahler, it was because the symphony seemed to him too fixed and traditional a form to accommodate the quintessentially "new" style of what he called the "modern musical lyric"—related to the song rather than the symphony or sonata: particularly the through-composed "Gesang" as opposed to the more formal "Lied" (its manner of extension and development Seidl strikingly compared to the elaborately engineered "flights" of modern iron construction).[24] Echoing ideas we find expressed in letters by Mahler, like that to Gisela Tolney-Witt quoted in the previous chapter—things he might well have discussed with him—Seidl saw the new lyric form as involving the disintegration of classical themes into motivic elements, reflecting "scientific progress in the study of the mind": "from the psychology of feeling to the physiology of emotion (extending now even into the finest of nerve-fibres). The *artistic* analogue to this process is presented by music in the far-reaching elaboration of the polyphonic orchestral texture to the point where all these motivic particles divide out into ever more intricately wrought musical structures."[25]

Seidl accordingly held that it was not *Darstellung* (representation) but *Einfühlung* (perhaps "emotional sympathy") that was the true character of musical representation in this style.[26] But whom, we might ask, was it *for*?

ARISTOCRATIC PESSIMISM

Not, alas, the stable boys to whom Richard Strauss wished to deny the vote and would certainly not have had seeing *Parsifal* on the cheap on a Sunday afternoon.[27] But then Strauss was a complex character and before the First World War, as I have indicated, had himself embraced the growing "public" for his music as more shrewd in its taste and discernment than conservative critics, like Hanslick, who rejected it:

Whatever is great can only be impeded in its victorious progress for a little while at the most, and can never be finally halted by the men behind the scenes: thus it was that the great public—the Voice of God—enabled even Franz Liszt to conquer malice and stupidity just as its enthusiasm enabled Richard Wagner in 1876 to defeat decisively all his critics, ill-wishers and detractors.[28]

And what was this "greatness" that the "great public" could discern, but not the malicious critics and "men behind the scenes"? To approach more comprehensively its manifestation in an extended symphonic work might be to account for the content and quality of the experience such a work was able to invoke in an audience whose access to complexity and intensity of musical communication relied on a heterogeneous mixture of musical effects, conventions of interpretation and performance, and its members' individual physical and emotional responsiveness as conditioned by a host of material and cultural factors.

A question closely related to the requirements of the audience for "modern" music of this kind was put by none other than Count Leo Tolstoy to the young Sergei Rachmaninov—a friend of whom I quoted earlier, lamenting the early eclipse of his fame and blaming "former agents of electrical societies." The story goes, as told by Rachmaninov and elaborated upon by Fyodor Chaliapin, that the composer had visited Tolstoy in January 1900 with Chaliapin (they were both twenty-six). Rachmaninov had previously sought support and advice from Tolstoy after the failure of his First Symphony but got little more than a pat on the knee and a "happens to us all" sort of comment. On this second occasion the two young men had performed Rachmaninov's song "Fate" (op. 21, no. 1), with its persistent allusion to the opening motif of Beethoven's Fifth Symphony. Rachmaninov recalled what followed:

> Tolstoy sat in an armchair a little apart from the others, looking gloomy and cross. For the next hour I evaded him, but suddenly he came up to me and declared excitedly: "I must speak to you. I must tell you how I dislike it all!" And he went on and on: "Beethoven is nonsense, Pushkin and Lermontov also." It was awful.... I never went back.... And just think, the first time I went to him, I went as to a god.[29]

Chaliapin's recollections of the occasion also attributed to Tolstoy, the great writer and fighter for the rights of the individual against the Tsarist bureaucracy, the following more direct question to Rachmaninov: "What kind of music is most necessary to men—scholarly or folk music?"[30]

One cannot imagine that this encounter did much for Rachmaninov's state of nervous depression, for which he shortly sought advice and therapy from the amateur musician and professional hypnotist Dr. Nicolai Dahl. He would dedicate the Second Piano Concerto to Dahl, so much did its completion seem to have owed to Dr. Dahl's ministrations. Might Rachmaninov even have conceived of the main theme of the first movement, with its initially burdened confinement to a narrow range of adjacent notes as a kind of Tolstoyan "folk" melody, for all that the rhetoric of the movement as a whole was directed so effectively to the urban and even *sub*urban "serious" concertgoer of the day? In his attempt to marry the popular with the "scholarly," Rachmaninov would soon fall victim to the Romantic discourse of high art as signifying and facilitating superiority over the consumers of music to whom Tolstoy seemed to want him to cater. Just as he would himself grow weary of his often-requested Prelude in C sharp minor, so the Second Piano Concerto has never been taken terribly seriously by intellectuals, for all its popularity—indeed precisely because of it. The discourse of Modernism was already establishing its reversed critical replacement of Tolstoy's opposition of scholarly to folk music with "serious" as opposed to "popular." In public the Second Piano Concerto of Rachmaninov can make haughty idealists of us all, perhaps in spite of ourselves. Theodor Adorno would accordingly refine his disparagement by implicitly tarring Rachmaninov with the brush of being able, with Tchaikovsky and Dvořák, to write only "medleys" of themes that (as he interestingly continued) "either were or seemed to have been borrowed from folk music":

> Whatever is not a theme in the sense of a nationally characterized single melody declines to a mere transition or, in the bad product of the species, to noisily blown-up fillers. But this upsets the idea of symphonics, of unity producing itself from diversity. . . . The sole remaining organizing factor is the schema, not work from within. The structures approximate the medley form. Song hits have become the heirs of nationally tinged thematics; the legitimate successor of Rakhmaninov is Gershwin.[31]

That was intended, even more effectively than Tolstoy, to administer a kind of critical coup de grâce to Rachmaninov, the Russian aristocrat with the dissolute father who had lost the family wealth—the composer who had to make do with being known as a "pianist," and who, by the time of his American exile in the 1930s was demonstrably "behind the times." He was also the compatriot and contemporary of whom Stravinsky (another Russian aristocrat turned post-Revolutionary émigré) quipped that at twenty-five "he became a very old composer indeed."[32] Much depends upon how we construct Rachmaninov's popular audience and what it was that they were hearing. Thinking of Leppert's reading of Grimmer's leisured aristocrats, we might ask if they were "contemplating" it at all. For an answer, watch Celia Johnson in *Brief Encounter* at that moment when she chances upon the Second Piano Concerto on the radio: her face registers a complex knot of emotions as she finds released within her the voice that tells the story she cannot openly tell her husband, Fred, as he does his crossword by the fire, the story of a love affair that nearly was, but couldn't be. Such uses of Rachmaninov have contributed to the scorn that is heaped upon him.[33] They might also be taken as documents of the kind of response his best works will receive both in and out of the concert hall—I think of the bored man I once sat next to at a performance of the Second Symphony who had been thrashing noisily through the pages of his program as if to find something to distract him from his boredom and anger at having to suffer all this for the sake of his more musically committed wife. A short way into the slow movement he stopped, and at the end muttered confusedly to her, "That was really pretty."

"Gloomy" is a more usual assessment—the kind of fated gloominess for which Rachmaninov might equally be celebrated. This ushers in the other trope of Rachmaninov criticism: to explain it all, quasi pathologically, in terms of his "background"—in terms, that is, of "decadence" in its social Darwinian sense. Leonid Sabaneyeff did this, albeit sympathetically. He was the critic I initially quoted on the agents of electrical societies. He had known Rachmaninov in Russia and in 1925 wrote about him admiringly, but also as irrevocably marked by Moscow's Bohemian social life, its restaurants, gipsy choruses, and its atmosphere "of continuous dissipation in which perhaps there was no merriment at all, but on the contrary, the most genuine, bitter and impenetrable pessimism.... Music here was a terrible narcosis, a sort of intoxication and oblivion, a going off into irrational planes. Drunken mysticism, ecstatic sensations against a backdrop of profound pessimism permeating existence."[34]

Now at least we are getting somewhere nearer to a sense of what Rachmaninov's music might "express"—in terms, I would suggest, that often match the criteria set by Seidl for his "Modern Musical Lyric" form. Listen, perhaps, to his remarkable tone poem *The Isle of the Dead*, after Arnold Böcklin, for an example from the period just before the First World War, when Rachmaninov spent time in Europe, honing his style in comparison with dominant German models like those of Strauss.[35] It was the period in which he produced the Second Symphony.

We might even go beyond Adorno and hear that symphony as a revealingly negotiated *engagement with* the now conventional, institutionalized form. "Folk music" à la Tolstoy it never is, but neither is it exactly "scholarly." Perhaps it is concert music—music that accepts the concert experience as one of movement toward those narrative-friendly teleological goals we have come to suspect, and not least when turned, as here, into the commoditized grand theme and experience of "flight" as the symphony's key experiential tasks.

Rachmaninov engages critically (and thus in "modern" fashion) with established form—with the symphony, first-movement "sonata" form, and the like—in a manner therefore best decipherable precisely in what have come to be called "programmatic" terms: involving narrative, protocinematic visualization and so on. We might even more positively identify these modes of decipherment not as outmoded relics of "unmusical" ways, but as the strategies whereby the nature of this critical and dialectical engagement with "form" might be described or communicated by the audience for whom it was designed: necessarily both inexact and precise, marked by subjective variances of perception and reception whose bodily and "emotional" character complements and complicates other conceptual and strategic maneuvers. The kind of description they might facilitate will always be in conversation or "dialogue" both with the composer's presumed intentions and with then contemporary modes of reception. Neither method of assessing "meaning" need cancel or be regarded as contradicting the other or claim greater authority. Similarly, the difficulty in arriving at, or even desire to avoid (particularly on the part of the composer) some sort of verbally articulate clarification of meaning need not be taken as demonstrating an intellectual lack or disability that could facilitate the mumbo jumbo of "ineffability." Such problems rather define the character and nature of reception in this case as a cultural practice that intimately involved the listener (particularly the lay, or "popular," listener) entering in public into a private imaginative engagement and sensual negotiation with the performed music. Such reception might be constructed of Berglinger-like narrative visualizations, might indeed involve both sensual and "out of the body" experiences, like Berglinger's vision of King David or those aroused, with evident authorial complicity, by any performance of Mahler's Second Symphony. In them the cultural and the personal are complicatedly entwined in a kind of enacted mediation that might at times be related more than merely metaphorically to bodily and specifically sexual experience. We refer relevantly to musical "climaxes," albeit without the physical processes involved in actual sexual activity—something which has facilitated their culturally driven descriptive association with "transcendence" and "spirituality" (while in truth providing us with means to better *understand* those very notions). The following account of the Second Symphony is offered as a way of evoking something of its popularly accessible "meaning" as a form of discursive entertainment, in all its complexity, without relying upon conventional music-analytical discourse, although some of its terminology will be used as appropriate (I refer to cue numbers in the score for those inclined to consult a copy; they may be ignored by those who are not, but can listen).

RACHMANINOV'S SYMPHONY (BEYOND ADORNO)

The Second Symphony's participatory roller coaster ride is prefaced by a darkly meditative, slow introduction that represents a convincing span of Seidl's "modern musical lyricism." Its subtly modulated emotional character offers a pessimistic gloss on all that follows, as if from the viewpoint of a voice-over narrator. From mournful solemnity it rises through half-despairing aspiration to an attempt at real melodic "flight" that almost takes off, only to fall back whence it had come. The start of the *Allegro moderato,* though derived from the same initiating material, comes with a palpable sense of relief. The given, even ritualized public task then takes over from the self-constructing responsibility of private "expression" like the cinematic "fade" into a narrative of the prehistory of the narrator's pessimism.

The key is still the gloomy E minor, but the Introduction's motif is now turned more comfortingly into a symmetrically-phrased and symphonically promising "theme," with a rocking and rustling accompaniment and even a potentially heroic, aspiring tail. The manner of the Tchaikovskian exposition is at once evoked, and if there is something almost over-literal about the extended, dramatic sonata form structure that we know we have embarked upon, it is a fact that we register with pleasure and anticipation. Rachmaninov seems to share it, freed now from the burden of private introspection as he embarks upon the symphonic "work" that the socially established form requires of him. The movement he creates is marked throughout by a lyrical impulse toward the kind of ecstatic climax that the form presupposes. If he cannot attain that climactic resolution out of private conviction, it is clear that the social "symphony" itself might be permitted to do so and provide its audience (among whom the composer himself is of course numbered) with the transcendent experience that its subject has relinquished. From that point of view, it is fascinating that the conventionally lyrical, "singing" second subject starts to realize the sequentially aspiring grand-thematic promise of the first subject's concluding tail only after five bars of music which, while still in 4/4, subtly evokes the manner and tempo of a waltz in G major—of a social dance, therefore, rather than a private song or aria.

The stretch of confident public aspiration that ensues achieves a codetta of real lyrical repose (from cue 10) before the predetermined logic of the symphonic business moves us on, and this time in the direction of the rhapsodic, freely evolving battleground of the anticipated "development section." A fascinating and even terrifying one it is, too. In conventional Germanic terms, there is relatively little real musical or tonal conflict in it, only the quasi-programmatic trappings of conflict. Viewed another way, it brilliantly underlines any suspicion that we may have that the true conflict within this work is not of the old-fashioned musical-metaphorical type at all, but is rather expressed in a tense confrontation between the fundamentally hopeless (and musically futureless) expressive truth of the introduction and the redeeming business of symphonic form, conceived in what might superficially be regarded as simply a series of "boxes to be filled." This, in effect, was a musical dramatization of the rift between art as idea (and ideal) and art as cultural practice to which I referred at the start of this chapter. Here, in the section of romantic-modernist sonata form least prescribed by structural models, the anticipated snatches of "expressive" first-subject material, whittled down into motivic building blocks of modulating sequential chains, are tossed along from the outset by a chill Sibelian storm wind derived from the germ motif of the introduction. As the progenitor of the first subject, it effectively monopolizes the whole development, overwhelming us at times with great howls of despairing emptiness, at others with fearfully materializing marches of the battalions of the dead. Even the attempted "recapitulatory" appearance of the subjectively generated first subject itself, fourteen bars before cue 18 (correct notes, but over a dominant pedal B) fails to reestablish its shattered equilibrium as we approach the apocalyptic outburst that ensues, which is effectively the climax of the development.

The point is reinforced at cue 20 by the restatement of the germ motif in the form in which we had heard it as stated by the cor anglais at the end of the introduction. What follows is the real recapitulation, but, in a masterly confirmation of its originally implied alternative rather than organically "transformatory" role, what we recapitulate is the second-subject material in a structurally appropriate, warmly consoling but in no way spiritually "won" E major. Formal convention alone now permits the Tchaikovskian-heroic, luxuriantly celebrated apotheosis of the sequentially aspiring subsidiary theme and its space of achieved repose, just as philosophical ones demand that the coda sweep us back into the storm of the development and a last conclusive cadence back in E minor.

When viewed in this way, taking the sense of alienated contradiction between its form and the impulse and manner of much of its musical material as its effective subject matter, the movement can be seen as a brilliantly concise exposition of what we might call the symphony's problematic premise (the self-destructive potential of subjective consciousness left to its own devices) and the possible shape of its solution. The "escapist" aspect of that solution is therefore the reverse of what is usually imagined. Rather than into inner fantasy, the escape here is into the socially endorsed form that demands its ultimately attainable, ecstatically transcendent "grand melody." The first really satisfying example of such a thing comes in the second movement, the Scherzo, where it sweeps us off our feet in gloriously snatched *"molto cantabile"* interludes in the threateningly violent exuberance of the piece. The grandest of all such melodies will be the goal and focus of the most public, and in a sense most formulaic, of all the symphony's movements, the Finale. First, however, comes the Adagio, which had so moved my concert neighbor, and in which the burden of tragic realism borne by so many of Rachmaninov's great melodies is exhibited in a remarkable manner.

Sabaneyeff, whose idiosyncratic insights into Rachmaninov's style I have already cited, had more to say in standard "decadent" vein about its "volitional impotence" and psychology: "As if in a torpid, hashish-state he, will-less and motionless, imagines visions full of fascination and beauty, and does not even wish to reach out for them."[36] Yet rather than being a self-indulgent function of such creative psychology, Rachmaninov's music arguably performs and demonstrates its troubling doubleness. The Adagio is certainly in some sense torpid, even "motionless": its main theme, after the rising incipit, is in effect just a decorated, four-bar scalic descent from upper to lower tonic. It is a luxuriant arabesque, a dying fall (it is notable how the harmony, by withholding the unaltered tonic chord of A major until the end, enhances the effect of direction toward the final note). But the expressive tension imparted by the arpeggios that terminate in rising appoggiaturas (strictly, decorated versions of the *descending* appoggiatura of lament, of course) suggest that theme *has* willed and still harbors wishes, just as Rachmaninov's strategy for its deployment in the movement ensures that we, the audience, strongly will its return. Once again he both relies upon and reinterprets symphonic convention; the latter postulates a lyrical slow movement of solemn intimacy, inviting sustained sympathetic involvement with what seems to be the composer's unmasked expressive voice—a soliloquy as it were "before the curtain." Yet we would anticipate no veristic recitative of chaotic passion, but a structured aria inherited from the eighteenth century's favored model of objectified and formalized, in a sense *socialized,* emotion.

The strategy of deployment to which I have referred is Tchaikovskian in its reliance upon a linked pair of themes: the intense and passionate opening melodic sentence joined to a more restrained, more bearably extendable subsidiary theme, whose rhetorical business is precisely that of a kind of delaying tactic, permitting the formal extension of the movement while ensuring always an element of spontaneous authenticity in its restatements of the primary melody, particularly in its anticipated climactic celebration. The gentle clarinet theme whose first statement begins in bar five, performs its function admirably, providing a long interpolation in what might have been a simple "A-B-A" presentation of the main melody. That structure is nevertheless picked up again at cue 47 in an eight-bar period whose business is to reintroduce the opening melody, now fortissimo and grandly scored—although still only four bars long. Its intimate authenticity as well as its fatal passivity, is reinforced and explained by a direct *poco più mosso* reference to the symphony's initiating motto from the first movement in a simple, sequentially descending version. It reminds us that the source of the Adagio theme's scalic descent is the symbolic motif of fatalistic subjectivity out of and against which the whole work has proceeded. The developmental "middle section" of the movement is consequently fascinating.

A slowed-down, quasi-canonic version of this motif from the first movement's introduction (it is now therefore seen to be "formalized') twice, as if in spite of itself, gives way to richly scored expostulations in the expressively "hot" manner of the main Adagio theme. The second of these ousts the introductory motif altogether and extends itself into a massive twenty-bar *Steigerung,* of increasingly transcendental bearing, that leads into the expected climax, where the main theme finally reappears in full C major glory. But now it is most significantly reduced only to its single initial bar, subsequently descending against darkly intoning horns and our introductory motif in its basic, dissolutionary semiquaver form. This quickly clears the stage of all the protagonists and leads to a general pause bar, after which the formally "correct," recapitulatory third and final section of the movement begins.

Once again the element of reinterpretation to which I have referred is most eloquently manifested. Just as the authentic expressive charge of the main theme has required that its main climactic statement be reduced to a single lyrical gesture that hardly has extended thematic status any longer, so its restatements in the closing section are presented now as explicitly nonvolitional recollections: as tonally migrating after-echoes of its original character (the fatally significant introductory motto from the first movement maintains a constant presence in the texture here). Formal balance is properly ensured, however, and the extended subsidiary theme fulfils its role by leading this time into a broadly scored section in which sequential statements of the opening bar of the main theme on one flute and one clarinet are drowned by a full string counter-melody that musters one last precariously poised fortissimo insistence on the opening of the main theme at the very moment that it seems finally to dissolve before us into a long-unwinding music of aftermath. In homage to similar passages in the first movement, only at the last does it attain a vision of beatific calm in the D major subdominant approach to a rich closing cadence in A major. At this moment, alone in all the symphony perhaps, the fatalistically downward-winding semiquavers of the introductory motto assume a merely lyrical, almost decorative role, as if in finally ensuring acceptance of the impotence of the subjective will, their work is done.

If that movement functions as a symbolic public baring of Rachmaninov's "inmost soul" that is both direct in outward manner and richly complex in its inner structural self-awareness, the Finale can appear crude, a kind of circus parade in honor of the Big Tune whose first appearance will be theatrically withheld until well into the festivities. Rachmaninov might appear now to slip wholly into the facile, "commodity" approach to symphonic writing that his detractors have tended to attribute to the whole work, if not his entire output. Here I would refer to observations I made earlier about the first movement, relating to the sense of creative relief that Rachmaninov had seemed to project at the outset of the *Allegro moderato*, where the socially and culturally endorsed formal manners seemed to lift from his shoulders (and from the first subject itself) the expressive burden of the introduction's more "realistic" introversion. From that point of view, the whole direction and intent of the symphony might be associated as much with the social *act* of the Finale as with the prior public *en*actment of the Adagio. If the concert-goer for whom the Adagio is merely a container for a sentimentally hummable tune has missed the "movement," the same habitué of the work is perhaps much closer to the heart of the matter when, at the beginning of the rumbustious proceedings of the Finale, his or her pulse begins to race in anticipation of the coming reward for long symphonic endurance. Does not the stereotyped merriment and portentous marching depend upon an unacknowledged principle of functional, affective redundancy? It takes us back to the very model of that older romantic modernist sonata type whose structure required clear, gesturally heightened articulation and whose emotional vitality depended upon the delayed attainment of transcendent flight: upon the "grand climax," the great tune. The opening celebration seems even designed to permit the audience to continue the process of relaxation and repreparation that has begun during the pause after the emotionally demanding Adagio. The new movement good-naturedly drowns the coughs, creaking chairs, and concluding conversations, giving us to understand that its initiating music forms no more than an advance guard for the eagerly awaited guest of honor.

There is something specifically processional (the potential ambivalence of which image is stressed for a time in the more darkly scored recapitulation) about the second theme. It acts as a "middle section" delay of the return of the opening material, which then works up a great lather of excitement until it is itself caught almost unawares by the briefly announced entry of the grand tune, in the surprising key of D major. Presented in Tchaikovskian triple octaves, over a resolute pedal D and replete with accompanying woodwind and horn chords in excitedly vamping triplets, it is indeed a splendid affair. Irresistibly it sweeps us off our feet and up through a warm layer of the flat submediant toward the aspiring figure in bar six. Yet even this grandest and most intentionally "consumable" melody in the symphony reveals its heart and true nature in the initial four-bar phrase by which it announces itself, and which we will most likely carry away with us at the end: an emphatically, gesturally physical descending phrase built out of a series of downward-swooping sighs of sheer abandonment: abandonment to fate, to ourselves, to things "as they must be" perhaps, while here signaling celebration and affirmation.

By reading the theme in this fashion we are approaching the paradoxically serious and "modern" way in which the symphony might be regarded as conservative: not on the crude level of stylistic fashion, but in the more precise, social sense that it tends to reinforce a social status quo while again also signaling the fated inoperancy of the individual will and private subjective experience. This message is significantly stressed in the ensuing direct reference back to the Adagio (the main theme with the introductory "motto" as counter-subject) and the still darker references to the introduction itself that are made in the otherwise purely functional development section. However, the social bonding that the Finale theme ensures even more clearly in its last, deliberately delayed apotheosis proves rationally groundless in a most striking way—depending upon nothing but the very emotional charge that it generates: the nostalgic recollection of a grounded togetherness that could gloriously signify childhood, love, the past, "mother Russia," or whatever.

We might conceive of Rachmaninov having taken Tolstoy's concerns so much to heart that the modernistically inclined subjective realism celebrated in this symphony, and many related works of the period, permits no illusory symbolic drama of musical resolution, of "work from within" (as Adorno put it), but rather represents a conscious process of constructing a bridge between himself as egocentric subject and the audience, of which social body he was also a member. The very forms in which he sought to "express himself" and win success were, as I have suggested, the creation and requirement *of* that audience. The grand Rachmaninovian melody, with all its "volitional impotence," may prove after all to have something of the quality, *pace* Tolstoy, of the new symphonic folksong of a culture in crisis. Perhaps it bears all the weaknesses and strengths of that culture in a way that, by being intentionally consumable and usable by it (rather than standing critically apart from it), sets out an alternative means of reestablishing the link between bourgeois artifice and popular, or "folk," art that had, in a sense, been Wagner's goal. As with Strauss, the particular "folk" concerned were, of course, precisely bourgeois folk, at heart if not in purse, and wearing neither the fake peasant costume of the nationalist nor wielding mythological swords, for all that they may have harbored fond memories of both.

Here was an aristocrat of sensibility, or "decadent," who was able to communicate that sensibility to the widest possible audience, who could exercise his romantic desire to "exult," as he once put it, more effectively in the institutionalized form, replete with Adorno's "noisily blown-up fillers" and "nationally tinged thematics," than in the more modern subjective representation of pessimistic "soul states" (the phrase is Rachmaninov's). He nevertheless also excelled in those and was no less committed to their expression, believing (as he told Olin Downes in 1919) that it was "possible to be very serious, to have something to say, and at the same time to be popular."[37]

COSMOPOLITAN ECSTASY

I will approach my second and more recherché late-romantic "conservative" from a different direction, from the viewpoint not so much of an expectant concert audience as of the passionate musical enthusiasm of a young Yorkshireman, himself a consumer of music (albeit from the cultural margins). He nevertheless appears to combine the roles of the musician as professional "authority" and the lay listener in a revealing and striking way. He was himself a naturally talented, if largely self-taught practitioner: a God-fearing church organist since the age of twelve, he happened to have perfect pitch. Thanks to the advent of the modern media, he was also part of a new, more disseminated audience for music, of which he was able to hear quite a wide range on records and on the radio. It is 1926 or 1927, and he was about twenty-one years old. Neither he nor history has told us whether, like Joseph Berglinger, he was vouchsafed visionary or transcendental experiences while playing the organ of a cold Sunday morning in Scarborough Parish Church, but he was getting to hear some more or less modern music that was, he discovered, able to move him profoundly in ways that appeared to run somewhat counter to his nature and would-be music-professional status. We know he discovered Elgar in this way and that he later wrote of his belief that the beginning of the second part of *The Dream of Gerontius* expressed "the mood which savours of the heavenly world wherein lies our destiny . . .—the most blessed felicity, by which I mean an active and loving rest in God."[38] He thus comes into focus as a petit bourgeois "spiritual" type whom we might easily mock. But other music was moving him, too, in the 1920s: the music of Delius, for example, who by then was blind and paralyzed and in the process of dying slowly and agonizingly from syphilis in his house in France.

Eric Fenby, our organist, would tell the story in his own way, and I let him speak:

> I had known on first hearing it that the music of this man was no ordinary music. It had moved me strangely and unaccountably. . . .
> When at last, after weeks of enquiries and disappointments, I was able to peruse the vocal score of his *Mass of Life,* I had stood spellbound in the little

music shop of my native town as I read that soul stirring and original passage for Solo Contralto which, rendered into English by Thomas Common, reads:

> "O Zarathustra! Beyond good and evil found we our island and our green meadow."

As I read on, a cold thrill ran through me at the magical entry of the chorus basses, singing sotto voce:

> "O Man! Take heed!. . . "

and my musings continued. . . . I knew nothing of Nietzsche. It was the music that struck me to the heart so that I could scarcely think for days.[39]

Sadly, nowadays the very mention of Delius's name can send some people running (it has even been deliberately used to disperse groups of young people supposedly bent on vandalizing ticket machines in railway stations).[40] Where it is invoked it has come to stand for the mythical passivity and self-indulgence of late-romantic music under the negative banner of "decadence." Fenby nevertheless went on to find out more and was so affected that he wrote to Delius offering to help him, becoming his secretary and amanuensis until Delius died in 1933. Fenby laboriously took down from dictation some of Delius's later music, which he subsequently wrote about in his extraordinary little memoir *Delius as I Knew Him*.[41]

It is important to point out that when Eric Fenby finally did learn something about Nietzsche, he liked what he learned as little as he liked the paintings by Edvard Munch and Paul Gauguin that Delius had around the house—as little as he liked Delius's irreligious scorn of his new assistant's faith or his tendency to make proclamations like "When a man tells me he likes Mozart, I know in advance he's a bad musician."[42] Delius had lived the life of a Parisian decadent. He had in fact been born in Yorkshire in 1863 to German émigré parents, been sent to Florida as a young man to manage an orange grove his father had bought, but had opted for music instead and had returned to Europe to study at the Leipzig Conservatory and take up the career of a composer; he also traveled widely in Scandinavia before finally settling in France in a village outside Paris with his painter wife, Jelka Rosen. Delius, at his best a master of Seidl's "modern musical lyric" style, seems to fit the model of a sort of English Des Esseintes of music—and we saw earlier how like an angry old colonel he could become in later life: inveighing against Russian impresarios, Parisian decadents, and the press. He had every reason to know about such things, being himself an atheist and

Nietzschean aesthete who seemed to be on friendly terms with every bohemian artist in Europe, including the Australian Percy Grainger. Claiming later that there "was no" English music, he was, in truth, ever the alien. It may even be wrong to claim Delius as an English composer at all. In a period of European music history still dominated by Germany, Delius had a following *in* Germany before ever in Britain (and then thanks to the work of Sir Thomas Beecham)—and it was in Germany, and in German, that many of his significant earlier works were published and first performed.

Apart from a series of striking orchestral and choral pieces like *A Mass of Life*, *Sea Drift*, and *The Song of the High Hills*, there were also operas from which we can learn much. They are now largely neglected for some easily accountable reasons. A couple of early examples were never staged; one was *The Magic Fountain* (1895), which climaxes impracticably in a part-balletic, grand-operatic revelation of the Fountain of Eternal Life at the end of a cinematic sequence of scenes that take us from a shipwreck at sea to a palm-fringed beach, a Seminole Indian encampment and a number of spectacularly different locations in the rich swamp forests of the Florida Everglades. Two of his finest stage works were *A Village Romeo and Juliet* and *Koanga*, both conceived in the 1890s, the latter, like *The Magic Fountain*, reflecting Delius's Florida experiences in ways that we must undoubtedly approach with caution. How closely did the hauteur of those assumed decadent manners of the aesthete match the model of the conservative aristocrat projected by the author of that article in *The Sackbut*, who in other circumstances might have been expected to want nothing to do with art of *any* kind? I turn here to *Koanga* as a work whose dramatization of a version of the "colonial" experience potently aligns late-romantic musical visions, aspirations, and lamentations with some provocatively revealing onstage musical theater.

The opera could be described as a powerful realization of an extraordinary scenario, but with a dreadful libretto. Douglas Craig and Andrew Page tried to rewrite it in 1974, so painfully did the original resound a vision of Africans, and particularly African slaves, that would have been encountered in Victorian drawing rooms in ways that now properly embarrass us.[43] Slavery may well have gone by the 1890s, but colonial-imperialist attitudes toward Africans had not, and a chorus of slaves singing "Come out, niggers" will of course no longer do (the text of the chorus is reproduced below). But beyond the language, whose meanings have changed, there lies a rich vein of Delius's experiences of hearing his Florida plantation workers in what he believed to be harmonically improvised renderings of slave songs and spirituals as night fell. Tolstoyan "folk" voices emblematically emerge through the nostalgic web of late-romantic lyricism and elaborately nuanced musical evocation. "Dark is the night. The distant voices call . . .," warn Koanga's escaped negro followers as their master prays to mysterious powers in the nocturnal forest, before enacting a ritual curse upon his former masters. Koanga, the Voodoo priest and African prince, had, following his treacherous enslavement, been shipped to America, where he would be tamed with a lamentable sexual bribe: he is offered the pretty mixed-race Palmyra in return for his cooperation. But on his supposed "wedding night" his white masters abduct Palmyra, who turns out to be an illegitimate daughter of the plantation boss's father-in-law (and is loved unrequitedly by his current overseer). Shocked and enraged, Koanga bitterly repents of what he now sees as unjustified treachery to his own people and escapes into the forest.

Here the problems multiply, many stemming from often ill-informed alterations to the 1880 source-novel, *The Grandissimes* by George Cable, in the rather bungled efforts to turn it into an opera libretto by Charles Keary with the involvement of Delius and others.[44] Apart from inaccuracies about the names of "Voodoo" (or vodoun) gods and numerous failures of dramatic logic, which Craig and Page tried to sort out, the characterization of Koanga himself is embarrassing for its tendency to present him as a creature whose evident nobility is associated with wayward impulsiveness; he repeatedly forgets or repudiates his African status and Voodoo beliefs at the merest sight or recollection of Palmyra, with whom he falls instantly and unconvincingly in love at first sight in act 1. But Craig and Page are right to observe that his part is nevertheless "imbued with great dignity throughout."[45] This contradiction is key to understanding what the opera is essentially "about" and how this strange attempt at an exotic, melodramatic opera (hardly uncommon in the nineteenth century) mediated something central to Delius's late-romantic nostalgia for his complicatedly conditioned experience of Negroes and "their" music (he had, typically, first encountered it in entirely fake form in black-face minstrel shows in Bradford before coming closer to its reality in Florida).

Structurally, the opera takes the form of a narrative flashback—a tale told by "an old slave" (Uncle Joe) to a group of white girls who have escaped from the all-night dancing in a *Gone-with-the-Wind*-style plantation house in Louisiana. They have heard the tale before, but want him to tell it again. As he begins, an orchestral interlude takes over and mist fills the stage. When it clears, we find ourselves in the world of his story and see the eighteenth-century plantation by night, with slave huts and sugarcane fields in the moonlight. More importantly we have heard, in the interlude, a fine piece of expansive scene setting in the midst of which has gradually emerged an idealized vision of one of Delius's great "American" themes, deriving from the world of Europeanized spirituals but generously signifying the space, the people, and "otherness" of an imagined American South that included his reimagined Florida. In the opera the theme returns to conclude the first slave chorus, which comes at the end of their onstage "awakening" as they are roughly roused from their slumbers. It is then soon heard *off*stage, coming now "from the fields"; the revised text as printed for a Beecham performance in 1935 ran as follows:

> Come out, niggers, come out to cut the waving cane,
> The moonlight shadows are faded and the day is back again.
> The humming-bird is waking, no nigger dares complain
> When once they please to call us to the fields of sugar cane.[46]

The powerful effect of the distantly sung version of this takes us to the heart of *Koanga*. It is really a dramatic symphony with interpolated enacted scenes whose theatrical logic is entirely subordinated to the larger musical drama in which the slave chorus moves from the foreground to the picturesque background, but remains the main protagonist. Its power and its threat are personified in Koanga, with whom Delius manifestly identifies as the tragic hero of the opera. His beloved Palmyra's mixed-race status is important in that it presents her with painful choices of affiliation attendant upon her belonging to both white and black races. When the escaped Koanga returns to claim her and release her from the curse he has put on the plantation, he is killed. Palmyra not only then stabs herself, but also first renounces her own Christian faith and embraces Voodoo. The opera concludes with an Epilogue—or rather, perhaps, with the extended orchestral interlude that leads *into* it. This is dominated by a new musical figure that had first appeared as a counterpoint to Koanga's own motif when Palmyra had observed to the plantation manager, after Koanga's brutal death, that he had "passed beyond your anger." The unfolding and transfiguring stages of its musical emergence lead us back through the mist to an Epilogue in which Uncle Joe now remains significantly silent and where the plantation girls console themselves rather tamely, rather shockingly, with the hope that the rising sun will make all well again and allow them to hope that "true love will find happiness." But the theme with which the orchestra closes the work is the one that we had heard in the very first interlude, the song of the slaves whose fate and whose brutal treatment apparently play no part in the girls' irresponsibly escapist fantasy. This unresolved doubleness of purpose has understandably led Eric Saylor to observe that Koanga "is not necessarily what it appears to be."[47]

The relevant questions have been implicit throughout this chapter: questions, I suppose, about the politics of those engulfing passions of our decadent late-romantic aesthetes and, indeed, their potential audiences. Christopher Small approaches a version of such questions when, early in his book *Musicking,* he reveals that he can hardly bear to listen to the *St. Matthew Passion,* "so powerfully, so cogently does it embody a myth that to me is profoundly antipathetic." "Marvellous music it is, indeed," he confesses, "but marvelous for what?"[48] At the end of the book he comes out with it: "Was even Mozart wrong? Is there something in the nature of the works of the classical concert repertory that makes the act of performing and listening to them under any circumstances go counter to the way human relationships should be?"[49]

It is an extreme question indeed, if what I am trying to do is to encourage us to become better historically informed about, and responsive to, late-romantic music. Should we just put it all back in the historical filing cabinet with a cautionary label attached: "We know where it led ..."? My treatment of these works that still move me and draw me into their historical world, as if speaking in a kind of vernacular, would be all too evasively "historical" if I were to ignore critical questions about their cultural and ethical character. As always, perhaps, it is the distant sounds, those distant voices in the night that tell us most.

The work to which we might turn to hear them at their clearest is one that is closely linked to *Koanga* and others of Delius's "American" works. This is *Appalachia*—not the earlier, and also fascinating, *American Rhapsody* of the same name, but the later, longer version first performed in 1905 and called *Appalachia: Variations on an Old Slave Song with Final Chorus.* Philip Heseltine notes that the original included a "prefixed note" explaining the title *Appalachia* as "the old Indian name of North America. The composition mirrors the moods of tropical nature ... so intimately associated with the life of the old negro slave population: longing, melancholy, an intense love for nature, childlike humour and an innate delight in dancing and singing are still the most characteristic qualities of their race."[50]

This hardly dispels postcolonial anxieties. A perhaps more accurate translation of the complete German text might read as follows:

> *Appalachia* is the old Indian name for North America. The work mirrors the nature-moods of the expansive tropical swamp of the great Mississippi River, which is so intimately associated with the fates of the negro slaves. Yearning and melancholy, an intense love for nature, co-existing with child-like good-humour [Heiterkeit] and an innate delight in dancing and singing are still the most characteristic qualities of these people.[51]

There is certainly something about this work that merits careful consideration, in the light of what I have suggested about *Koanga*. *Appalachia*, too, begins with what sounds like a nature mood, a subdued evocation of dawn, followed by an opening *allegro* section in which, as the sun rises, an already peculiarly "American" sounding social bustle arises (anticipating both Copland and Bernstein). Gradually we catch parts of the relatively simple little theme on which the often submerged variation structure is based. Submerged, that is, in an apparently freely evolving structure that approximates to the "psychological form" of Arthur Seidl's modern musical lyric in its apparently improvisatory episodes and ever more mysteriously and poignantly nuanced chromatic harmony. Some of the variations are sprightly and clear in outline; others, particularly toward the end of the work, seem to speak in the voice of a troubled listener: the often ecstatic Delian effulgence grows ever more harmonically mysterious and painfully nuanced, and the conclusion of individual variations is marked by the sound of distant choral voices. At first it is just three bars of "la, la, la" for pianissimo tenors and basses. You can hardly hear them; were they even there? Later they are there again in the distance, sounding more Victorian, more English, and politely pastoral—"out there," where the "others" are supposed to be according to colonialist preference, but sounding rather like our friends and neighbors in theatrical fancy dress.

But where was Delius? Physically, one presumes, on his comfortable veranda. But how did he conceive his audience (if at all) or, indeed, his overheard singers? Who might each group include or exclude? The end of the work is provocatively moving given both what had and what had *not* happened at the end of *Koanga*. Where even *does* *Appalachia* end? we might ask. It had almost seemed to close in F major, the key of most of the central part of the work. Here the orchestra stops, and we at last hear the unaccompanied choir sing the "original" song (which is closely related to one of the act 1 choruses in *Koanga*). The distant voices are suddenly foregrounded. There follows, "Misterioso Lento," a wonderfully reflective coda, bringing the work to a close in A flat (it had opened in E flat major). Now we hear the singing voices once again, pushed as if finally back into the cadential margin whence they had come, singing a distantly wordless "ah," *pppp*.

"Dark is the night. . . ." But once again the voices do not *stay* distant here; it is *not* over. The theme resumes yet again, *Lento* and in A flat minor, in the woodwind. Shortly we are back in A flat major for the real final chorus, led by a baritone solo, his part marked *"popolare."* Later versions of the score stipulate that he must be placed with the chorus and *not* in a detached position of conventional musical power beside the conductor.[52] I would propose that what follows is as near as Delius could be expected to get to a practical apology for the end of *Koanga*, and to realizing something approaching a more "authentic" voice for the Negro workers he had heard in Florida. Here their words of hope and old pain are profoundly affecting, as they sing of parting, death, and possible reconciliation. The voices that the work had apparently tried to contain and "place" seem now to break free, their final lamenting "ah" a sad indictment to all of us who might have been listening with a patronizing smile. Undone by historical plot and the gentrified poetry they sing, they are truly and triumphantly "envoiced" (as Carolyn Abbate might have put it);[53] the sopranos even chance a perilous *fortissimo* high C at the climax on "scented woods":

> *Solo:* Oh Honey I am going down the river in the morning.
> *Chorus:* Heigh-ho, heigh-ho, down the mighty river.
> *Solo & chorus:* Aye! Honey I'll be gone when next the whippoorwill's a'calling.
> And don't you be too lonesome, love and don't you fret and cry;
> For the dawn will soon be breaking, the radiant morn is nigh,
> And you'll find me ever a'waiting.
> [Heigh-ho]
> And you'll find me ever a'waiting, my own sweet Nelly Gray!
> [La, la, la . . .]
> T'ords the morning lift a voice
> Let the scented woods rejoice,
> And echoes swell across the mighty stream.
> [Ah! Ah!]

It might be imagined that a Christopher Small would be eager to express skepticism. Delius's implicit response across the decades came not long after that outburst about Parisian decadents and press agents in his 1920 article in *The Sackbut,* which had continued: "Music is a cry of the soul. It is revelation, a thing to be reverenced. Performances of great works are for us what the rites and festivals of religion were to the ancients—an initiation into the mysteries of the human soul."[54] We still have something to learn from this wayward early-twentieth-century master of late-romantic music at its most publicly vulnerable and nuanced, its most ecstatic and yet nostalgic. Delius's "mysteries" of the human soul existed in close proximity to both its cruelty and its sadness. If *Appalachia* is a work still worth attending to, it is for the moving complexity of the mysteries it reveals, the narratives it both invokes and rejects.

Eric Fenby's initial response to *A Mass of Life* was to value its "music" over its (to him) largely incomprehensible words; his subsequent discovery was that those words and the deeper significance of that work were, together, less congenial than he would have wished. Here was a "modern" music antipathetic to his upbringing and the whole tenor of his relationship with the art he practiced and yet which spoke to him with a profound and perhaps latterly troubling directness. His ambivalent devotion to Delius, in spite of his love for Elgar, was a profound testament to the complexity and power of late-romantic music. No less so was the actual late reconciliation between Delius and Elgar, another great late-romantic who would visit Delius in 1933, bringing gifts that included recordings of music by yet another: Sibelius—to whom we shall return.[55]

CHAPTER 3

Sunsets, Sunrises, and Decadent Oceanics

I listened, I heard, and never did such a voice
Come from a mouth or strike upon an ear.
At first it was a sound, large, immense, confused,
Vaguer than the wind in the forest trees,
Full of ringing notes, of soft murmurs,
Sweet as an evening song, strong as a clash of arms,
When violent fight engulfs the squadrons
And blows, furious, from the trumpets' mouths.
It was a music ineffable and profound
Which flowed and vibrated ever round the world.

—Victor Hugo, *Ce qu'on entend sur la montagne*

My reading, in chapter 1, of Richard Leppert's argument in *The Sight of Sound* suggested that the represented and culturally privileged Music of which he writes there typically performs a key social task akin to repression. Discursively and practically it apportions power unevenly between masculine "contemplation" and feminine "performance," at the expense of genuine musical attention on the one hand and the pleasure of unrestrained bodily engagement on the other (something associated with the threatening disorder of the popular sphere). This is a view that seemed aligned with Christopher Small's critique of the ethos of the public symphony concert devoted to "great, dead composers." My interest here in a particular area of the repertoire of such composers, the so-called late-romantics—who arguably followed uneasily in the footsteps of the great dead without ever quite securing their cultural power or authoritative status—has in a sense led me to step slightly back from Leppert's panoramic "something else" and to return to the new-musicological mode of deciphering "particular musical texts" that he had associated with Lawrence Kramer and Susan McClary (here I might reference in particular the latter's provocative readings of Tchaikovsky's Fourth Symphony and Brahms's Third).[1] My inclination is to want, above all, to remain attentive to the complex subjective character and content of the sort of reception which I suggested Fernand Khnopff's mother, listening to Schumann, might have been embarrassed to reveal to the painter. Rather than her shielded eyes demonstrating what Leppert describes as a "horror of the body" of the performer (thus obscuring the unseemly bodiliness of the music's utopian import), I would argue that they might rather be *protecting* the inward, private character of her response, which could even have embraced the very bodiliness she is anxious to conceal. The social character of such listening is hardly freed from the problematics of which Leppert writes so persuasively, but is richer, less empty of meaning or the contemplative involvement that he had earlier doubted was even *required* by music of the great dead for it to perform its cultural work.

My interest in the "late-romantic" repertoire—with which Leppert does not, in all fairness, directly engage in *The Sight of Sound*—requires the specificity of that familiar label, not to regulate or limit my field (as historical categories like baroque or classical may seek to do) so much as to avoid more critically tendentious ones like *maximalizing* or *decadent*. These, I would propose, are relics of the propagandistic discourse of Modernism which I have sought to avoid, preferring to nuance the disparities and contradictions, as much as to reveal the apparent consistencies within my chosen field. Mahler, Rachmaninov, and Delius, for example, were evidently three very different composers, who catered, perhaps, to the tastes of distinct, if overlapping, audience constituencies, for all their aspirations to universality. As individuals they were different in temperament, background, class, and nationality. However, to link them in a reevaluative study of late-romanticism in music need entail no evasion of those differences, which might be manifest in numerous individual characteristics of their respective works. Sharing the broad syntactic and grammatical features of advanced tonality, those differences in style and nuance could in all probability have been recognized and "read" by their contemporaries as easily as could stylistic differences between Tolstoy, Proust, and Mann by any broadly literate reader of novels, whatever the reader's personal taste. It is, then, at the level of the performance and modes of reception of these composers' works that their cultural-historical affinity is perhaps most clearly seen. All three created compositions for large orchestras that were inevitably intended to be heard in large concert halls or opera houses whose institutional character as sites of musical consumption and entertainment were broadly similar (and the categories "consumption" and "entertainment" might, of course, be modified by a range of more or less value-laden historical descriptors, from "moral and spiritual edification," through "the acquisition of cultural capital" to "mere distraction").

The architecture and internal arrangements of halls and theaters may have differed in a variety of ways, as would details of the layout, performance protocol, and even tuning of the orchestras and singers involved. Still, it would be fair to say that from London to Paris, Amsterdam to Vienna, as far as Budapest or Moscow, or back across the Atlantic to New York (all cities in which Mahler himself incidentally conducted), the concert experience would have been broadly recognizable as similar and the audiences behaved in broadly similar ways. Across large parts of the developed Western world symphony concert and operatic listening habits would also have been comparably mediated by advertisements, journalistic reviews, inexpensive "pocket" or "study" scores, piano reductions and analytical music guides for use in the home—all of which contributed to the thought, debate, and writing about music that enlivened its broadly cosmopolitan character as a cultural institution.

But we have to say more, guided above all by the wealth of material and information about concert life gathered by the historian William Weber in his exhaustively researched work on European musical taste and practice. In the light of that work (and of the many other cultural historians he draws upon), we are obliged to nuance any account of the apparent dominance of one broad "kind" of concert culture by taking note of the contestation over taste within it that is evidenced above all, in the nineteenth century, by the almost simultaneous emergence not only of what Weber calls the "imposing hegemonic status" of classical music by the 1860s, but also of the threat that classical idealists sensed was being posed by the spread of more popular musical entertainments.[2] These were supported by a no less impressive industry of agents, publishers, and performers that overlapped with and often eclipsed that supporting so-called serious music. Weber catalogs a variety of ways in which the ostensible hegemony of classical music in "criticism, pedagogy and civic ceremony" was decisively contested, for example, by "concerts of popular songs designed for the general public."[3] He stresses that the resulting rivalry between "classical" and "popular" musical cultures failed in the late nineteenth century to reinforce any clear sense of class differentiation between their taste communities. Weber nevertheless quotes Bernard Shaw as an example of what he calls an "idealist" who, in the early 1890s, bemoaned the threat of mass culture signaled by the many "miscellaneous" concerts of songs and shorter pieces that attracted "a vast number of people without definite musical ideas, loosely strung good-natured creatures who are attracted solely by the names of the performers."[4]

Who now would not prefer to sympathize retrospectively with those "loosely strung good-natured creatures" rather than the haughtily stern and serious devotees of classical music, with its formal ways, its stamp of civic and even state authority, and its devotion to high-principled edification over mere entertainment? This, of course, is where the cultural character and reception of late-romanticism proves so interesting, as its producers, ostensibly sharing and often disseminating no less serious and stern ideals, worked to gain a foothold in the canonic repertoires of the established orchestras and opera companies. Critical reception suggests that while their successes might have modeled and anticipated the interventions of high-minded modernists to come, before the First World War such composers were no less open to being castigated, like Mahler and Rachmaninov in their different ways, for their *lack of affinity* with classical music, for their inability to compose "real" symphonies and tendency to indulge not only their own emotions but also those of the popular masses to whom they were deemed to be pandering (the implication being that genuine "classical music" was associated with more discriminating refinement and connoisseurship). That difference is significant.

This is where we might return to the literally mediating role of Romanticism—popularizing the "serious" and taking serious the popular—in its foundational construction of "classical music" in the early nineteenth century. Elsewhere in William Weber's work we are reminded by him of the close association of the "rise of musical mass culture with the elevation of the classical masters."[5] It was not just a case of the latter being shored against the ruin threatened by the former. The late-romantic symphony arguably reveals itself to be a key site for the compositional mediation of this tension between high and low, the serious and the popular, and to have been threatened by the newly dominant generic and aesthetic values of the culture upon which its existence relied. A century after the decade (the 1860s) in which Weber locates the achievement of "classical" music's hegemony, Carl Dahlhaus, in his 1967 *Esthetics of Music,* was still happy to define musical "greatness" by means of the twin criteria of "monumentality and the idea of difficulty, of not immediate accessibility."[6] Is it any wonder that late-romantic symphonists were riven by doubts about themselves? (A significant few of them, including Tchaikovsky, Dvořák, and Elgar, were unceremoniously dismissed by Dahlhaus in that same essay.) Tormented by high- and historically minded critics, some were driven to create almost deliberately "unsymphonic" symphonies, like Delius in *Appalachia*—a work whose defining qualities might arguably be characterized not as monumentality and difficulty so much as subtlety and accessibility. In the subtlety lay the mark of self-consciousness in their art. This was, in fact, no less a mark of its Romantic modernity than was the vernacular accessibility of its strategies and meanings. The contradictory agendas of public discourse about music might still seek to hide or even deny access to such meanings.

SYMPHONIC CONFUSIONS

The first performance of the twenty-eight-year-old Mahler's First Symphony in Budapest in 1888 was perhaps a key event in the historical unfolding of the special problematics of the late-romantic symphony. These arose out of its being caught between aspirations to difficult Beethovenian "monumentality" (Dahlhaus's formula was really only a tendentious shorthand theorization of what Schumann was getting at in "Florestan's Shrovetide Oration") and "programmatic" renderings of the symphony's formal structure as narrative, or as drama, in ways that were directly accessible to a lay audience—an issue behind which lurked not only the old mystifications of official Aesthetics, but also more contemporary anxieties about the threat of mass culture as involving a "desecration" of the classically ineffable (that was really not ineffable at all to a self-appointed professional elite).

Mahler, to return to the First Symphony, had presented the work in its earliest form with a mysterious title: "Symphonic Poem in Two Parts"—after which he listed the movements (at that time five, like Berlioz's *Symphonie Fantastique*), indicating that the penultimate movement was in the style of a funeral march (like that in the *Eroica?*). By 1888 everyone knew what a "symphonic poem" was. It had nearly become the dominant new form of the New German School in Liszt's hands in the 1850s: the one-movement symphony (often not much longer than the concert- or opera-overture that it most resembled), whose "meaning" was advertised in a piece of prose or poetry that was printed in the score and outlined the dramatic, narrative, or philosophical content of the piece. A title often named the work's protagonist or the subject of its depiction (as in Liszt's *Tasso: Lamento e Trionfo* or his *Orpheus, Prometheus, Hamlet* and so on).

In Mahler's case the audience was given only a generic title ("Symphonic Poem") and structural hint ("in two parts"; the disposition of the movements between the two parts was also indicated). While the five movements and the title advertised the young composer's apparently intentional affiliation with Berlioz and the New German School, the absence of any actual "program" or further guidance as to the work's content or meaning was oddly confusing—not least in the presence of the performed work. Critics openly questioned Mahler's apparently perverse decision to *conceal* his program: in spite of the pastoral tropes, stylized birdsong and folk dance allusions of the first "part," and in even greater spite (as one might put it) of the audience's inevitable confusion when faced with the bizarre goings-on of the "funeral march" and the epic but somewhat inchoate drama of the Finale.[7]

The critical reaction instructively confounded Mahler's apparent decision to opt for a judicious pleasing of all camps—specifically those of the Schumannesque "classical" idealists and the "popular" hermeneuticists. The latter were given license to hear narrative and see images but no clue as to what they might actually be. Of course if he *had* decided (as he later did) to provide some kind of detailed "program," Mahler would have been a ready target for the idealists and preachers of ineffability. Instead of appreciating his decision to let the "readers" construe the meaning for themselves, they accused him of obfuscatory concealment. This was not a game one could easily win.

Liszt himself certainly had not done so in the 1850s; but then his struggle to establish himself convincingly as a "serious" composer in Weimar was always a critical hostage to the historical character of his long association as a pianist with the more popular world of virtuosos and Italian opera.[8] This was in spite of his attempts as a performer to educate his popular audience in the ways of "serious" music (given that he was a Romantic "classicist" at heart, who knew his Beethoven) and of his symphonic poems' choice of subjects from high-flown poetry, history, and "classic" literature. Hanslick did not help, of course, but there were those who grasped what it was that Liszt was trying to do—Wagner, for one. The "New German School" stone he set rolling was in fact to gather a great deal of momentum (moss, for some) during the latter part of the nineteenth century.

So many of the most interesting late-romantic composers, from whose number Debussy and Sibelius will occupy the greater part of this chapter, were thus ever caught "between" the symphony and the symphonic poem, trying at their boldest to fuse the two in a way that spoke profoundly of the underlying cultural politics of the confusion and its roots in Romanticism. The contemporary *fleurs du mal* of that confusion (as some would have regarded them) blossomed profusely in the soil of the debate over musical "meaning" which was also a cultural-political debate about the contested rights of the "popular" and "classical" taste communities. The "aesthetic" debate was always a kind of sham, a cover for what Richard Taruskin comes closer than many to explaining in his Oxford History section on Liszt's symphonic poem *Les Préludes* (1854). That work's public association with some high-flown poetic thoughts by Alphonse de Lamartine about the meaning of life has been demonstrated to have been the product of Liszt's second thoughts about this piece—the music having originated in some movements of choral music called collectively *The Four Elements*. For all his musicological inclination to hold on to the contestability and negotiability of musical meaning, Taruskin points out that "associative meanings of all kinds . . . are virtually by definition conventional, hence artificial"[9]—something applicable not just to music but to all sign systems and all language, of course. We should be clear that "ineffability" is itself just another sort of associative meaning.

Taruskin's longtime intellectual sparring partner, Lawrence Kramer, has made a valuable point in his fine essay on Beethoven's *The Ruins of Athens,* apropos the whole heated debate about musical meaning and interpretation, observing that "music begins living up to its potential for critical inquiry, its capacity to be read, the moment when we realize that reading and listening are not antithetical. Listening is a reading, too. Representational listening is not a compromised or lower form; it is just an explicit one."[10] The more precise relevance of all this to our period may be clarified with reference to some of those debates about musical meaning, in which the fascinating, if all too frequently forgotten, critic Paul Bekker figured variously as protagonist and respondent. I referred to him in the previous chapter as a target of the conservative composer and polemicist Hans Pfitzner around 1920. In that same decade, the author of that offending book about Beethoven and the "poetic idea" in music had responded appositely to the idealist and conservative mystifications of Heinrich Schenker's "analytical" work on Beethoven.

Thanks to the more recent work of Matthew Pritchard, we learn that Bekker's response to Schenker's monograph on Beethoven's Ninth Symphony was to side less with Schenker, as self-appointed successor to Schumann, than with the nonprofessional late-romantic listener.[11] Such a listener might even, Bekker ventured, have a better understanding of the Ninth than the authoritarian analyst: "I can analyse Beethoven's Ninth Symphony harmonically and thematically, right down to the last details, and yet inwardly may stand further from the work than some listener who knows not the first thing about compositional technique."[12] The politics of this matter were clarified in Schenker's (originally unpublished) response: "[Bekker] appears to rely for support on the widely-read *Frankfurter Zeitung*, in whose service he is engaged. But that . . . is only a daily newspaper and, secondly, only a democratic paper. And so I can say boldly that I am stronger than Bekker and his paper—his shield—because I am engaged in the service of the aristocracy of genius."[13]

Never more than in this period were the politics of music-aesthetic hobbyhorses so startlingly clarified. They performed a tense, confusing, but oddly creative role in the period in underpinning the ascendancy of late-romantic symphonic music as the supreme art of sharing in public ostensibly "private" experiences, aspirations, and intimations—variously intellectual, emotional, and bodily; sometimes grandiose, sometimes of the utmost intimacy and complexity—in the certain knowledge that official criticism could do no more than deny that music was a medium in which *anything* could really be revealed, save the lack of class, the lack of "genius" of its perpetrators.

"LATENT" AND REVEALED CONTENT

It was in this way that what Taruskin, writing about Shostakovich, has called "latent content" (implied but not clarified, and therefore apparently negotiable) came to play so central a part in late-romantic symphonism.[14] It was also in this way that the reconstruction and clarification of musical meaning in the public domain by a composer like Liszt was to present such a critical problem to those who might have wished to keep the lay bourgeois public firmly under the control of the aristocrats of genius. Perhaps the underlying social and cultural politics here help us no less to understand something of the reason why Schenker's scorn of the unmusical masses was oddly appropriated by Second Viennese School modernists and the avant-garde that they inspired. All of them tended, like Adorno and Dahlhaus, to be unceasing in their disparagement of various of their late-romantic forbears, construed as ineffectual bourgeois liberals who still believed naively in the Romantic mission and possibilities of Art, whose highest achievements, post-1918 modernists might retort, would nevertheless be left to *them,* as anti-bourgeois revolutionaries whose only remaining move could be to reappropriate the aesthetic values of the "aristocrats of genius" whom they had deposed, but to do so in the interest of a "higher" democracy. That, of course, would exclude their late-romantic progenitors and the mass lay audience which they had served (did they construe its members as uniformly bourgeois?).

This ventured, admittedly somewhat tendentious reading of the situation leads me to concentrate deliberately here on two composers who have been treated with more interest and sympathy by their modernist and avant-garde successors than the more obviously elitist-seeming (and often -acting) Rachmaninov or Delius. Debussy and Sibelius are certainly much more likely to feature in the early chapters of those progressively orientated histories of "Musical Modernism" or "Twentieth-Century Music." To reinterpret these two figures as significant exemplars of late-romantic symphonism is thus a deliberate provocation: one that leads me to recall my suggestion in the previous chapter that there might even be some sort of equation between the late-nineteenth-century symphony concert experience and that of the music of twentieth-century mass culture. My polemical impulse there, aroused somewhat by Christopher Small, was reinforced by the nature of the dismissive tropes often employed by critics of the late-romantic project. Of course the comparison ignores significant differences in register and social constitution between the two types of musical practice and has little to do with any crudely empirical totting-up of audience numbers for, and wider cultural impact of, say, Rachmaninov as opposed to Delius, or either as opposed to Beethoven or the Beatles. My assertion remains that all of the composers I am discussing here were contributors to an ultimately transnational project of refining a "modern" style of post-Wagnerian (and indeed post-Tchaikovskian) tonal music, experientially direct and expressively complex, for an orchestra of a size that would have been unthinkable without the public symphony concert as a stable cultural institution. This also, of course, required an audience of musical consumers prepared to pay for tickets, buy programs, piano arrangements, and study-scores—the last two being things that Eric Fenby could still access in a local music shop in Scarborough in the 1920s (as well as being able to experience both established and newer music on records and in radio broadcasts). Was he, and were they, consuming these things for purely "social" reasons, to accrue cultural capital? That I very much question, as I would question the longer-term historical relevance of James H. Johnson's suggestion that increasing silence in the mid-nineteenth-century concert hall was a function of audiences' need to concentrate on something they did not know how to "listen to."[15] Were those audiences really made up of Shaw's "loosely strung, good-natured creatures," hitherto attracted "solely by the names of the performers"?

It is certainly clear that class and the commoditized image of decadent aristocratic idealism were often rather deliberately part of the product they were consuming. Delius and Rachmaninov matched the image and both had their day and their admiring audiences—that very fact playing a significant part in their vigorous cultural "othering" by the "serious" versus "popular" opposition as it became repoliticized and reappropriated by high-modernists preaching the "collapse of tonality." Richard Taruskin has provided his own compelling historical account of this as being at once to claim the idealist high ground and to exclude all but the most soberly attentive and undemonstrative audiences *from* it, referring, for example, to the Schoenberg circle's post–First World War "Society for the Private Performances of Music" in Vienna.[16] In a sense their aim turned into the one of aggressively historicizing and putting a plague on all late-romantic houses, reviving the old bourgeois put-downs of "decadent," "fin de siècle," and so forth. But in shipping them all off to a critical gulag where their voices would become ever more distant, because (it was hinted) they were all really singing devils, the Schoenberg faction performed a discursive critical maneuver that we are not obliged to accept. Nor should we accept its implied construction of the wider audience as simply naively susceptible or mindlessly philistine.

We can, of course, now see that that essentializing move was profoundly indebted to Romanticism. As a product of the ostensible idealism of Schumann's *Davidsbund,* it had been implicit in the selective misanthropy that had assailed Wackenroder's Joseph Berglinger when coming out of his transcendent musical experiences, only to find himself among "the most vulgar of vulgar people." It was a fantasy elitism (since Berglinger was really one of them) like that of Huysmans's Des Esseintes—who was just a character in a novel, after all. It was nonetheless one that was bound up with productive tensions both within society as a whole and within late-romantic musical culture. One such tension was hinted at in my double-image juxtaposition of Friedrich's solitary artist-dreamer on the mountain heights and the grand metropolitan symphony concert in which the fruit of such dreams is laboriously presented and "performed" for gain and social advancement, just as Friedrich's painting might itself be displayed, perhaps purchased and redisplayed in ways which would subtly nuance its contextual meaning and its maker's name and reputation.

Another, related tension was manifested precisely in the way in which Taruskin's "latent meaning" was mediated by those for whom recent music around 1900 was something by which they were genuinely moved, excited, or "carried away" (that phrase being echoed in 1950s and '60s popular culture by the related notion of being "sent" by music that inspired you to hear it and feel it again, and again, and again). Their eagerness to clarify and comprehend their experience as something shared, related to something perhaps "expressed" by the composer (as conventional talk had it), fed the desire for confirmation and reinforcement that fueled the general appetite for "programs" and reported "statements by the composer." All such things, as I have suggested, were part of the wider Romantic discourse about music which was engaged in an unfolding process of construal and construction of what serious music, "classical music," was—a process that for most of our composers, and certainly for performers like Liszt, Rachmaninov, and Mahler, was one in which creativity and its contemplation fed on each other in ways that heightened the "Berglinger complex" of art-enthusiasm leading to a desire more fruitfully, and ever more effectively to recapture and model that enthusiasm in new art. Its public failure, through uncomprehending initial reception, might thus break the bond between aspiration and realization and lead to self-doubt and even alienation. The experience of art could be both gloriously ideal and disappointingly deceptive; we are returned to distant sounds and singing devils.

It is for this reason that the programs of "programmatic" works of late-romanticism are as important as the confused first audience for Mahler's First Symphony suspected. Of special relevance to the two composers I shall be exploring in the rest of this chapter is the prefatory program to what came to be numbered as the "first" of Liszt's symphonic poems. Its French title—*Ce qu'on entend sur la montagne* (1850–57)—is often reduced in Germany simply to "Berg-Symphonie" ("Mountain Symphony"); it derives from the Victor Hugo poem that is printed at the head of the score, a part of whose opening section forms the epigraph to this chapter. It is another dream, a kind of "vision," in which the poet offers a discursive paraphrase on an actual experience of nature. He sits high on a coastal mountain, the sea on one side of him and an inland valley on the other. Like many nineteenth-century "programs," not least those of the Romantic-classicist Liszt, it outlines a kind of developing allegorical definition of music—or rather, we might say, of the new music of the mid-nineteenth century.

At first the poet indulges in textbook idealism of a neo-Platonic hue. Here Nature—all he sees and hears of it from his vantage point—is associated with an idealized music:

> a music ineffable and profound
> Which flowed and vibrated ever round the world,
> . . .
> the world, encompassed in the symphony,
> As it floats in air, floats in harmony.[17]

Our poet becomes absorbed in contemplation of it, hearing "ethereal harps," yet being "lost in that voice as if lost in a sea." This, in essence, is the eighteenth-century Sublime. But shortly the poet begins to hear more in the sound, to hear *two* voices:

> One comes from the seas: song of glory! blissful hymn!
> It was the voice of the waves talking to each other;
> The other, which rose from the earth that we inhabit,
> Was sad: it was the murmuring of man.

Initially the poet tries to reunite the two voices in a "great concert," as if in effective counterpoint with each other. As he contemplates them, however, their difference and even opposition becomes ever more troubling:

> And I asked myself why we live on earth.
> What, after all, is the purpose of all this?
> What can the soul do? Is it better to exist or to live?
> And why the Lord, who alone can read His book,
> Mingles eternally in a fatal marriage
> The song of Nature and the cries of Humanity?

Once again we seem to be preparing the ground for Mahler's Second Symphony, and perhaps the Third (with its "redeeming" celebration of "all life" in a genial inspiration that will weld the two voices back together again). The *Berg-Symphonie* itself is a fascinating, if not wholly convincing exploration of a kind of sonata duality that refuses to "resolve" in transcendent unity, while generating much Beethovenian storm and stress, along with the tremolando "misterioso e tranquillo" susurrations of a protean Nature that open the work. Timeless "existence" against time-bound "living"? Variously mediated evocations of nature were always more than merely picturesque evocations of the pastoral in late-nineteenth-century music. In fact they grew bleaker and stranger as the late-romantic project unfolded and expanded across many national boundaries (for all that "nature" readily signifies specific landscapes and nationalism in one kind of standard historical narrative). Nature certainly sold (as still it does), and not least, in our period, because artists, poets, and composers came from the same milieu as their consumers, whose urban preoccupations and escapist aspirations they shared.

I stress that it was always potentially more than the conventional pleasure of evoking or "representing" Nature in all its registers: from the pastorally welcoming to the inspirational and liberating "wide far distances—the great solitude" of Delius's *Song of the High Hills*.[18] Further still beyond that lay the terrifying sublime of Sibelius's *Tapiola*. Arnold Schoenberg's own great late-romantic cantata, *Gurrelieder* (1901–13), began allegorically with an expansively evoked sunset and ended with a chorally hymned sunrise: positioned there as the evocation of a "real" Nature in spring, celebrated in "modern" Nietzschean fashion as replacing and transcending the old-romantic mythology and religious fantasy of the love story of Tove and Waldemar.

If the seriously philosophical side of German Nature is represented there, as it was in Liszt's *Berg-Symphonie*, reminding us of its intended relationship to the idealized construction of cerebrally spiritual "classical music," we should remember that late-nineteenth-century critics were nonetheless ready to mock the "musical philosophy" of Mahler and Richard Strauss—particularly in those composers' Nietzsche-inspired masterpieces of 1896 (the Third Symphony and *Also sprach Zarathustra*—to which Delius's *A Mass of Life* was added between 1899 and 1905). Such criticism tended to avoid engaging with the intense and exciting kind of musical experience they purveyed—which was, in a sense, both part of the "philosophy" and what concert audiences sought. This, as I have suggested, was also a matter of physicality, intimacy, and even eroticism. The latter was celebrated in the period no less in the more marginalized, if still commercialized, realm of songs and the solo piano miniature.

Such things were often reckoned to comprise the part of a composer's output that was more pragmatically linked to the ready market for domestic music, purchasable (if not always performable) by amateurs. The case of Chopin is interesting here, as are the piano works of some of his late-romantic successors, like Rachmaninov's friend and contemporary the mystical eroticist Alexander Scriabin (composer also of three remarkable symphonies and the 1905–7 *Poem of Ecstasy* for the grandest of late-romantic orchestras). Debussy, too, might be associated with the late nineteenth-century's re-reading and reappropriation of Chopin. The widespread popularity of that early master of Seidl's "new musical lyric" style rather annoyed Theodor Adorno, who explained it in terms of what he called the "socialization" (meaning the popularization) of Chopin's often feminized expressive pathos, designed for the overrefined "soirées of high society." In this case, Adorno thought, reception probably confused rather than illuminated the true relationship of music and class, the true "social sense" of Chopin's music.[19]

Chopin's end-of-century popularity certainly seems to have been related to the consumably decadent sensuality of esoteric late romantics like Debussy and Scriabin, in their different ways. It also effected a sort of rapprochement with the more widely consumed salon genres. The popular-serious tension nevertheless lurked, as did late-romantic theorists intent upon resolving it. The notorious Polish novelist and sensualist Stanislaus Przybyszewski even produced in 1892 a contribution "Zur Psychologie des Individuums" entitled *Chopin und Nietzsche,* in which the composer and the philosopher were closely compared as what he called *Rauschkünstler* (artists of "intoxication" or "ecstasy'): as protagonists of the "new art."[20]

The implied character of that new art reflected one of the central models of dramatized and "physicalized" musical form, whose meaning was most often left "latent," although the handsome younger Liszt seems to have recognized it as part of his own audience appeal. The model was precisely one of eroticized sensuality, even explicitly sexual representation and expression that readily mobilized mass cultural worries in the higher-minded critics of late-romantic music. Thanks to Lawrence Dreyfus's recent book on Wagner and eroticism, one might think here of Clara Schumann's revulsion when she heard *Tristan* for the first time: "It was the most repulsive thing I have ever seen or heard in my life. To be forced to see and listen to such sexual frenzy the whole evening in which every feeling of decency is violated and by which not just the public but even musicians seem to be enchanted."[21] High-minded critics were ready to sympathize with her, in even more forthright terms. William Tappert went so far, in 1876, as to denounce

Wagner's more overtly "sexual" music not only as "immoral and noxious" but as appealing somehow only to decadents and (of course) women. "Hysterical wenches and nervously effeminate men" was his precise, and revealing, formulation.[22]

DEBUSSY'S OCEANICS

For all his anti-Wagnerism, Debussy's music was often accused of appealing to a similar kind of audience. For reasons, perhaps, of national-political pride, he publicly distanced himself from Germanic intellectualism and symphonic grandiosity in favor of a supposedly French sensuality, as if sympathizing and siding with Nietzsche's later anti-Wagnerian proclamation: "Il faut méditerraniser la Musique!"[23] But his own late-romantic credentials included a mode of idealism that was manifested in his desire to encourage public mystification of the craft of composition, which was to be rendered "invisible" like the technology and orchestral apparatus of Bayreuth or the modern cinema. Investing in the uniqueness of artistic vision, Debussy was ready to observe that socioeconomic success "spoils an artist for me, such is my fear that he will become merely an expression of society."[24] Expressing his own proto-"modernism" in the following, entirely post-Wagnerian and late-romantic fashion, Debussy wanted his music to sound "as if not written down":[25]

> Like the art of an enquiring savage discovering music step by step through his emotions. Nor is there ever a question of any particular form; at all events the form is so varied that by no possibility whatsoever can it be related to any established, one might say official, form, since it depends on, and is made up of successive minute touches mysteriously linked together by means of an instinctive clairvoyance.[26]

In the spirit of this aesthetic credo, rich in implication, I can hardly avoid quoting again what is perhaps Debussy's most famous denunciation (as "Monsieur Croche") of conventional practitioners of his art, presumably of Germanic inclination or origin: "Musicians listen only to the music written by cunning hands, never to that which is in Nature's script. To see the sun rise is more profitable than to hear the *Pastoral Symphony*."[27]

My first specific example of Debussy's luxuriously consumable realizations of his aesthetic project as outlined in such statements must take us back to the sea, in this case after the sun has set. . . . The moon is up and the sea evoked is gentle, rocking, alluring; it rises and falls as, imaginatively or actually, we consign ourselves to its motion, variously caressed and buoyed up by its directionless swell. We "give way" to it as if consigning ourselves to maternal arms. And then we hear voices: mysterious female voices, indeed, wordlessly humming or simply exhaling as in a musical sigh—to themselves? For us?

Debussy's *Sirènes,* from the *Nocturnes* (first performed in 1901), is almost too good, or perhaps "bad," to be true in this context. Here is a piece of alluringly "decadent" late-romantic music (I am going to abandon all the other more usual labels) that nevertheless seems to carry its own health warning for the musical hedonists it would have delighted. It explicitly invokes those Sirens who lured sailors to their deaths in Homer, suggesting that its decadence might be so thematized as to turn it into irony or even back into a prototypical form of modernism. Or perhaps we might see it as the "anti-Finale" of the *Nocturnes*' implied three-movement choral symphony that was deliberately subverting Beethoven and Germanic absolutism with a programmatic piece of knowing French sensuality. In his great early novel of bourgeois German life, *Buddenbrooks,* Thomas Mann had even proposed that where mountains represented Nature for healthy spirits (but let us not forget Strauss's *Alpine Symphony* and all that lurked in *its* shadow), the sea was the landscape of choice of sick, world-weary souls.[28] Remarkable indeed, given the fin de siècle commodification of decadence as peculiarly French, is the extent to which a large part of Debussy's output even seems to have been programmed as if to illustrate or "realize" those few pages of Huysmans's 1884 novel *À Rebours,* chapter 14, in which Des Esseintes's literary tastes are cataloged: from Flaubert and Verlaine through Baudelaire and Gautier to Mallarmé (*L'apres-midi d'un faune* is lovingly described) and Edgar Allan Poe: "with his chaste, ethereal amours, in which the senses had no share and only the brain was roused."[29] Huysmans tells us that this writer's works occasionally left Des Esseintes "with his hands trembling and his ears cocked, overcome, like the unfortunate Usher, by an unreasoning fear, an unspoken terror."[30] Although Debussy never completed his opera based on Poe's *The Fall of the House of Usher,* its atmosphere often shrouds some of his most sensitive and dreamlike works (it is surely there in the gloomy vaults of the castle of Allemonde in *Pelléas et Mélisande*).

It is precisely relevant here to refer once again to another German, to that friend of Thomas Mann, Theodor Adorno, who would later become a trusted musical adviser for his novel *Doctor Faustus.* In the jointly authored *Dialectic of Enlightenment* of 1944, Adorno and Max Horkheimer would dwell famously, and extensively, on Homer's tale of

Odysseus and the Sirens in their uncompromising analysis of how the project of Enlightenment came unstuck in the "entanglement of myth, domination and labour" that marked the bourgeois commodity economy.[31] The cunning Odysseus permits himself to listen to the Sirens, while roping himself "impotently" to the mast and requiring his labor force—his oarsmen sailors, who "know of the song's danger but nothing of its beauty"[32]—to stop their ears with wax, meaning of course that they would not even hear his own perhaps self-destructive cries for liberation:

> The oppressor is no longer able to escape his own social role. The bonds with which he has irremediably tied himself to practice, also keep the Sirens away from practice: their temptation is neutralized and becomes a mere object of contemplation—becomes art. The prisoner is present at a concert, an inactive eavesdropper like later concertgoers, and his spirited call for liberation fades like applause. Thus the enjoyment of art and manual labour break apart as the world of prehistory is left behind. The epic already contains the appropriate theory. The cultural material is in exact correlation to work done according to command; and both are grounded in the inescapable compulsion to social domination of nature.[33]

We recall that in Homer, as Circe warns Odysseus, the Sirens "bewitch everybody that approaches them": "There is no home-coming for the man who draws near them unawares and hears the Sirens' voices. . . . For with the music of their song the Sirens cast their spell on him, and they sit there in a meadow piled high with the mouldering skeletons of men."[34]

But how, more precisely, might we figure the aestheticized Sirens in Adorno and Horkheimer? Are they to be unmasked as femmes fatales, primal muses or primal artists? Or do they just give voice to unmediated desire? It is possible that Debussy steals a march on the critical theorists. After all, the Sirens—always female, like mass culture and second subjects—lose out somewhat in Adorno's and Horkheimer's dialectical analysis of the implications of Odysseus, his sailors, and even Circe. What *is* their "practice" in respect to passing sailors? In the brief explanatory text about the *Nocturnes,* apparently by Debussy himself, *Sirènes* is described as follows: "It is the sea and its fathomless rhythms; then, amidst the waves silvered by the moonlight, the mysterious song of the Sirens is heard, laughing before it passes away [*s'entend, rit et passe le chant mysterieux des Sirènes*]."[35] The song of *these* Sirens is "mysterious" rather than fatal. And rather than them being a static threat to passing vessels, *our* voiceless passivity as an apparently disengaged, listening audience is stressed. Do these Sirens present no threat?

Or might the "laughter" heard in their song even suggest that it is perhaps the Sirens who are in motion and going somewhere, laughing. At us? The fact that their song is "mysterious," alluring, and somehow dangerous puts us in a relationship with them in which we are perhaps required to act and even call them back as they disappear. Might we then imagine that they are not committed Sirens at all but reconstructed modernists heading off to book advance tickets for *Le Sacre du Printemps*? Or are they, rather, laughing at us for our inability to be anything other than safely passive "consumers" of their music? Are they challenging us to live more dangerously, to be drawn into their world of sensuous abandonment, rather than simply to die on the rocks beneath them?

Debussy's mysterious and enthralling music of nature is never susceptible to a pat or easy reading. And if the composer-conductor is one model for the enchained oppressor in the myth for Adorno and Horkheimer (Adorno's account of "The Orchestra" in his late *Introduction to the Sociology of Music* further suggests this), I cannot resist reminding their shades of the disaster of Debussy's attempt to conduct the first performance of the *Nocturnes* in London. When he completely lost his way in *Fêtes*, he tried to stop the orchestra by furiously tapping the stand but found that his labor force, far from being oppressed, were doing fine without him and carried on to the end of what was apparently a rather good performance.[36] And in spite of the evidence of Debussy's ostentatiously "decadent" hauteur that could easily match that of a Delius, it is well worth recalling that touching little story about how, after he had been made a Chevalier of the Légion d'honneur, Debussy had gone to see his old father in the suburbs, wearing the ribbon under his coat. Standing on his scrap of front lawn working on his boots with a waxing brush, his father was first made aware of his presence by Debussy's deliberate cough and then by the dramatically revealed ribbon of honor. He had embraced his son, belaboring him on the back with both boot and waxing brush; Debussy seems to have been delighted by his father's protestation. He told a friend that in that moment he believed he "could feel pride at having been good for something."[37] It is always worth knowing where antipopulist decadent aesthetes really come from.

At the very least such information can remind us how complex the art-life relationship was in this period, and how in Debussy's case we might in fact be dealing with another special instance of the Rachmaninov model of a composer who really could be both popular and "have something to say." Further illumination might be found in Debussy's celebrated belief in music's power to "evoke imaginary scenes" while at the same time mocking those conventionally trained musicians (as Debussy himself was, of course) who "listen only to music written by cunning hands, never to that which is in nature's script." As always it is the quality of the evocation of what the modern city dweller feels deprived of that such art offers, as much as art "in itself." While Debussy may have elevated even saleable miniatures like his piano preludes to the level of rarefied *Rauschkunst,* some of his major works did speak effectively to a wide and varied audience—*too* wide for some of the countesses, aesthetes, and even conventionally social operagoers who were taken aback by the widespread enthusiasm for the ostensibly rarefied experimentalism of his opera *Pelléas et Mélisande.* This led to their having to sit in sight of, or even close proximity to, the sometimes fragrant but generally down-at-heel young devotees of the opera—"those who were sixteen to twenty when it first appeared"[38]—for whom, as Jacques Rivière put it, *Pelléas* represented "a miraculous world, a cherished paradise where we could escape from all our troubles. . . . I say this not as a metaphor: *Pelléas* was for us a particular forest, a particular region and a particular terrace overlooking a particular sea. We could find refuge there, knowing the secret door, and the outside world had no hold on us."[39]

By contrast, *La mer* distressed and pleased Debussy's widely constituted audience in contradictory ways in 1905: confusing some of the decadent escapists but seeming a touch more decent to the critics and *salonistes.* M. D. Calvocoressi found Debussy's inspiration here "more masculine [mâle]. The colours purer and the outlines sharper."[40] Roger Nichols has summed up the response: "Even those who found the work incoherent and 'unseaworthy' could no longer fall back on the old charges of femininity, lassitude or decadence. . . . More recently investigations by Roy Howat have confirmed that *La mer* is indeed most carefully constructed."[41]

So, we need worry no more then. Investigative musicologists can always be trusted to find "cunning hands" where composers want us to hear unmediated nature, to identify "masculine" construction instead of "feminine" fantasy and abandonment. It is what is expected of them. In this case, of course, they are also reseating Debussy on his pedestal as a pioneering modernist, whose decadent disdain for mass culture is thus almost taken as read. This, of course, is where *Sirènes*' thematization of the character and problematics of late-romantic musical pleasure proves so fascinating, precisely for its physical and sensuous character, its bodiliness, which engages the manners of "popular" music listening as defined by Frith, as if in opposition to that of the somberly undifferentiated intellectuality of "classical" listening. In fact the mode of popular listening is engaged no less interestingly and paradoxically in *La mer,* which, rather like Rachmaninov's Second, is a symphony "about" symphonics—here perhaps about not wanting to be "a symphony" at all; Debussy even subtitled the work, with studied modesty, "Trois esquisses symphoniques," Three Symphonic Sketches.

Among the many masterpieces of poetic musical evocation in this period there are few to match the first movement: "De l'aube à midi sur la mer." Its minutely detailed record of the psychological nuances of a mind intent upon losing itself in contemplation of nature succeeds in re-creating the quality and structure of an experience of unfolding revelation that bypasses most of the conventional mannerisms of naïve tone painting. The title is totally appropriate in its indication of a progression "from dawn to midday," from darkness to light. We begin where the *Nocturnes' Sirènes* may have wanted to position us: in submissive accommodation to the stillness of a calm sea at dawn. Responsive listeners may gradually imagine themselves consigned to a waveborn journey whose goal is not the merely physical ecstasy of Scriabin, but one whose character and elemental context may even hint at a spiritual oneness with the universe that has its own charge of authentic "mystery." The almost ritualistic attainment of this experiential state depends upon what feels like an intuitive, uncharted structural journey that seems to demand something more than traditional analytical labeling. A curious sense of trancelike suspension is attained at cue 11 and is then subtly intensified, like a coiling spring, through the succeeding "rituenuto" over many pages in which the music seems to pierce veil after veil of deepening mystery until the miraculous calm of bar 122, anchored to a bass pedal A-flat. The sensuous state of total passivity gives way (like a becalmed boat slipping out of the mist) into a brief but stunning coda. The wound energy of the movement is released in a dionysian celebration in which the formerly rather "clever" closing augmentation of bar 76 becomes an awe-inspiring gesture of bare, primeval fifths.

The listener is clearly intended to be left reeling at the close of this movement, which provides a directly comparable artistic experience to the more notoriously aggressive one which Stravinsky was to offer Paris in 1913, in the manner of the garishly pagan Russians of *Le sacre du printemps*. Both works seem to come from somewhere significantly outside the European tradition and consequently represent comparable goals of a radical modernism. Decisively closer to that European tradition, in Debussy's case, and more suspiciously dependent upon "cunning hands" perhaps, is the second movement of *La mer*. Subtly realized as its tone painting is, and so Analysis-inspiringly complex its structure (as we have seen), it is much more easily typecast than its predecessor in terms of traditional models. The title alone—"Jeux de vagues"—is a touch trite in its homage both to the symphonic scherzo and to the salon world of the early-Romantic genre piece. It is difficult to suppress the nagging question: What possible interest can we have in the "play of the waves" so soon after experiencing ecstatic communion with the very in-itself of the Sea? As a picturesque scherzo in the best Romantic manner (specifically that of the Russian School; the equally watery Scherzo of Tchaikovsky's *Manfred Symphony* is a not-so-distant prototype), this movement justifies the epithet "symphonic" in the work's self-conscious title in an apparently regressive way. Of all composers, Debussy seems the least likely, and in this of all works, to feel any need to pander to the conventional symphonic audience (whose "philosophical and artificial attitude" he had specifically condemned in 1901)[42] to the extent of giving them a break from the serious business in a cleverly entertaining "intermezzo." And yet he does.

The lengths to which Debussy went to confuse the outlines of an underlying Scherzo and Trio somehow calls attention to it and gives the game away. In the first movement the very clarity of its idiosyncratic form is what, by comparison, is so telling. While on the one hand the music seems here to begin with a naturalistic lack of concern for formal manners (where even does it properly get under way?—at cue 16?—at cue 19?), as the movement progresses not only might the occasional touches of real "Tonmalerei" embarrass modernist sensibilities (as at cue 20), but the increasingly apparent delineation of however arcane a formal structure, dependent upon repetition and development, seems at odds with the real inclination of the material and requires the generation of a new thematic type (initially from around bar 82) whose wholly Western and nineteenth-century "waltz" characteristics dominate the long quasi-recapitulation from cue 33. The gradual emergence of the waltz is technically fascinating, but the fact that it precipitates us into the balletic world of *Jeux* is a function less of the movement's progressive aspect than its regression to an older representational aesthetic where natural elements perform in three-four time a far from natural dance. Lacking the philosophically charged humor of Mahler (whose minueting flowers and clog-dancing animals have far from respectable intentions), Debussy here almost consigns his masterpiece to the programmatic "Nature" moods of the salon—but he has deliberately kept something back, in the manner of the best popular symphonists. Up-to-the-minute late-romantic technology of experiential evocation is employed and the reward, when it comes, is remarkable.

In reading *La mer* as a symphony in all but name, I am approaching it rather as what Britten scholar Christopher Chowrimootoo (alluding to Derrida) might call "a symphony *under erasure*," a late-romantic, cyclic Franckian symphony masquerading as a more esoteric set of "symphonic sketches" in the modern manner.[43] It even has first movement material returning in the Finale, whose programmatic and pictorial title, "Dialogue of the Wind and the Sea," hints at the possibility of a kind of sonata duality, a "contest" even, in the old Germanic, Beethovenian manner. We certainly do not need a Roy Howat to point *this* out; any bourgeois concertgoer might recognize a prop-box musical storm when hit full in the face with tremolando tritones in the double basses, driving rhythms and buffeting horn figures. What is really fascinating is the main theme, which we might almost hear as a sort of "second subject" to the complex of "storm" motifs. Its initially tight chromatic oscillation around the dominant seems to emphasize its lyrical potential as a melody with a real sense of having somewhere to go. Toward the end of the movement it will take us there on late-romantic wings as emotively grand and symphonic as anything else in Debussy and much in Rachmaninov. But it is before that heady flight that we are vouchsafed an esoteric epiphany—we, that is, the decadent seekers after escapist "experience," à la *Pelléas,* whichever part of town we may have come from, no matter how cheap the seats we have been able to afford. As *Sirènes,* so too *La mer* constructs us here as suddenly static, sedentary observers of a represented miracle—and the visual dimension of the experience should be stressed. The wind dies, the sky clears and at bar 157, as in a wide-screen D-flat major panorama, defined by very high and very low string pedals "plus calme et très expressif" (the high harmonics might remind us of Mahler's First), we hear (or do we see?) the theme to which I have referred. In fact we hear what sounds like its original form, its ideal essence, now shimmering in the distance, outlined with tentative refinement (Debussy requiring its first four bars to be held back a little) by a flute and an oboe in unison, but in two different rhythmic articulations, the tremulous oboe tracing in repeated notes the outline of the flute's visionary melody. It is as if time ceases and we gaze for a moment beyond it, entrusted with a fragile vision of something beyond all our certainties.

GLIMPSING THE ABSOLUTE

This extraordinary realization of what I might call a Joseph Berglinger moment, recalling our tragic romantic hero's climactic musical visions, leads me to venture more about late-romantic musical epiphanies and the complex issue of the visualized inner listening that they often seem to have entailed. It is an aspect of nineteenth-century programmaticism that has received too little attention. Of course, there is sparse historical evidence to work on. The listeners are long gone and the topic easily gets confused with psychological conditions like "synesthesia," which is not what I am talking about here. I have, however, discussed elsewhere the numerous examples of nineteenth-century composers—Wagner was a leading exponent—who glossed their narrative descriptions of music in ways that I can only describe as protocinematic (phrases like "we see" and "there appears before us" pepper Wagner's elucidations of Beethoven as much as of his own music).[44] And there are images like that reproduced in James H. Johnson's book *Listening in Paris*, which shows musical listeners, perhaps satirically, with beatific expressions, eyes closed on an inner vision (in that case of Beethoven's Seventh Symphony).[45] We have all seen such listeners, and perhaps surreptitiously been them. To find more we might briefly move north. Where Debussy could already construct his audience as spectators of his musical realizations of "nature's script"—moving and changing like the clouds in *Nuages,* the colors and patterns of the waves in *La mer,* or the wordless female chorus of *Sirènes*—the Finnish symphonist Jean Sibelius might be regarded as a veritable cinematographer of late-romantic musical narrative. He was, however, no less troubled by those dualistic worries about its populist character and potential while wanting to "say something serious" (whether in Rachmaninov's or in a Beethovenian sense). That serious something seems always to have been linked to the Romantic goal of piercing the veils of transcendent truth in ways too solemn to be spoken of in mere words, or in words other than those of spiritualized romantic idealism. Here is Sibelius writing to a friend about the Fifth Symphony: "I'm already beginning to see dimly the mountain I shall surely climb. . . . For an instant God opens his door and His orchestra plays the Fifth Symphony."[46]

Sibelius, of course, came to be seen by some in the period as a relatively marginal and marginalized Finnish "nationalist," although his domination of European and American concert platforms for parts of the mid-twentieth century tells us something else—as does his entirely standard, nervous late-romantic awareness of the cultural politics of public statements about musical meaning in the age of New Music. He was no less aware of the danger of being marked down as the composer of shorter popular concert items of the sort that had led Mahler (interested though he was in him as a person) to write Sibelius's music off as that of a "national" composer producing mere commodity items: "kitsch spiced with a national sauce prepared from those 'Nordic' harmonies" (as Mahler rather cruelly put it in a 1907 letter to Alma).[47] As a result, Sibelius often presented himself in the no less standard role of the misunderstood Artist living in the heart of the Finnish forest, his position really one of pure idealism: celebrating the "profound logic" of Absolute Music and bringing to the public the starkly modernist Fourth Symphony, which he clearly regarded as a response to German and wider European maximalism and decadence.[48] For this reason he seems to have welcomed that symphony's unpopularity like a Nordic Delius protesting "against the compositions of today." Where other modern composers were mixing "cocktails of every hue and description," Sibelius characterized his Fourth as "pure, cold water"; there was, he said "nothing, absolutely nothing of the circus about it."[49] Never were the complicated discursive politics of being an effective communicator of visionary musical passion so manifest in this period.

There are various ways in which we might compare Debussy and Sibelius—not least, of course, in terms of explicitly Debussyan works like Sibelius's sea piece *The Oceanides* (1914), or more complicatedly in respect of a piece like the sadly neglected *Nightride and Sunrise* (1907). No less Debussyan was he in his often idealistic manner when discussing the craft and calling of the composer as being more about improvisational intuition, "inspiration," than responding to cultural models or producing works that that might pander to audiences' ephemeral taste for "national romanticism" of the *Finlandia* kind, or tone poems, or salon-style pieces like the *Valse Triste*. Yet all of those things he did and had done very well indeed. He had also certainly lived the decadent life in his day, as we know from Axeli Gallen-Kallela's *Symposium*, his great self-portrait in the company of Merikanto, Kajanus, and the young Sibelius, all of them evidently visited by an alcohol-induced, fin de siècle vision of Osiris (see figure 2). Let me turn (dare I say it?) to

Sunsets, Sunrises, and Decadent Oceanics | 77

FIGURE 2. Akseli Gallen-Kallela, *Symposion*, 1894 (private collection). Those witnessing the alcohol-induced vision are (from the left) the painter, Akseli Gallen-Kallela, Oskar Merikanto (head on the table), Robert Kajanus, and, far right, Jean Sibelius.

"the music itself" for a moment, to demonstrate how and why he emphatically belongs to the loose network of composers I am concerned with here—which of course entails demonstrating that "music itself" always exceeds culturally dominant notions of what that "itself" might actually or properly be.

In the case of the already-mentioned Fifth Symphony (1914–19) we are faced with a First World War work whose escapist and theatrical aspect always caused someone somewhere some kind of embarrassment—not least among ardent Sibelius analysts, armed with voice-leading graphs, of the kind whose pages I have seen and heard fluttering like the Sibyl's wings in the rows of conference attenders, their import no more easily decipherable. The perpetrators of such things have generally fought to pull Sibelius out of the popular and nationalist gutters, as if refighting the battle of Schenker versus Bekker. I know one who claimed to have devoted himself to counting dominant sevenths in Sibelius; who knows what might come of that? Most recently there was James Hepokoski, bravely confronting those inspirational swans that had flown over Sibelius's house, but inventing "rotational form" in order to keep them, and Sibelius, in manageable aesthetic order.[50] But listen to the first significant climax of the Fifth's first movement, in which an inverted derivation of the "scotch snap" figure, adumbrated in the second figure of the movement's opening bars, returns four bars after cue D in magnificent style. Here the Berglinger inner eye surely opens upon something like a cinematic "point-of-view" shot, as of someone having climbed a tortuous incline or been pulled by a slow locomotive up a mountain railway to a place where a panorama of welcoming grandeur suddenly greets us. Who needs analysts to guide us *here* (for all they might tell us about the technicalities of the engine)?

Of course, we might with full justification seek additional guidance as to what critical conclusion we might finally reach about this music, and this composer, who became unwillingly enmeshed in some dispiritingly interesting critical battles in the 1940s. I suspect that sensitivity to gesture and what one might almost call musical "comportment" would have to play a part in any relevant analysis of this music that can walk, stride, and even dance with the subtlest agility (one might compare Debussy, Scriabin, and Sibelius in this respect, but voice-leading graphs would not be the tool). For all that Sibelius was, or became, an emblematic patrician Artist, personally somewhat aloof and remote after the First World War, there is something about the generously inclusive, festively swaying gait of that arrival in the Fifth Symphony that I cannot conceive of finding heavy or authoritarian—which is perhaps why the suddenly revealed major-mode landscape seems so welcoming.

Some would argue that to suggest this is unwittingly to pay homage to the Singing Devil, a role in which Theodor Adorno bad-temperedly cast Sibelius in his notorious 1938 "Glosse über Sibelius."[51] Dan Grimley has suggested that Adorno was provoked not least by the pro-Sibelian writings of Bengt de Törne, Constant Lambert, Cecil Gray, and Ernest Newman, which he had encountered in England during his brief sojourn in Oxford.[52] Glenda Dawn Goss has relevantly added that he might have been no less inspired by the Sibelianism he would have found flourishing on his removal to the United States in 1938, the year in which the "Glosse" was first published. Adorno might well have imagined, before discovering the evidence at first hand, that American democracy would have duped itself with mass-mediated "music appreciation" supplied by liberal critics like the Sibelius-worshipping, but Mahler- and "modernism"-hating Olin Downes. Both Downes and Adorno overstated their particular cases by means of available discursive moves, but Adorno's ill-tempered tirade contained some relentlessly gritty observations (the adulatory German reception of Sibelius in the 1930s—to which Sibelius was not, alas, unresponsive—needs to be factored in to our reading of what lay behind his relentlessly tendentious essay):

> The earthquake that found its expression in the dissonances of the great New Music has not spared the old-fashioned, lesser kind. It became ravaged and crooked. But as people flee from the dissonances, they have sought shelter in false triads. The false triads: Stravinsky composed them out. By adding false notes he demonstrated how false the right ones have become. In Sibelius the pure ones already sound false. He is a Stravinsky malgré lui. Except that he has less talent.
>
> His followers want to hear nothing of all this. Their song echoes the refrain: "it's all nature; it's all nature." The great Pan, and as needed Blood and Soil [Blut und Boden] too, appears promptly on the scene. The trivial is validated as the origin of things, the unarticulated as the sound of unconscious creation.
>
> Categories of this kind evade critique. The dominant conviction is that nature's mood is bound up with awestruck silence.[53]

Adorno's position (entailing also an unfavorable comparison of Sibelius's with Debussy's "nature" music) invests so much in the cerebral Hegelian narrative of Austro-German modernism's dialectical advance that he could have reacted in no way other than exasperatedly to the contrary position of Olin Downes, who had subsequently helped to popularize Sibelius in radio programs in the United States. Downes's apparently regressively slanted adulation of Sibelius might well have been implicated in Adorno's scornful reference to essays on the composer "in which he is praised as the most significant composer of the present day, a true symphonist, a timeless non-modern."[54] Writing of his first hearing of the Fifth Symphony, Downes had expressed himself as follows: "It was with apprehension and relief that this music was heard by the writer. It had, of course, met with wide approval. But there had been signs of a possible decadence in the Fourth Symphony, and a man of Sibelius's power, a composer with his unique possession of the spirit of heroic tragedy, could ill be spared."[55]

This almost presents Sibelius as a member of the local golf club who had been rumored to have been seen frequenting Schoenberg concerts. So much for the "pure cold water" of the Fourth Symphony. Had it been polluted by off-the-peg modernist perversity? The polarized critical discourse of modernists versus conservatives during the interwar years was intensified in the 1940s, in a manner that must surely be reckoned a key factor in Sibelius's own self-criticism that may have brought about the notorious "silence" after *Tapiola* and his tragic destruction of the Eighth Symphony.

As for the Fifth, well—what Hepokoski has called its "*Rosenkavalier*" status in Sibelius's output has consistently positioned its admirers as regressives and reactionaries.[56] Even some of *them*, like the English Sibelian Cecil Gray, writing in 1943, always had doubts about the Finale theme's worrying similarity to what he referred to unspecifically as a "popular music-hall song of some ten years ago" (which would still have positioned the song as having appeared more than a decade after the completion of the Fifth).[57] So what *do* we do with it? Probably what hosts of Sibelians have done for a long time: forget the critical contortions of modernist and antimodernist cultural politics and listen—but not uncritically.

Never was a work of this period in fact more bitterly and laboriously hewn and reworked through at least three different, but fascinatingly interrelated versions during the dark years of the First World War and the civil war that followed the Russian Revolution and Finland's independence. The great "swan hymn" of the Finale, whose accompanying processional chords Tovey notoriously and rather improvisationally associated with the swinging of "Thor's hammer," has always seemed too "in your face" for advanced critics, too blatant in its crowd-pulling sunset-glories.[58] Yet I question whether we need to assume that that crowd would *necessarily* have missed the subtle and complex craftsmanship of Sibelius's transitions and transfigurations. At times these involve a kind of experiential counterpoint that is often anything but escapist—as toward the end of the Finale in the version that was premiered in 1915 on the composer's fiftieth birthday. For those who know the work in its more familiar, final form, there will be some surprises—passages later reduced and tightened to epigrammatic terseness appear here in more extended and sometimes startlingly bold form.[59] But what is emphasized in this passage, as we in fact move toward the final peroration (longer and grander in this version) is the insistent engagement of the strings' threnody of bleak lamentation, even as the sunset splendors return—in fact growing more dissonantly pained and questioning as "God opens his door" on the distant horizon. Only slowly does it accept and merge into the affirmative vision to which Sibelius has led us, like an assiduous tour guide who has saved the best view for the last—not, I think, because he wants to impose it on us, but to share it with us, at whatever cost. Here Sibelius reveals an Absolute Music that is in reality what it had probably been for half a century, a theater of the inner eye and the solar plexus as much as of the ear. Not to "see" and viscerally "feel" this music is surely to miss its historical character, not least as a late realization (and perhaps resolution?) of the tense standoff between the voices of Nature and Humanity that had inspired the first of Liszt's symphonic poems over half a century earlier.

CHAPTER 4

Making the World Weep (Problems with Opera)

> We fight the good fight of the cloakroom, justify our claim to art by showing our ticket at various points, and are shown to our velvet-covered seat amidst the assembled throng. The smell of perfume, the sound of chatter, satin corsages that creak at the seams, disagreeable faces—the faces of people who are manifestly incapable of either a good sentence or a good deed. And then, up there, the ideal world to which one gazes . . . , swiftly intoxicated by the music, with shame and questioning in one's heart: can it be good, can it be sublime, if it also appeals to all those other people as well?
> —Thomas Mann, "Versuch über das Theater," 1908[1]

Turning now to the field of nineteenth-century opera, where late-romantic music's dramatic stories and scenic skills were played out live on stage, along with the "symphonic" orchestral discourse they had variously provoked or "realized," we are obliged to confront the ogre. I refer not to the genre, but to Wagner, whose influential presence as a composer, often considered the most notorious "singing Devil" of them all, has of course already been invoked. As the late-romantic most widely, tendentiously, and also meticulously studied (the literature continues ever to expand), any serious engagement with him must almost inevitably be attended by anxieties, both scholarly and critical. Perhaps they might be clarified, if not overcome, by my readopting an autobiographical mode and once again entering the frame of my study.

For I am, I must confess, a "Wagnerian"—in the rather specific nineteenth-century sense that I have not only been long obsessed by his music dramas; I have also, no less relevantly, made the pilgrimage to

Bayreuth. This I may have done more frequently than I should care to admit, if Jewish critic Norman Lebrecht's recent account of his own "accidental" visit can be taken as any kind of yardstick. Citing its "madness, its black history and its cherished aura of exclusivity" alongside the Nazi history of Bayreuth and the alleged racism of the Wagner family (which still controls the festival), Lebrecht resolutely "wanted no part of this circus."[2] The trip had been necessitated by an arranged interview with a conductor, who offered him tickets, and it surprised him. The amphitheater-like *Festspielhaus* clearly came as a revelation:

> The lights go down and what follows is a silence unlike any other, a silence so profound that it qualifies as a musical sound. The orchestral chords that emerge shrink the auditorium to pocket size. . . . The acoustic is incomparable to any other musical space on earth. I enjoy the opera with a depth of concentration that is hard to sustain in less perfect surroundings. I feel privileged to be here.
>
> This intensity is a Bayreuth miracle. Never have I sat amongst so rapt and motionless a crowd.[3]

Lebrecht subsequently develops a degree of respect for the "democratic town of Bayreuth," but nevertheless vows not to return while the Wagner family controls the Festival: "it will remain tainted by crimes against humanity."[4]

Perhaps one cannot be any grade of Wagnerian now without some degree of ambivalence. Lebrecht pitches *his* ambivalence as between the intensity of the experience (despite the frequent inanities of *Regietheater* production style—a matter to which I shall return) and what he knows of the history of the theater and the political affiliations of the Wagners. A different kind of Wagnerian ambivalence is expressed by Thomas Mann in the passage I set at the head of this chapter (it was in fact *Die Walküre* that he was about to experience from his "velvet covered seat" in or before 1908). It too has an ethical dimension, but in spite of Mann's own frequently articulated distaste for Wagner's writings and (in the 1930s) for the dark tendencies of his politics and his anti-Semitism, the most striking aspect of Mann's ambivalence in that essay is that it precisely reproduces Joseph Berglinger's Romantic inability to square the exquisite intensity of his musical experiences with the mass of the "disagreeable" and apparently uncouth members of the audience in whose presence he had to enjoy them. However, rather than rescuing his friends from it all and leaving, like Schumann's Florestan at the Shrovetide performance of Beethoven's Ninth, Mann perseveres, borne up by those "wonderful hours of deep and solitary happiness amidst the theatre throng," of which he would write elsewhere.[5] He is subsequently troubled no less by Wagner's implicit complicity *with* that throng, and by the underlying character of *Der Ring des Nibelungen* as a "supreme piece of puppet theatre, with its uncomplicated hero!"[6] He seems to be on the verge of turning back to Nietzsche, or anticipating Adorno, and criticizing Wagner's Art as prototypical mass entertainment. Instead, like the "decadents" with whom he mercilessly and humorously peoples his stories and novels, he turns *on* that audience and accuses its members of not really being genuine Wagnerian "Volk" at all: "The theatre seems to have become a lost cause only since it became a pastime of the vulgar bourgeoisie, who are the true representatives of an anti-romantic and unpopular democracy who are to the genuine middle class as the modern masses to the 'real, genuine' people."[7]

This of course reveals less about Wagner than about himself, as one of Carey's "intellectuals," and the future author of *Reflections of a Nonpolitical Man* (1918). There he tended to side with "Art" (decadent or otherwise) against the unwashed masses of a philistine democracy—a position which took him most of the Weimar years to write and think himself out of.[8] Yet the later Mann, the novelist and canny humorist, knew well what he was about, having penned part of the short 1911 essay "Coming to Terms with Richard Wagner" (from which came the line about the "wonderful hours of deep and solitary happiness") on the notepaper of the Grand Hotel des Bains on the Venice Lido, on whose beach he assumed the persona of the famous writer Gustav von Aschenbach. ("Remote on the one hand, from the banal, on the other from the eccentric, his genius was calculated to win at once the adhesion of the general public and the admiration, both sympathetic and stimulating of the connoisseur.")[9] There Aschenbach would be found gazing at a beautiful young Polish boy (whose real-life original even claimed to remember Mann watching him).[10] He was falling in love with him and thus precipitating Mann's projected symbolic demise: as Aschenbach, as a victim of his own art in the novella *Death in Venice* (also 1911).

This, of course, is a way of positioning Mann very much as a self-conscious, "late-Romantic" kind of modernist of that period—an estimation reinforced by his subsequent popularity (demonstrated not least by the extraordinary success of *Buddenbrooks* in 1901–2, and then of *The Magic Mountain* in 1924). As in other cases we have considered, decadence could be an integral part of that product—as in *Death in Venice*, where it is over-determinedly emphasized as the (tragically) acceptable face of its opposite: the Nietzschean iconoclasm of a politically revolutionary modernism. Indeed, Aschenbach's "decadence" is explicitly diagnosed by Mann as a function of the bourgeois writer's lack of the very self-knowledge that he, Mann, was demonstrating in *Death in Venice*: on the one hand perilously accommodating conservative bourgeois disapproval of Aschenbach and his emergent sexuality and sensuality, while on the other implicitly accepting that same decadence in himself as a marker of all that distanced him from the "vulgar bourgeoisie." He would similarly wish to distance himself from anything other than anti-Wagnerism of the ambivalent, delicately balanced kind that he evoked in that "page and a half of the choicest prose"[11] (as it is described in *Death in Venice*), which was Aschenbach's little piece of beach writing, thought to have been the same "On Coming to Terms with Richard Wagner" in which he, with Aschenbach, emphatically presented his love of Wagner as of a kind that was "long devoid of belief" in him or in his ideas.[12] It was even one which envisaged the descent of Wagner's star "in the skies of the German mind" in favor of a "new classicism" which Mann believed to be "on its way."[13] He nevertheless added:

> Even so, when some chord, some evocative phrase from Wagner's work impinges all unexpected on my ear, I still start with joy; a kind of homesickness, of nostalgia for my youth, comes upon me; and once again, as of old, my spirit succumbs to that clever and ingenious wizardry, full of yearning and cunning.[14]

UNSETTLING OPERA

It is as one uneasily inspired by Mann, as much as by Wagner, that I cautiously reenter the frame of the present study, in homage to the Wackenroder/Berglinger tradition in which *Death in Venice* itself sits, in order to focus more directly on the nature of the Wagnerian experience offered by the July 2012 public dress rehearsal in the Bayreuth Festspielhaus of director Stefan Herheim's production of *Parsifal*. I was seeing it, as a guest of a member of the Festival Chorus staff, for the third and last time (it was the final year of the production run). In many respects it was a manifestation of the kind of *Regietheater* (or "director's opera") that Lebrecht describes with reference to the "faux modernism" of Hans Neuenfels's *Lohengrin*, with its chorus dressed as rats and the swan appearing "as a piece of white sanitary ware."[15] Herheim's *Parsifal* was complicatedly referential of other productions, other kinds of theater, and added complex layers of symbolism on the levels of dress, the use of scenic effects (including lighting) and both live and prerecorded video projection. Each of the three acts was set in a different period of relatively recent German history: act 1 around 1900, act 2 in the interwar "Weimar" years (it featured a cross-dressing Klingsor with a Marlene Dietrich wig); act 3, scene 1, evoked the bombed-out aftermath of the Second World War; act 3, scene 2, was set in the postwar "reconstruction" period, in the Bonn Bundestag.[16]

What distinguished this *Parsifal* from the general run of *Regietheater* opera productions was firstly that its referential range extended beyond the usual devices, whose interpretive license and alienating effects often perform a deliberate modernist countervailing of the composer's or librettist's scenic instructions. These are rejected as representing, perhaps, an uncritical naturalism that facilitated a form of naïve sympathetic pleasure which reinforced, rather than highlighted or interrogated, the ideological character of the original as "entertainment." In this light, *Regietheater* represents an extreme heightening of the kind of aesthetic self-awareness I have proposed as being already an integral feature of late-romanticism. It was certainly true of the first *Parsifal* in 1882, with its return to symbolic ritual and the invocation of religious mysticism, framing Amfortas's role in the Grail Hall as master of ceremonies of a form of enacted "redemptive" art-fantasy: the "wounded" priest of the Grail whose revelatory task causes him intense pain and anguish. Herheim and his designer (Heike Scheele) also reinforced the implication (a modified borrowing from Syberberg's famous film version of *Parsifal*) that the whole work is peculiarly and particularly Wagner's own historically determined self-projection as the Artist of a "higher" form of opera (or "music-drama")—a *Bühnenweihfestspiel* as Wagner called it. They therefore set much of the opera variously inside and outside a clearly identifiable simulacrum of Wagner's Bayreuth mansion "Wahnfried." In the external scenes of Act I, for example, we looked from Wagner's grave (the deliberately reconstructed prompt box) toward the rear elevation of the house; in interior scenes the action was situated in the grand drawing room and library of Wahnfried, with its broad semicircular bay window giving onto the garden.

The enacted Prologue movingly presented the death of Herzeleide in a great central bed which featured in most of the opera's scenes (up to and including act 3, scene 1); she was attended by servants, a doctor, and the child Parsifal, who touchingly retreated into play from the emotional intensity of his dying mother. All of this fitted in with the interpretive style of other such productions, although the sensitivity with which Herheim's moved with the pace and character of the music was immediately striking; here Wagner's score was forcefully turned into the "cinema music" that Adorno mocked it for prefiguring.[17] More specifically, this production offered the three-dimensional verisimilitude of a partly naturalistic set that often permitted the simultaneous depiction of interior and exterior spaces. It even evoked specific places (often with the use of video projection) and an external, and peopled, natural world, with real trees, in a way that few other modern producers would dare to do. Two instances in act 1 will suffice to illustrate my point.

The first was a moment of astonishing naïveté and charm—rather like the visual realization of an escapist moment in a Mahler symphony as described by Adorno in one of his more unguarded moments.[18] For all the scenic and technological complexity of the production and the black wings that the late-nineteenth-century burghers, male and female alike, all wore as they milled about the busy stage like fallen angels, the production's moments of scenic "magic" were unlike anything I have experienced in any theater since the grand London pantomimes of long ago, to which I was sometimes taken with my sister by our parents or favorite aunts as a special Christmas treat. What happened in Herheim's *Parsifal* was as follows: During Gurnemanz's explanatory conversation with the young esquires, in the "forest" of the Wahnfried garden (while Amfortas is bathing in the offstage lake), he recounts the story of Klingsor's crimes and theft of the Spear. This occasions further questions from the Third Esquire, to which Gurnemanz responds by explaining that the Holy Grail and Crucifixion Spear had been entrusted to Titurel by angels, who had descended with these objects of mystical power which would protect the knights of Monsalvat. During this passage Herheim seems to have allowed himself to engage in an imaginatively "open listening" to Wagner's musical depiction of this event and then realized its ostensible symbolism by having a large Christmas Tree appear in the windows of the Wahnfried drawing room, while snow began to fall across the stage. As this continued, a semicircle of attendants gathered around the prompt box "grave" with small, glowing handheld lanterns. Nothing in the production suggested irony or subversion here; Herheim permitted himself to realize on stage what the music had led him to "see": a naïve, even sentimental image of a Christmas gathering at Wagner's grave. One might think of it as an evocation of Mann's recalled "puppet theater." The tableau was held for no more than a minute or two, but its effect was utterly disarming, perhaps because so unexpected. Can we be permitted such nostalgic, and ostensibly regressive, indulgences in a modern production of Wagner? More was to come.

No modern presentation of *Parsifal,* act 1, can fail, at the end of the first scene, to trigger the inner eye and some intimation of what the first audience in 1882 was intended to see: Gurnemanz leading Parsifal to the nearby Castle of the Grail. As the great processional sequences of the orchestral interlude lead inexorably toward their goal, a large area of unscrolling painted scenery was to create the illusion of "imperceptible" change, more specifically of lateral movement out of the forest, through a door in a rocky wall, and into ascending passageways which lead finally to the "mighty hall" which "loses itself overhead in a high vaulted dome."[19] Pictures of Joukovsky's original set design (the original was used in Bayreuth into the 1930s), adorn most program books, as if to make up for what now we never quite see. But Herheim worked an extraordinary theatrical miracle. As the interlude unfolded, the walls of the Wahnfried drawing room (into which the action had once again moved) began imperceptibly to recede. The ceiling rose and columns began to curve inward as if to form arches. At my first visit to this production I hardly dared hope that, just for once, something like the original set might in some way be evoked. To my astonishment, the transformation indeed continued, with all the machinery of the theater being employed to effect a seamless illusion. As finally the bells rang out in steady tread, the upper front edge of the proscenium itself now began to rise, to reveal indeed Joukovsky's great dome with limelight streaming down from above. I can only describe it as a moment of the nineteenth-century theatrical sublime, realized with twenty-first-century machinery that seemed to "play" the old theater as the great instrument of dreams and wonderment that it truly was (if not always, it must be said, with such success). The sense of pleasurable relief and, indeed, historical privilege at being permitted to experience something like this once more was overwhelming. Hours later at the opera's end, the audience resolutely sought to break the Bayreuth dress rehearsal code of no curtain calls, by applauding with astonishingly un-German abandon. The stage curtains remained resolutely shut, but Herheim himself eventually stood to acknowledge our energetic enthusiasm. There was nothing passive about that.

MODERNIST ANXIETIES AND ERASURES

I write about Wagner in this rather personal, rather unmusicological and even seemingly uncritical way with the deliberate intention of bypassing the weighty seriousness of more conventional scholarly discourse about Wagner, in which the residue of two distinct historical responses to his work lie sedimented. To both of these I am in fact sympathetic. On the one hand there is the "idealizing" tradition which takes Wagner, his works and his writings, as seriously as he appears to have wanted them to be taken: as the highest of high (might we not add "German"?) art. On the other hand, there is the skeptical tradition that goes back to, and beyond, some of the first 1876 festival visitors—like Tchaikovsky, who wrote critically about the *Ring* cycle, was considerably bored, but did acknowledge its "marvellous stage settings and production."[20] The great line of Wagnerian skeptics began most resolutely, perhaps, with Nietzsche, leading on through a host of early-twentieth-century critics to Adorno's brilliant Marxist analysis of Wagner's bourgeois pretensions in his 1937–38 study *Versuch über Wagner (In Search of Wagner)*. In that study the exceptional "critical moments" in the composer's project are set against an unrelenting stream of bracing assessments of Wagner's underlying bourgeois amateurishness. As a music fanatic who crossed the threshold of the footlights to set his own visions before an audience, he then "beats" that same audience into submission, both literally as conductor and figuratively as the increasingly fanatical ideologue of German nationalism and anti-Semitism and the anticipator of manipulative, mass entertainment cinema.[21]

It will nevertheless be clear that I am concerned precisely to fix upon and even celebrate that mass cultural aspect of late-romantic opera, Wagner's not least: to reclaim the protocinematic mass entertainer Wagner, whom Adorno (and, before him, Thomas Mann) often set up rather as a mock ogre, a figure of fun, in spite of all the evidently pleasurable and often overwhelming experiences of his works that they had "once had" before siding with Nietzsche and confronting Wagner's politics and all that was prefigured therein. That critical tradition must be taken seriously (as must the film noir shadows of the Führer and Winifred Wagner in the Festspielhaus, even today). *Regietheater* productions less boldly generous than Herheim's, for all their formulaic tiresomeness and predictable "unpredictability," must be associated with an essentially modernist move to reclaim Wagner for a new kind of "high" artistic purpose in their effort to appropriate his critically deflated, reinterpreted works and erase the historical, contextual, and "popular" theatrical element in association with the (compromised) "pleasure" that it, and they, might appear to dispense.

Interesting, and rather thought-provoking in this respect, is the language employed by Ellen Lockhart in a recent essay on, of all supposedly unlikely things in this context, Puccini's 1910 opera *The Girl of the Golden West* (*La Fanciulla del West*). While the comparison between Wagner and Verdi, his exact contemporary, has often been invoked (and was in the period), the one between Wagner and Puccini was in fact no less frequently discussed between 1900 and 1930 for reasons that have precisely to do with anxieties about mass culture as threatening to, or in competition with, "high" culture. This was particularly evident with respect to the Germanically biased comparison between Wagner as representative of German "Kultur" and Puccini as master of melodramatic and sentimental Italian "hits." But Lockhart's comparison has more specifically to do with practical and performative aspects of their continuing legacy as *reflecting* their respective critical stature.

Adopting deliberately commercial terminology, she considers the more recent fate of the "House of Wagner" as compared to the "House of Puccini." She refers specifically to the liveliness and fluidity (or otherwise) of the ongoing reception of each as evidenced in the relative liveliness and hermeneutic diversity of the production history of their works: "The House of Wagner has thrived in the past few years, with an abundance of new productions and something like a reformed critical apparatus: a Wagner for the new age, detached from oppressive totalities and final solutions."[22] Wagner, she goes on to explain, has enjoyed revival and re-reading, as indicated by the richness and diversity of his performances (from Patrice Chéreau's *Ring* to Katharina Wagner's recent *Meistersinger,* for example) and also by the renewed, more positive critical evaluation of him by French theorist Alain Badiou (in his 2010 *Five Lessons on Wagner*).[23] The House of Puccini, on the other hand, seems to have languished: "Puccini has had no recent apologist of Badiou's stature, nor, indeed, has there ever been critical approval to equal the popular one. His operas have long been dismissed as haphazardly constructed and semantically thin: in other words, inhospitable terrain for the hermeneutic wanderer."[24]

In fact Lockhart's essay on *La Fanciulla del West* fails quite to focus its own agenda as regards Puccini, whose mass cultural status and aims she seems intent upon stressing, without examining them more closely—fascinating as her material on *Fanciulla* and its "authentic" staging (after Belasco's original) undoubtedly is. She does, however, offer some valuable material for a critique of the proposed opposition of a hermeneutically inspiring Wagner to the hermeneutically static and somehow "fixed" Puccini (given the supposedly overliteral, "statistical" aspect of his "realism"). Her key observation is that the hermeneutic "*jouis-*

sance" of more recent Wagner reception, and his critical reevaluation by Badiou, rely on a negative privileging of the visual and scenic aspects of his music dramas. These above all are considered to require revitalization, in a way that indeed positions the critical, modernist impulse of *Regietheater* close to a kind of reidealizing of the operatic text. This works well if that text is constructed unhistorically, as consisting primarily of words (in the libretto) combined with "abstract" music whose original scenic "look" and realization in the bodily movements of real actors and singers placed in specifically evoked locations may be dispensed with as (she quotes David Levin here) so much "antiquarian bric-a-brac and conventional, grandiloquent stage business."[25]

In a sense this underlying and potentially regressive aspect of *Regietheater* has well-established roots in Romantic idealism, not least that of the passionate, impecunious Wagnerians of the upper, or "fourth," gallery who were pictured, with a mixture of sympathy and gently implied humor, in a Pauline Eigner illustration for a 1900 edition of *Jugend* that used to be on display in one of the cases in the old "Cabinet of Kitsch and Curios" in Wahnfried. It showed various individuals leaning on the curving rail and gazing down to a distant stage (unseen from the artist's viewpoint); others are sitting on the floor below the rail, one with his back to the stage, head sunk in passionately internalized response to *Tristan* act 2 (the caption simply read "O sink hernieder, Nacht der Liebe, gib Vergessen das ich lebe!"). This link between avant-garde staging and the *culturally* "antiquarian bric-a-brac" of Romanticism (as one might call it, again after Levin) points to something interesting about the changing configurations of Wagner reception, as much as of Puccini reception. It is strongly hinted at in Lockhart's counter-intuitive suggestion that *Regietheater* has *detached* Wagner "from oppressive totalities and final solutions"[26]—also her suggestion that Badiou's recent, and certainly significant, attempt to reclaim Wagner from the tendentiously political readings of Lacoue-Labarthe and others strikingly presents itself in a little book whose cover bears no representation of a performance of Wagner, only a page of the score of *Siegfried*.[27] Is it not equally interesting, given the implied alignment of that choice with "old" musicological ways, that Badiou's vision of a new, more open and positive critical approach to Wagner might involve reinstating him in a renewed notion of "high art"?[28] His argument is subtle and important, and I find myself in agreement with much of what he has to say about Wagner. But certain affiliations of his language, and of the strategies Lockhart has spotted in the broader work of *Regietheater*, lead me to return to the history of post-Wagnerian opera, particularly in the era of modernism.

OPERATIC PASSIONS AND CONFUSIONS

The problem of being an opera composer, particularly a German or Austrian one, in the wake of Wagner was surely comparable to that of being a symphonist in the shadow of Beethoven a generation or two earlier.[29] Given that fact, it is all the more striking that the period from around 1890 to the Second World War was a rich one for opera in Germany, and not only for ongoing performances of Wagner, alongside a varied historical repertoire based on Mozart, Beethoven, Weber, and some of the "lesser" romantics like Lortzing and Marschner (French and Italian grand operas by Rossini, Verdi, Meyerbeer, and others might also be added according to local taste). So busy a period of opera consumption was it that younger composers might arguably have celebrated their good fortune to be working at a time when the difficulties and expense of staging *any* opera proved surmountable in the interest of new and novel pieces that might attract audiences. A considerable number of substantial new works made it to the stage in this period; a surprising number were also successful, even becoming "popular" in their different ways.

After Humperdinck's *Hänsel und Gretel* (1893), the operas of Richard Strauss, who was deemed a rather wild "modernist" of decidedly late-romantic, "decadent," and salable hue before the First World War, began to establish themselves in the repertoire from *Salome* (1905) and *Der Rosenkavalier* (1911) onward. Hans Pfitzner's *Die Rose vom Liebesgarten,* premiered by Mahler in Vienna in 1905, and his 1917 magnum opus *Palestrina* in particular gathered an esoteric if somewhat conservative following, along with some of the operas of Max von Schillings (notably *Mona Lisa,* 1915). Nor should we forget the often annoying (to conservative critics) importation of other "foreign" novelties into German operatic culture from the 1890s, indeed like the enormously successful operas of Puccini and the younger Italian *"veristi"* led by Mascagni and Leoncavallo. Often compared to them (both favorably and less so), the Austrian Franz Schreker (of whom more in chapter 6) became genuinely popular in the Weimar years in the wake of his 1912 success with *Der ferne Klang.* The Swiss pianist-composer Eugen d'Albert first established his operatic reputation with *Tiefland* in 1903. Another Austrian, Erich Wolfgang Korngold, had begun delighting the

Viennese public before the First World War as a child-prodigy composer, under the guidance of Schoenberg's friend Alexander Zemlinsky (himself a fine opera composer), but Korngold's 1920 *Die tote Stadt* was a genuine popular triumph that readily established itself in the repertoire of German opera houses.

The fact that Schreker, Korngold, and Zemlinsky were wholly or partly of Jewish origin is sadly relevant to the dire historical events that finally brought the Nazis to power in 1933 and would eventually precipitate the Second World War. Before that apocalypse, they would engineer the effective shutdown of Weimar culture in all its diversity, obliterating most of its prominent composers' works, too, for nearly three decades. The gradual rediscovery of them in recent years would also turn up forgotten "Zeitoper" hits like Ernst Krenek's *Jonny spielt auf* and even some of the rich crop of operettas that had drawn pleasure-seeking crowds with their frivolity, their tunes, their sentimental nostalgia, and often satirical edge.

I shall return to this repertoire and the anxious questions raised about the threat posed to opera by the cinema, even in the heyday of the "silent" era before the advent of sound in 1927. Those anxieties highlight to what extent opera may actually have functioned as a preparatory form of mass culture. For the moment I wish to recall the once dominant modernist narrative that relegated more or less all of that lively and passionate cultural activity in and around opera houses to the margins and footnotes of a story of historical "progress" and development that had its focus elsewhere. It led from Wagner, of course, and the early Strauss operas (meaning *Salome* and *Elektra*) more or less directly to the Expressionism of Schoenberg and Berg, whose interwar experiments provided the building blocks of a new modernist canon in the 1950s in which Schoenberg's experimental music theater pieces *Erwartung* (1909) and *Die Glückliche Hand* (1911) gained belated positions. Comparisons were drawn between them and symbolist operas such as Debussy's *Pelléas et Mélisande* (1902) and Bartók's *Bluebeard's Castle* (1911), which were admitted to this canon as "forerunners" of a new kind of alternative high-culture opera. This had also, in a sense, been presaged in the early *Regietheater* Wagner productions of the 1920s (like the Berlin Kroll Opera's notorious *Flying Dutchman* in 1929).[30]

One of the most secure positions in this select, modernist canon would be gained by Alban Berg's opera *Wozzeck,* premiered in 1925 and a few years later taken up as what became a widely successful challenge to the supposedly irresponsible theatrical hedonism of those popular operas that it was often hailed as supplanting. Now it is readily coupled with Berg's posthumous *Lulu*, after Wedekind, which was, however, never performed in Berg's lifetime and played no active role in the cultural world of which I speak, other than as a retrospective mirror (as we have come to see it) of some of its central fears and tensions. The question to ask of *Wozzeck*, as we consider this emblematic alternative to those distanced sounds and singing devils that were critically conflated into a single force of deadening regression, is what we are to make of its pessimistic political radicalism and naturalism, mostly couched in the musical language of atonal "expressionism"? How conclusive *was* its triumph over the world of Wagnerian late-romantic opera?

In volume 4 of his Oxford History, Richard Taruskin's treatment of *Wozzeck* betrays productive unease. It is an opera that evidently both impresses and troubles him. He is, of course, sharply focused and helpful on what the problem might be—and has been *felt* to be by some few critics among the opera's otherwise vociferously convinced admirers. The problem as he presents it has to do with Berg's apparent conflation of modernist irony on the one hand with, on the other, what he calls a "vitalist" commitment to the political illumination that he wants his audience to gain through sympathy with Wozzeck's tragic plight.[31] Another question then arises. What *should* we make of those virtuosic underlying "forms" (symphony, suite, "inventions," etc.) that Berg clearly acknowledged but claimed not to want the audience to notice, heeding rather just the "idea" of his opera? Much has been made of them in the literature; the fine old Böhm recording with Fischer-Dieskau and Evelyn Lear came supplied with a booklet that itemized them all in a rather fearsome-looking diagrammatic grid that covered a full page, with headings such as "1. Akt—Wozzeck und die Umwelt (Exposition)—5 Charakterstücke" and "2. Akt—Dramatische Entwicklung (Peripetie)—Symphonie in 5 Sätzen," and so on.[32] Are we convinced that these forms are "ironic"? A quotation from T.S. Eliot is offered by Taruskin as possible elucidation (perhaps there is irony in his own intention here?). Eliot observed: "It is the function of all art to give us some perception of an order in life, by imposing an order upon it."[33]

The source of this Taruskin cites as Herbert Lindenberger, who was venturing a suggestion about Berg's operatic shaping of the rather chaotic dramatic material Büchner had left behind at his death in 1837. Might we note, a little nervously, Eliot's idea about "imposing an order" on *life* and then be struck by Taruskin's typically direct and apposite follow-up question: "Did that consoling sense of order jibe with Berg's avowed purpose in *Wozzeck* of exposing a social problem? Or was it just a palliative?"[34] He goes on to suggest that the act of merely "exposing" a social problem could be tantamount to voyeurism and all too close to the titillation offered to "gawking men" by Puccini's suffering heroines: a pleasure socially regressive because rationalized as pity: vice masquerading as virtue. He proposes that just such a viewpoint might explain Joseph Kerman's scornful dismissal of *Wozzeck*'s act 3 tonal interlude in *Opera as Drama* (a book even more comprehensive in its lack of sympathy for Puccini, we might recall).[35]

Perhaps I am alone in finding the musical form Berg "imposes" upon life here decidedly *un*consoling in its suggestion of high culture agency masquerading as diagnosis. Might it not even be understood as symbolically driving and *determining* Wozzeck's fate as much as simply "revealing" it? We know, of course, that Berg was a curious representative of John Carey's "intellectuals." Left-leaning in his politics, an almost textbook practitioner of late-romantic concealed programs, Berg nevertheless found the eventual popular success of *Wozzeck* (from 1929) so distasteful that he had to be consoled by none other than Theodor Adorno.[36] Taruskin thus deftly hits a significant nail on the head by speculatively reducing Berg to the level of Puccini. In the modernist narrative he is always good for a cautionary comparison. As Ellen Lockhart points out, no card-carrying apparatchiks will take you aside on *Puccini's* account—after all, he was a case, he was Italian, he had a bit of a thing for weak suffering women and, well, he was and always has been loved by those to whom Stravinsky alluded when (as Taruskin dutifully reminded us earlier in his *Wozzeck* essay) the composer of *Le Sacre* had observed: "What disturbs me about *Wozzeck*, a work that I love, is the level of its appeal to 'ignorant' audiences."[37] Clearly, being exposed to *Wozzeck*'s social message need not constrain us from mocking ignorant audiences and music that communicates all too directly with them—like the tonal interlude in act 3, like Puccini's. In fact, Lockhart's point about Puccini lacking critical support is somewhat out of date. Verdi scholars who first ventured into the dense critical undergrowth of Wagnerism that surrounded Italian opera, eventually, once they could lay down their machetes, turned to Puccini and have long been making access roads into the hermeneutic and critical analysis of Puccinian opera.

Some German and Austrian critics also took Puccini seriously during those same years of *Wozzeck*'s early fame. We can learn a good deal from them about the politics of consumable musical passion at that time. Their approach certainly reveals that early-twentieth-century opera was, as I have suggested, enough of a going concern, its audience still sufficiently wide and diverse, to support an unequivocal evaluation of some of its character and products as "popular": even, in the late-twentieth-century sense of that term, as a form of mass culture. High-culture criticism of Puccini has always suffered in some degree from the awkwardness of that Stravinskian assumption of the popular audience's "ignorance," which might be taken to reflect back on the composers and works that move and excite them. The pioneering leader of post–Second World War Puccini scholars, the Austrian (and Guido Adler pupil) Mosco Carner, felt obliged to begin his important 1958 study of the composer by categorizing Puccini as "an artist who bore the authentic stamp of genius but who for some reason failed to cross the boundary into the realm of absolute greatness."[38] Another Austrian, a friend and biographer of Gustav Mahler, had nevertheless made his peace with the Italian in a still more revealing way. This was Richard Specht, whose *Giacomo Puccini: The Man his Life and Work*—dedicated to Alma Mahler and published in 1932, the year of Specht's death—was introduced explicitly as "an admission of error on the part of its author, and as such an act of atonement."[39] Specht explains in it how he had long subscribed to the prevailing mistrust of Puccini's "shameless theatricality," before diagnosing that mistrust as Wagnerian blindness to the specific, non-Germanic nature of Italian opera, or rather something that transgressed German boundaries of what might be accepted as "art":

> People, even serious people, are fond of Puccini, but they do not profess allegiance to him as they do to Wagner or Mahler or Richard Strauss. When men of merit confess their liking for his music, they always do so with a touch of embarrassment, just as they might be ardent readers of Eugene Sue or Conan Doyle without quite liking to admit it.[40]

Later in his admiring study of the composer (in which he too felt obliged to categorize Puccini as a "minor master of the first rank"),[41] Specht isolates one aspect of what was likely to be problematic for a Wagnerian about that "shameless theatricality," for all that it might also have marked Wagner's works in ways that I have indicated. Writing about *Manon Lescaut,* he admitted that non-Italians were astonished by the fact that Puccini had appeared onstage to acknowledge applause in the middle of that opera's first act at its premiere in Turin in 1893. The incongruity of Puccini appearing "in modern [dress], surrounded by the singers in their stage attire" was clearly uppermost in his mind, as he supplied his own explanation:

> The contrast between the Festival Theatre at Bayreuth, on the one hand, with its hidden orchestra and prohibition of applause during the progress of the piece, or even of curtain-calls, and the Italian opera house on the other, where on occasion it is possible to encore even a death-scene, a conductor who refuses to do so being liable to be pelted with fruit, is significant not only of two different national temperaments, but also of two different ways of approaching life in general.[42]

Had Specht experienced *Verfremdung* in the wrong theater and without Brecht's assistance?

Another influential German critic, who was less convinced but prepared to devote quite a lot of space to Puccini, was Adolf Weissmann (1873–1929). He published a German monograph on Puccini as early as 1922, but of more immediate interest here is the still earlier essay on Puccini included in Weissmann's scurrilously amusing little book, published in Berlin in 1920, called *Der klingende Garten. Impressionen über das Erotische in der Musik*.[43] Its mocking tone and naughtily direct illustrations by Michael Fingesten (figure 3) conceal a critical experiment which takes its place in a line of post-Nietzschean and (by 1920) early Freudian texts on sexuality and the Dionysian in music, which included Przybyszewski's *Chopin und Nietzsche*. Half satirically, half-seriously, Weissmann elaborates a thesis that music is primarily an expression of human sexuality. As with Przybyszewski, *Rausch* is the vital commodity here, associated allegorically with Dionysus, sponsor of music and the nocturnal erotic and opponent of what Weissmann calls the ordered polyphony of "light" practiced by Palestrina or Bach. So, Mozart represents eternal puberty, in which eroticism, metaphysics, and virtuosity form a "triunity"; Chopin deals in a "goalless," hermaphroditic sexuality of yearning without fulfilment; Wagner attempts to join Dionysian, "revolutionary" sexuality with bourgeois idealism and homely morality. Those who once mocked Susan McClary's bold association of musical style and processes with gender and sexuality in *Feminine Endings* would do well to note that others had been there, more than half a century earlier.[44]

The elements of an intriguing style-based criticism already lurk in all this, not least when Weissmann proposes that Puccini loses his way between "true" erotic expression and mere theatrical effects (a standard trope of course) thanks to the dual influence of American "business" and the deadening effect of the bourgeois. But Weissmann was impressed

DER
KLINGENDE GARTEN

IMPRESSIONEN ÜBER DAS EROTISCHE IN DER MUSIK

MIT 10 BILDBEIGABEN VON
MICHEL FINGESTEN

VERLAG NEUE KUNSTHANDLUNG
BERLIN W / TAUENTZIENSTR. 6
1920

(a)

FIGURE 3. Adolf Weissman, *Der klingende Garten: Impressionen über das Erotische in der Musik*, Berlin 1920. (a, *above*) Interior title page designed by Michael Fingesten. (b, *opposite*) Image by Michael Fingesten for "Chopin."

by Puccini's "cosmopolitan restlessness," which he saw as steering a peculiarly Italian path around Wagner's "metaphysical eroticism, which congeals into the pathos of bourgeois people":

> To be Wagnerian in the midst of the earthy voluptuousness of the cantilena; to marry number and leitmotif; to permit the human voice once again to float as queen over an augmented but transparent orchestra—that could be the way for Italian opera. A non-metaphysical woman will laugh at all Brünnhildes, will appease the consciences that Germanism for a while excited and confused.[45]

In *Madama Butterfly*, however, Weissmann felt that the victory of bourgeois America over the naïve little Italian girl represented a capitulation to the spirit of American-style capitalism and turned Puccini into a salesman in musical effects, his voice evidently that of a singing devil:

In the hotels and cafes he whispers in the Kapellmeister's ear: With my notes you will conquer. In New York, London, Berlin, Paris—the same spectacle of seduction by Puccini's cantilenas. . . . The refinement in the mix of passion and brutality—which sounds a thousand notes of remorse over the lost delicacy of *Bohème* and yet which is the real Puccini—through its success the opera-writer contaminates the world. Even in Germany it scares all metaphysics out of people's souls—people who don't experience intoxication [Rausch] but want to imagine it of themselves in order to get its effect.

"Puccinismus" has become a sickness[46]

But what an interesting one, in the present context. Popular, persuasive, modern, yet a victim of bourgeois modernity, Puccini seems to link the refined and the plebeian, the evidently feminized historical "case" and transcendent manipulator of emotions who prompted urgent ethical questions about the nature and future of music as an art form in the public domain. Most particularly, Weissmann provides authority from the period for a move I made in the previous chapter, inspired not least by Richard Leppert's *The Sight of Sound*, to invoke more specifically the body and bodily reaction to orchestral and even "symphonic" music as linked not only to the facial expressions of those French listeners invoked by James H. Johnson, but also to the physicality of response that Simon Frith, citing John Blacking, had associated specifically with twentieth-century popular music. The musical body dances, languishes, strains, and pulsates in many of the critical and descriptive tropes, positive and negative, applied to the broader late-romantic or romantic-modern repertoire—we might also recall those passive, *sweating* bodies Bertolt Brecht explicitly invoked in his scornful 1935 description of just such a bourgeois audience ("transported into a peculiar doped state, wholly passive . . . helpless and involuntary victims of the unchecked lurchings of their emotions").[47] Weissmann, and perhaps Specht too, saw that audience not only as being seduced but also liberated, even "de-Germanized," in some way by musical experiences of the kind dispensed by Puccinian opera and, perhaps, Debussyan and Rachmaninovian symphonies. In the opera house there certainly need be no question about the reception of narrativized musical experience in visualized and, indeed, embodied dramatic terms. Where in the symphony concert the passionately energetic conductor might act as a focus and channel for the physicality of the experiences he was invoking from his players, in the opera house that role was taken over by an entire cast of dramatized bodies interacting, loving, hating, and even killing each other or themselves.[48]

I am reminded here of Peter Brooks's approach to what he called the melodramatic imagination in his 1976 study of that name, reintroduced in 1995 with a new preface that seems to echo Richard Specht:

> What we have learned, in the different spheres where melodrama has been studied, is that the melodramatic mode no longer needs to be approached in the mode of apology. We know about its limitations, its easier effects and its more inauthentic thrills, but we have also learned that it is an exceptionally supple and adaptable mode that can do things for us that other genres and modes can't. Perhaps melodrama alone is adequate to contemporary psychic affect. . . . The study of melodrama has come to be an engagement with an inescapable and central form of our cultural lives.⁴⁹

In positing the popular, post-Revolutionary French melodrama as a primary referential "source" of modern literature and the novel, Brooks's coinage of the phrase "melodramatic imagination" might encourage us to toy with the idea of an equivalent "late-romantic imagination" as a source and comparative reference point for the whole field of modern music in the West.⁵⁰ And while it cannot exactly be said to have derived from an originally popular form, its inexorable appropriation by and descent *into* the popular sphere, forced by the ascendance of the new "high" art of interwar modernism, offers a provocatively fascinating comparison.

My interest in late-romantic symphonics led me through decadence and the reaction against modernism and the New Music to a geographically widely spread mode of musical experience that we might recognize in its internally "felt" and visualized, as much as in its programmatically verbalized, narrative character—something I have suggested resides at the heart of the Wagnerian music drama, for all its ostensibly idealized earnestness. In Puccinian opera I find myself initially inclined, however, to emphasize not the manifestly important visual and material aspects of the experience so much as its *symphonic* aspect, particularly in light of the comparison with those subterranean "forms" in *Wozzeck*.

SUOR ANGELICA

As in a late-nineteenth-century symphony or symphonic poem, a Puccini opera will adopt a musical manner that both foregrounds and contextualizes expressive subjectivity, sometimes accommodating conventional forms or lyrical genres (most obviously those of Italian opera), but utilized within a wider dynamic structure dependent upon the pleasurable dramatic deployment of set-piece climaxes and grand melodies.

To consider how closely these might work together and, indeed, with the visual realization of the stage drama, on which I concentrated in my comments on Wagner's *Parsifal*, I deliberately turn to one of Puccini's less well-understood but recently reexamined one-act operas—the central portion of *Il Trittico: Suor Angelica* (first performed in 1918). It is, indeed, a pleasure to see that Andrew Davis tackles *Il Trittico* head on in his recently published book *Puccini's Late Style*. I will refer more specifically also to the analytical and critical work of James Hepokoski and some more curious readings of Puccini ventured by Arman Schwartz.[51]

Set in a convent in the seventeenth century, *Suor Angelica (Sister Angelica)* evokes an exotic enclosed world: the vulnerably all-female one of a convent in which, however, an extremely disturbing series of events unfolds—events which are decidedly "modern" in the way they are dramatically explained. As in a mode of melodrama, the central character finds herself in a situation that induces an extreme emotional crisis of the kind that will give rise to an outpouring of emotionally charged memories and protestations: an explosion of agonized lyrical rhetoric that would, as we say, move the very heavens to open. In this opera they do, and are clearly seen to, at the climax of a tautly directed symphonic structure that is certainly not hidden, like Berg's. Here the "form" is shared with the audience as the basis of an aesthetic experience whose message concerns not repressive order but the mercilessly dramatized *dis*order that pours back into the saintly and sequestered life of Sister Angelica from the "real world" outside. To follow the symphonic analogy for a moment: we might describe the opera's structure as an implied three-movement one (Andrew Davis links his more detailed analysis to the seven titled "tableaux" of Forzano's libretto). On this reading, a kind of lyrical *Allegro moderato* with slow introduction presents an unfolding, sometimes *scherzando* picture of convent life, foregrounding the devout Sister Angelica, who has a way with flowers and herbs. This is followed (cue 42) by a central *Andante sostenuto*: a confrontation between Angelica and her chilling aunt, the Princess (La Zia Principessa), who comes, among other things, to reveal that the adored illegitimate son whose conception had led to Angelica's enforced retreat to the convent, has died. The delicate thread of fond hope that had sustained Angelica in her devout life (exemplary, by comparison with some of the other nuns) now snaps. The Finale takes the form of a kind of monodrama for Angelica alone: her fervent prayer to the dead child, her grief-stricken resort to self-administered herbal poison, her anguished repentance, and her miraculous vision of the Virgin Mary with a fair child who steps toward Angelica as she dies.

That all these things should happen during the hour or so in which we gaze into the convent's world is in itself the result of a generic concern for the play of heightened dramatic effects and situations—what, in terms of the late-romantic imagination, we might simply call "music." At first the effects are the locational and temporally cumulative ones of a typically Puccinian "social symphony," the boldest examples of which will be found in the virtually sonata-structured bustle of *La Bohème*, act 2, and the terrifying first act of *Turandot*. Here, a sequence of relatively discrete sections, often with a thematic motif or focusing musical gesture, that evoke lyrical piety, the strictures of convent life, the humor, and later the devoutly pious and gentle Angelica herself. As the sequence of recitative-linked sections advances, the "music" becomes more directly involved in the action. At first it *is* all "atmosphere" and the background accompaniment to conversation. Then come little moments of foregrounded lyrical excess, like the Monitor's blessing as she bids the sisters "play a while" in the late sunshine; this inspires eight bars of tender, almost Verdian cantilena for the orchestra alone as Puccini's protofilmic underscore invites and encourages us to become subjectively involved with the operatic picture. As the scene progresses, the sense of musical continuity and unity becomes more pronounced. Subtly recurring material leads us not so much to puzzle over motivic meanings or associations as to feel that this dramatized span of time is as organized as a Rachmaninov symphonic movement or an act of *Wozzeck*, except that Puccini hides nothing from his audience, while being arguably no more consoling. Even the identificatory manipulation is open for all to see, whatever level of expertise or Stravinskian "ignorance" we may bring to the work.

Angelica's first, momentarily show-stopping arioso ("I desideri/"Yet our desires are but the flowers of the living") focuses our attention upon her as musical-dramatic protagonist and begins the long preparation for her central scene with the Princess, where at last the broader symphonic span is interrupted by an authentically "verismo" confrontation of striking expressionistic modernity (note, for example, the harmony preceding cue 44). Angelica's central outburst is grounded by a repressively obsessive, writhing chromatic ostinato accompaniment. It might, incidentally, be proposed that for a popular audience, perhaps any audience—and arguably for Puccini himself—Angelica's evident former nobility (she has come from a "good" family) is leveled or erased by her ostracism, as would have been intended; she becomes *déclassé,* however unhistorically (given what is known of the powerful reinforcement of class distinctions that often marked the culture of individual convents). The opera can even be read as presenting an allegory of the appropriation of its passionate expression and emotional rhetoric by a mass audience. In this "operatic" convent, everyone can seem as equal as the members of an audience in a darkened theater or the victims of a Mahlerian apocalypse. With the princess's departure we are returned to the symphonic argument proper, whose goal is now, of course, the concluding "Miracolo" that has been so consistently misunderstood. Let me first quote Mosco Carner: "The closing Miracle, however, occurs only on stage. Despite the chorus of invisible angels with "celestial" orchestra offstage, the Hymn to the Mother of Mothers or *Marcia Reale* remains an expression of pasteboard religiosity. To convey mystic ecstasy and the cathartic power of Divine Love lay beyond the composer's powers."[52]

What, one might ask, is a "real" miracle supposed to sound like? Bach, Palestrina, *Parsifal*? It depends, of course, on who you are, where you are, and when you are, and Puccini is here concerned with the mind of a distraught Italian woman, not yet thirty, the driving force of whose theological speculations has been guilt over a sexual misdemeanor not countenanced in polite society. Should we be surprised that her beatific vision is a touch corny, inspired by memories of the youthful vitality and color of a Mediterranean religious procession, with its flowers and swaying effigy of the Madonna?

Arman Schwartz's recent essay on the opera seems rather self-defeatingly intent upon a reading of Angelica's aria addressed to her own dead son as mixing reflections of early twentieth-century experiences of radio transmissions and the fad for séances. I am bound to suggest that the sentimental and "melodramatic" conversation with dead loved ones is as common a response to close bereavement as the Princess's report of her own supposed "devotions" and spiritual communion with Angelica's late mother is manifestly manipulative emotional blackmail, preying upon Angelica's emotional vulnerability. James Hepokoski's reading, in his extended and authoritative analytical study of *Suor Angelica*, is much more open to the ambiguity of Puccini's intention in the concluding scene. Is it, he asks (as Carner had), a "real" miracle or just a staged realization of what is in fact a hysterical vision with which the dying Angelica briefly consoles herself, and perhaps us?

My own reading would interpret this whole concluding scene as a masterpiece of Puccini's art, which provides an invaluable key to the nature of its intended psychological effect: Before the *Miracolo,* Angelica, now in an extreme state of shock, gives voice at last to her set-piece outpouring of unbridled lyrical rhetoric that draws no less than two effectively new melodies from Puccini. First, once the Princess has departed, there is the "Ora che sei un angelo del cielo" ("Now you are one of the angels in heaven")[53]—a desperately loving prayer to her dead child ("speak to me, speak to me, my loved one!"). After Sister Genevieve's attempted but misguided intervention ("Our Lady has heard your entreaties"), Angelica's still shocked mind shifts suddenly into a more inward, "mysteriously exalted" mood. To a second expansive melody, she exclaims: "La grazia e discesa" ("Her grace has descended upon me, bringing peace passing all understanding. . . . My course I see clearly before me!"). This course, is, in fact, suicide, which she childishly conceives as a way to heaven and her dead child. She poisons herself after the orchestral and scenic description of night (the accompanying stage picture showing the moon rising and a "cupola of stars above the chapel"); appropriately enough this is a grand restatement of the visionary prayer to her son.

The Miracle itself, after the horror of Angelica's recognition of her mortal sin in taking the poison and her cry *in extremis* to the Madonna, could indeed be interpreted as a hysterically generated vision from within her own mind. But this is opera as a magic theater of revelation and transformation. She gazes at the radiant chapel and the white-clad child whom the Virgin pushes gently toward her (the angels singing a "gloria" to the marchlike motif that we had first heard after the Monitor's admonition "Our blessed Lady's watching!" five before cue 7). As this happens, the soprano taking the part of Angelica is directed to utter two audible sighs of entranced ecstasy (high Gs followed by a descending wavy line). Arman Schwartz hears these oddly as "horrible unpitched moans";[54] Hepokoski rather more convincingly hears them as combining "shivers of religious ecstasy" with "sensual pleasure."[55] A less literal reading than that of either Schwartz or Hepokoski might note that she stands for a moment, with us, outside the picture she has perhaps created, with Puccini's help, as the transforming, musically recapitulatory climax of the opera, toward which its every part had tended. She is of course overwhelmed by it. As a film director might thematize the intended effect of the camera's "gaze" (Anthony Perkins peering through the hole in the wall into Janet Leigh's motel room in Hitchcock's *Psycho* is a celebratedly dark, masculine example), so Puccini seems to demonstrate the effect of the seductive feminization that Weissmann had attributed to him. We might see this as a key example of late-romantic self-consciousness of its own strategies: here positioning us, the audience, as sympathetically drawn into Angelica's mind, her "point of view," to see operatic theater in all its unlikely, transforming magic and just for a moment to cry "Ah!"

The subtle psychological realism of this conventionally least "realistic" scene in the opera directs our attention to the broader musical, indeed magical or even ritualistic theater in which Puccini is always openly engaged behind the fashionably veristic facade.[56] He typically relied upon a stock of ordinary characters that he could nevertheless transform and, as it were, musically ennoble, if only for a while, by releasing from them what we experience as "great" music: as the sign of a passionately lived inwardness that is the match of that of any mythical king or princess. He might elsewhere bestow such music directly upon them, as when Cio Cio San is preceded up the hill by those intentionally magical augmented chords that rise by sequential steps, telling us that someone not quite of this world is approaching. And then there is Minnie, in *The Girl of the Golden West,* who bursts into her chaotic saloon bar after a gunshot and to a skyrocket of a melody that tells us she is absolutely no ordinary manifestation of what Emanuele Senici has wonderfully called the operatic "Alpine virgin."[57]

FEMALE PASSION AND THE HERMENEUTIC WANDERER

Thus returned to Puccini's women, we are returned also to a central issue of the politics of passionate musical expression—something which grants late-romantic aesthetic practice a key position in the regulation of the modern economy of private revelation in the public domain. I deliberately invoke here the language of Richard Sennett, who was addressing these matters in *The Fall of Public Man* at around the same time that Peter Brooks was confronting melodrama in the 1970s.[58] The psychoanalytic approach developed by Mosco Carner in his pioneering Puccini biography tended to symptomatize Puccini's art with reference to the composer's sexual fancies and foibles (not to mention the fact that his own sister was a lifelong member of such a religious community as that depicted in *Suor Angelica*). That approach can be seen to accommodate a longer tradition of Puccini criticism which for earlier German writers could primarily be accessed under the larger essentializing mode of "national character." It would not, however, be with the intention of masking or evading deeper questions of sexual and public politics in

Puccini if I suggest that the tendency of much of the critical discourse about him so far alluded to has been to engage in a kind of normatively feminizing disparagement of an art that may both regulate and transgressively cross the border between public and private, mass culture and high culture. I cannot avoid referencing here Joseph Kerman's famous disparagement of *Tosca* in *Opera as Drama,* not just as a "shabby little shocker," but in the specific terms of his rejection of the work's final musical gesture.[59]

It might be recalled that Tosca has murdered the chief of police, Baron Scarpia (her would-be rapist), thinking to have entrapped him into freeing her politically imprisoned and tortured lover, Cavaradossi. But Cavaradossi really is shot; Scarpia seems to have scored a posthumous victory for patriarchal power. As Tosca, whose crime will inevitably soon be discovered, leaps from the parapet of the Castel Sant'Angelo, the orchestra, in Kerman's cruelly memorable phrase, shouts "the first thing that comes into its head"—just like a woman, we infer, a hysteric. Even Mosco Carner, whose final thought was that the "Scarpia" motif "would have provided a far more relevant ending," echoes Kerman's literalist complaint that Tosca herself had not previously even heard "E lucevan le stelle" (a central figure from this aria is what the orchestra actually "shouts"). He oddly fails to point out that she never in fact *does* hear it, having fallen to her death almost before the first bar has been restated. The theme belongs primarily to what in cinematic jargon we would call the orchestral "underscore." In fact it is first heard purely orchestrally as it announces Cavaradossi's arrival at the place of execution as a ceremonial funereal lament. Only subsequently is it appropriated by him as sung melody in his aria, which interrupts the writing of his last letter to Tosca as he recalls one of their evenings of "sweet abandon" together—precisely what makes life seem all the more precious: "And desperately I die [*E muoio disperato*], / And never before have I loved life so much." The fate that claims them both *could* have been given Scarpia's signature; but how much more moving it is that it was not, that Scarpia's *grand guignol* chords had audibly "dissolved" into the night at the end of act 2 (their distant trace is just audible in the dawn prelude to act 3).

Puccini's problematic unfinished masterpiece *Turandot* engaged richly with *Tosca*'s preliminary exploration of the sexual roots of power and manipulative public passion and could merit a whole other chapter. Its completion may have defeated him precisely because he was trying to achieve the impossible. His intention seems to have been to dramatize the inexorable equalization of power relations between the male and female leads, but his beheading (read castrating) femme fatale is not only, in Weissmann's terms, very far from being a "non-metaphysical woman"; she also derives a kind of moral authority from the fact that she is avenging the rape of her ancestor Lou-Ling. Her numinously regal character arises not least from the fact that she is so conclusively marked as "other" to her alter ego: the faithful, tortured Liù, who kills herself for love.

Roger Parker discussed this opera, and Berio's attempted recomposition of Alfano's ending, in one of *his* Bloch lectures.[60] So I will not dwell further upon why the strength and clarity of what has gone before surely militates against the idealistically fanciful resolution that the libretto offers—whose contemporary reception by at least one critic (as we know from Alexandra Wilson) relished the prospect of Turandot's inevitable and proper capitulation to male force in terms that perhaps all too relevantly linked misogynistic patriarchal triumph with what Roger Parker appropriately calls "fascist virility," after Barbara Spackman.[61] One might almost put it that fate saved Puccini from completing *Turandot*, from leaving behind a work that might have contradicted in so awkward and even so crude a manner the vulnerable avowals Puccini constantly made, not only about his desire to speak to and please a mass audience, but to do so in a manner that deliberately embraced his own feminization and that of his music.

Dante del Fiorentino quotes Puccini tantalizingly in his entirely personal but nonetheless provocative memoir of the composer. Here, for example, he is quoted by del Fiorentino as protesting, "I have tried to write for the people. I would have written for the Negroes if I had known them better, . . . They have accused me of being sentimental, saying that sentimentality is a kind of weakness. Well, I prefer it that way. I am incapable of creating anything that does not come from the heart."[62] Elsewhere del Fiorentino describes Puccini's tendency to compose on an old upright piano, in his old clothes, in a favorite café in Torre del Lago, surrounded by the peasants and fishermen who were his drinking companions. Of Arnaldo Gragnani, who acted as a kind of butler-retainer in Puccini's villa, del Fiorentino records Puccini as saying: "If I can make him sing it while he is drying his nets or working in the garden, then I know I have written something the whole world will listen to."[63]

We know from Puccini's published correspondence that his vision of the conclusion of *Turandot* (1926) was of "a great duet. These two almost superhuman beings descend through love to the level of mankind, and this love must take possession of the whole stage in a great orchestral peroration."[64] Puccini's triumph and his intractable problem was that he had (as Alexandra Wilson has also observed)[65] instructed librettists Adami and Simoni at the very outset to create what almost sounds like an opera not about Turandot, but about the later-added character Liù: "Put all your strength into it, all the resources of your hearts and heads, and create for me something which will make the world weep. They say that emotionalism is a sign of weakness, but I like to be weak! To the strong, so called, I leave the triumphs that fade; for us those that endure!"[66]

Perhaps, given what I have said about *Suor Angelica* and its "Miracolo," we should most relevantly regard *Turandot* as about *Calaf*: the stage-struck outsider-observer and would-be participant in its alluring and yet "inhospitable" fantasy world of grand and brutal pageantry, driven by a beautiful and vengefully passionate woman.[67] We might even see Calaf as a personification of Lockhart's "hermeneutic wanderer," who takes it upon himself to solve the riddles of this realm of Art, which, like Joseph Berglinger, he might have been better advised to "enjoy . . . rather than to practise" (in the sense of entering into it, perhaps of confusing art and life?). Puccini's failure to realize that finally enacted triumphant immersion could be interpreted as reflecting the deeper underlying modernism of his vulnerable late-romantic desire to want to "make the world weep." We are nevertheless a long way here from Schoenberg's dictum: "If it is art, it is not for all, and if it is for all, it is not art"[68]—as far indeed as was Wagner in *Parsifal* or in the *Ring* cycle, for all that the conventional elitism of "grand opera" may historically and discursively have reclaimed what he was seeking to communicate, both to and for the same heterogeneous audience. It was an audience that would, in the 1930s, defect in large proportion to the movie houses. There theatrical, melodramatic excess was still to be experienced in abundance.

CHAPTER 5

Late-Romanticism Meets Classical Music at the Movies

> Composers of music for movies and advertisements consistently stake their commercial success on the public's pragmatic knowledge of musical signification—the skill with which John Williams, for instance, manipulates the semiotic codes of the late-nineteenth-century symphony in *E.T.* or *Star Wars* is breathtaking. . . . It doesn't really matter that academic disciplines have tried to insist that music is only music, that it cannot mean anything else. In the social world, music achieves these effects all the time.
>
> —Susan McClary, *Feminine Endings*[1]

When the latter part of the previous chapter was first delivered as a lecture, an awkward but fair question came back from the audience. Was I in fact proposing that Puccini should be considered as transparent, as hermeneutically impenetrable as we have seen Ellen Lockhart suggesting that critics and directors have found him to be ("inhospitable terrain for the hermeneutic wanderer")? Her ironic suggestions as to how reinterpretive *Regietheater* stagings of Puccini operas might be done convince me that the precise nature of the text that is being "reinterpreted" is what we should really be questioning here. Following Lockhart's lead, my suspicion is as follows: that by readmitting the stage directions and scenic descriptions that were an integral part of the original score, part of the "work" indeed, we are precisely *not* refusing or canceling hermeneutic license, but rather shifting the parameters within which it might play. This is not to constrain it so much as pull it back into a perhaps more truly critical, more truly "hermeneutic" mode. It is easy to praise experimental productions that resist conventional readings—but how conventional *were* those resisted readings? Are we shadowboxing with a poorly grasped construct? What indeed *was* the meaning of these late-romantic visions and passionate performances in these spaces, supported by this music and against these backdrops? The latter might have been of mountains or underground caverns, of a seashore or the interior of somewhere claustrophobically deprived of any sense of what is beyond it, be it a hovel or a palace—these things cannot be "read" if they are simply dispensed with. Something of the history of Germanically orientated musicology's fraught earliest engagements with opera of any kind lies at the heart of this problem (we recall that Hanslick had even placed *any* setting of words outside the category of "music," properly defined).[2] Back in 1979 Catherine Clément analyzed the dire results of that awkward engagement as a kind of patriarchal idealism that insisted upon a purification of opera by suppressing almost everything except the music. She has accordingly been accused of silencing and avoiding it in her account.[3] What is overlooked is her consideration of the role of opera first of all in its popular guise as an extreme form of irrational entertainment, deliberately set apart from the rational, the real:

> In a world where the unconscious takes up so little room, where so much is made of spoken words, as if they meant what they said, with no past and no roots, we have the opera, where the conscious part, the part played by words, is forgotten. No doubt it is because opera is the place for unformulated dreams and secret passions . . . the less one hears the words, the greater the pleasure.[4]

Clément's ironic purpose was of course in part a feminist one, focused on *reading* the conveniently forgotten words of those once-disregarded libretti; it was orientated antiromantically toward Brecht. She was troubled by the suppression not only of opera's words, but also of its cumulative dramatic "meaning," however interpreted. Contributing to that meaning were the female passions that opera often foregrounds as mysteriously inarticulate, just as their female subjects are killed off for reasons that, by being consequently obscure, we are unable fully to fathom and must therefore thus tacitly accept. Carolyn Abbate's bold alternative was to foreground the performative aspect of opera and suggest that its women may indeed be "undone" (in Clément's sense) by the plot and music of the male-authored work, but as performers wrest "the composing voice away from the librettist and composer."[5] Clément's underlying instinct is nevertheless worth noting: that by suppressing some part or parts of the works we affect to "enjoy" we are depriving ourselves of the critical ability to divine the historical meaning of the whole, whether benign or questionable. Those much-maligned scenic intentions, for example, might be no less significant, their erasure no less compromising for any fully critical approach to opera than one that either overlooks or overemphasizes "the music" (whose late-romantic definition was precisely inclusive of things experienced or "seen" in dramatic or narrative arrangement). Indeed, if pressed to clarify the comparison between *Wozzeck* and an opera like *Suor Angelica*, I would venture that Berg's hidden "forms" seem almost deliberately to invite idealizing Analysis, meaning professional elucidation and description of those concealed-but-advertised musical structures, almost as a way of distracting or closing off any impulse to genuine hermeneutic critique of the opera (although I suggested that Richard Taruskin had opened the gate—dare I say a window?—to just such a critique).

My broader point in the previous chapter was that Puccini has suffered from an exaggerated form of the blanket, one-move hermeneutic critique of late romanticism (branding it decadent, maximal, feminine, "typically Italian," or whatever). Rather than revealing some impenetrable operatic essence, I would prefer to reject the kind of ideological prejudice that in fact blocks the more flexible, reception-orientated hermeneutic approaches that I have been exploring with respect to late-romantic works like those of Mahler and Rachmaninov, like Debussy's *La mer* or Delius's *Appalachia*. From a fabricated, "purely musical" perspective, we have seen that those works too might be dismissed as hermeneutically unrewarding, so clearly were they deemed to be self-evidently "just" mad, or bad, or merely sad according to arguably erroneous criteria. Thus might a prevailing modernist aesthetic systematically exclude the popular, nonprofessional audience and its modes of reading and experiencing the complex symphonic and operatic works that were written for it.

I have, of course, proposed that a persistent effect of the aspiring visionary inwardness aroused by the nonprofessional public experience of art, in spite of Romanticism's paradoxical hostility to the public sphere, was to generate a curious anomaly: As the musical style of romantic modernism sought ever more elaborate and refined ways in which to recapture and indeed intensify that Romantic experience, so its practitioners discovered that they were living the very contradiction that came to plague Joseph Berglinger and that would draw Thomas Mann's fictional composer Adrian Leverkühn into alienated mockery of the techniques that he "sees through" in the Third Act Prelude to *Die Meistersinger*. These become for him *"good for parody only"* if he is to avoid falling with them, like Joseph Berglinger, among the "most vulgar of vulgar people," even as he perhaps hypocritically manipulates them.[6] All conventional art, like Puccini's for Weissmann, seemed to become a kind of sickness susceptible to ideological complications which modernist asceticism and parodic knowingness alone might ward off. Leverkühn becomes transformed into what his no less fictional biographer, Serenus Zeitblom, later (in chapter 24) describes as "a music-lover who had tired of romantic democracy and popular moral harangues and demanded an art for art's sake, an ambitionless—or in the most exclusive sense ambitious—art for artists and connoisseurs."[7]

In *Doctor Faustus* Mann was trying, in a piece of complex, late-romantic fiction, to come to terms with the ascendancy of high modernism (and we might note the implied political coloration of Leverkühn's idealism), even while he was still privately playing *Tristan* to himself on the piano before retiring—knowing and understanding all he did about Wagner in his exile in Los Angeles. Regretfully, and tortuously, he had known it (as he knew his Nietzsche) long before he left Germany in 1933.[8] Down the road in Hollywood, however, not a few of his former countrymen were, willingly or skeptically, assisting in the widest dissemination of the late-romantic style in popular entertainment movies, where its "unheard melodies" (to recall the significant phrase used by Claudia Gorbman as the title of her pioneering study of film music)[9] were indeed beginning to "conquer the world." This they were doing with Puccinian efficiency, and in musico-dramatic performances which precluded any directorial rearrangement of their "look" or locations, since these very things are fixedly integral to what film is—as perhaps a key source for the retrospective understanding of late-romantic music's "meaning" and expressive range.

Lest I be accused of falling into the trap of utopian idealization of what was going on in Hollywood, however, I must point out that down that road life was none too easy, and many of the composers who took it would have wanted to evince more sympathy with Berg than with Puccini and would, as we shall see, aspire endlessly to return to what their cultural background insistently presented to them as more authentically "pure," "absolute" music—or at least, that was what they said. To them, and to you, I would rather say "hold on"—let us stand back and consider how we might best approach film music, indeed how and why we might approach mass entertainment film at all.

CARING FOR THE POPULAR

In discussing Puccini I referred briefly to the way in which modern academia began nervously to approach mass culture forms in the 1970s—like Peter Brooks in his critically refined but really quite bold study of melodrama: revealing to academic gaze a popular form whose efficacy, style, and form, as much as its celebrated (or mocked) "excess," proved demanding of historically informed hermeneutic study for some rather significant historical reasons. Here I shall again seek assistance from a scholar working outside the ideologically hedged and harassed territory of conventional musicology. The American philosopher Stanley Cavell has frequently returned to Hollywood movies for no less serious reasons than Peter Brooks to French melodrama.

Let us consider a specific Hollywood movie that Cavell has written about on more than one occasion, here in his 1996 book *Contesting Tears: The Hollywood Melodrama of the Unknown Woman*. The film I am thinking of occupies two extended chapters of the book and is Warner Brothers' 1942 *Now, Voyager,* directed by Irving Rapper and starring Bette Davis.[10] The titles sequence begins in what was by then a standard fashion, with the Warner Brothers signature fanfare: it leads into a passionate string theme that accompanies the written titles and the still, painted images of a modern liner at sea that form the changing background to the names of the cast and so on. Comparable in many respects to the opening of Puccini's *La Fanciulla del West*, it is an angular theme betokening both storm and stress and the promise of romantic passion and excitement to come: an adventure whose beginnings will be set in a grand house where only the grandfather clock's chiming briefly terminates the musical flow, in a domestic interior richly representing "class," comfortable living, and security against the rain falling in sheets outside. We smile even as we settle back in our seats, aware that Leverkühnian irony will be expected of those of us foolhardy enough to try to speak about such things—but not by Cavell (who actually says nothing about the music of the film). He puts it as follows:

> Nothing much to me would be worth trying to understand about such a film as *Now, Voyager*—one of the great films of 1942, one of the four or five most popular films of the period . . . —unless one cares for it, cares to find words for it that seem to capture its power of feeling and intelligence, in such a way as to understand why we who have caused it (for whom it is made) have also regretted it, why we wish it both into and out of existence.[11]

Musicologists are, of course, not always ready to admit to caring for the things they study, or at least factoring such care openly into the process *of* their study. We may nevertheless feel that a particular effort of care is required to cope with that film's famous ending. Bette Davis, as Charlotte Vale, has adopted the late, unwanted daughter of a married man and his wife—a man with whom she has had a significant, life-changing love affair. He has opted not to leave his wife—he feels he cannot; she has opted to do without him, to settle for "friendship," based now on a surrogate family tie. The life she then faces continues to confound feminist and other kinds of critics, who cannot decide if she is victim or agent, a tragic or a triumphant heroine as she utters her famous line, after the no less famous lighting of the double cigarette: "Don't let's ask for the moon—we have the stars" (see figure 4). Even Max Steiner's hasty late-night short-score annotations for Hugo Friedhofer and his team of orchestrators, on a document reeking no doubt of more than two cigarettes, evince both an intense engagement with the detailed effects intended—"Hugo! This needs "lightening," *spread* but not *loud* (a *reminiscence*)"—and a parodic humor that seems designed to evince more skepticism than sincerity, for all the signs of end-of-work excitement and even pride: "Slowly and mit Schmalz" / "(con *schmalzo*) *Hugo! Give your all!!*" / *FINE* Also "the END"!! / Lieber Hugo!! DANKE FÜR ALLES!! Viele KUESSE—Shostakov-*Steiner!*" (see figure 5). Cavell, who takes the film very seriously indeed and sees Charlotte as a descendent of Nora in Ibsen's *A Doll's House,* adopts a characteristic mixture of earnestness with sympathy for the unconvinced:

> Issues in melodrama tend to be laid on with trowels: caring for them depends upon whether you can care about matters that demand that openness or extravagance of care. If or when you cannot take such matters this way, then you cannot take such things, for example, as *La Traviata* or the Tchaikovsky *Sixth* or the *Revolutionary Etude* or the tales of E. T. A. Hoffmann or *Titus Andronicus*. And of course there are moods in which you cannot take them, not with the extravagant seriousness they elicit, perhaps one can think of it as extravagance without excess.[12]

Feeling no need to scorn the admiring audience for such things, Cavell seems open to the possibility that such effects are examples of manipulative structural and narrative closure of the most "in-your-face" kind, while also being something that merits and repays intense hermeneutic interest and effort. From a musical point of view we might put it that the late-romantic form reliant upon subjective expressive

FIGURE 4. Bette Davis and Paul Henreid, preparing for the final line of *Now, Voyager*.

nuance, structural climaxes, and transcendent flight (is it is simply "escapist" to evoke the structural effect of climactic "Rausch"?) is here, even more securely than in opera, provided with a specific, visualized dramatic explication. The movie itself could be thought of as extending out of and feeding back into the fractured and fragmented "symphonic" score: as a programmatic narrative realization of it as drama. This allows us to experience a kind of virtual late-romantic symphony or opera that underpins and also justifies the repetitions and discontinuities in the underscore that audibility of the dialogue and clarity of musical effects may have necessitated.[13] The titles sequence gestures and their rhetoric are accordingly compact, emphatic, and urgent—more *Fanciulla* than *Tristan*, more Tchaikovsky than Bruckner—but there remains a sense that Steiner is somehow "performing" as much as underpinning and giving dramatic continuity to the movie that he will have been the last to see and hear in its original unmusicalized state. In such a way we might perform a gripping or moving story that we read aloud to family or friends. In the process Steiner created a mixed stylistic work combining elements of modernism within a late-romantic frame, rather as Andrew Davis has described the late Puccini operas.[14]

Appropriated by mass culture, late-romanticism becomes effectively invisible to either "high" or "low" taste. Claudia Gorbman's phrase "unheard melodies" thus proves retrospectively almost allegorically appropriate to a style that perhaps became as déclassé as Angelica in Puccini's one-act opera (in my "unhistorical" reading) and as unintentionally threatening to the bourgeois or even petit bourgeois institution of opera from whence it came. This was something Schoenberg envisaged in Cannes, oddly enough, in 1927, the year when film acquired sound and its actors started to "speak." Echoing Stravinsky's scorn of "ignorant audiences," but going rather further, he put it thus:

> "Art for everyone": anyone regarding that as possible is unaware how "everyone" is constituted and how art is constituted. So here, in the end, art and success will yet again have to part company.
> The erosion of the theatre began as the emotions of the people acting on the stage came to absorb more and more of the audience's interest.... The characters represented necessarily became even more ordinary, their emotions even more comprehensible to all. The result is that nowadays one sees on the stage almost exclusively the kind of philistines one also meets in life, whether they are supposed to represent heroes, artists or men-in-the-street.
> The opera is in a comparable situation. It has less to offer the eye than film has—and colour-film will soon be here, too. Add music, and the general public will hardly need to hear an opera sung and acted any more.[15]

Schoenberg "goes further" than Stravinsky in specifically aligning the ordinariness of the characters of popular emotional theater with the "philistines one also meets in life" and with audience comprehensibility. The quirky implication is that audiences might better submit to the incomprehensible actions of higher mortals who, like *Wozzeck*'s doctor, no doubt have or embody esoteric "theories." Such dramas evidently invite expert *analytical*-hermeneutic explanation of their buried revelations (in which we are required to believe); what is not clear is why such an interpretative project need have had nowhere to go with emotional works that figured recognizable and comprehensible people (be they vulgarly extraordinary or heroically ordinary) who are set in motion in musical-dramatic texts that can themselves be read and understood by most, if not all, of the "ignorant audiences" for whom, as Cavell reminds us, they were produced.

Of course a Marxist model immediately presents itself, given the institutional constraints imposed upon and accepted by Hollywood throughout most of the so-called classic era up to and into the McCarthyite 1950s. The hermeneutic enterprise should certainly seek

(a)

FIGURE 5. Manuscript pages from Steiner's score for *Now, Voyager*. (a, *above*) The penultimate page. (b, *opposite*) The final page. (Brigham Young University Film Music Archive, reproduced by permission of ALFRED MUSIC, © 1942 [renewed] WARNER-OLIVE MUSIC LLC [ASCAP]. All rights administered by UNIVERSAL MUSIC CORP. [ASCAP] Exclusive Worldwide Print Rights Administered by ALFRED MUSIC. All rights reserved.)

to identify the guiding hand of authoritarian ideology, subtly or unsubtly mediated by such deliberately populist strategies as were demonstrably in force in, say, the German film industry during the Third Reich. But this process threatens a self-reinforcing circularity that can perhaps be broken into only by the kind of detailed critical work that

Late-Romanticism Meets the Movies | 119

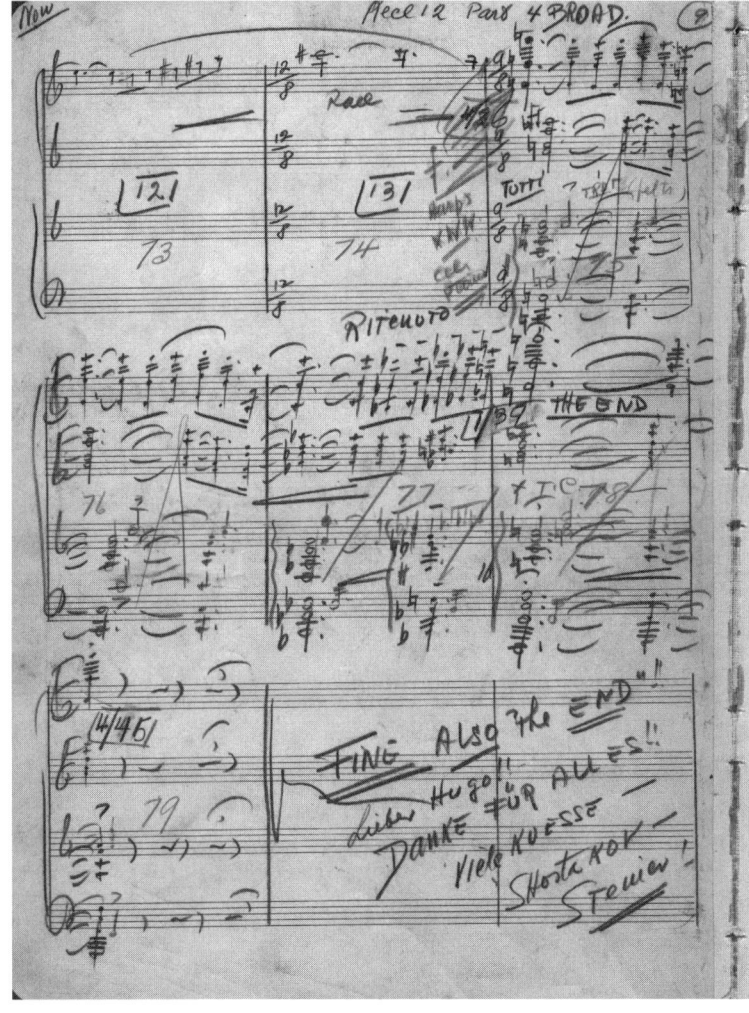

(b)

Cavell and many others have long been doing in the field of popular cinema. We might even begin here by reconsidering some aspects of the work and career of a composer now regularly cited as demonstrating in practice the force of (shall we call them Schoenberg's?) hostile prejudices and prejudgments about popular cinema and its cultural effect: Erich Wolfgang Korngold (1897–1957). In him we encounter a case apparently so transparent that hermeneutic elucidation is "taken as read," as unnecessary because we know (don't we?), or know at least that Korngold himself *saw* his move into Hollywood film composition as precipitated by political events. Of those, he was a shocked victim when Hitler marched into Vienna and annexed Austria into the greater German Reich (along with members of Korngold's family, whom he worked tirelessly, and indeed successfully, to liberate so that they could join him in America).

We know, too, that Korngold had been lucratively holidaying in Hollywood from 1934 (when he had been invited to arrange Mendelssohn's music for a film of Max Reinhardt's production of *A Midsummer Night's Dream*). We also know that his initial resistance to scoring *The Adventures of Robin Hood* in 1938, before the *Anschluss* helped make up his mind, was driven not by any blanket hostility to the film industry, but by his belief that it was the wrong kind of movie *for him:* "I am a musician of the heart, of passions and psychology; I am not a musical illustrator for a 90% action picture. Being a conscientious person, I cannot take the responsibility for a job which, as I already know, would leave me artistically completely dissatisfied."[16] The idealism expressed here was of a specifically *late*-romantic hue (we note the "passions and psychology"), and we should not forget that Korngold, an avowed admirer of Puccini, had always had problems with full-blown modernist versions of romantic idealism like Schoenberg's.[17] The "monomaniac" obsessiveness and seriousness of the Schoenberg circle had led Korngold, with Joseph Marx and Hans Gál, to set up an alternative event following the 1923 Salzburg Festival: works by Schreker, Strauss, and Zemlinsky were foregrounded in programs that constituted one of the last organized public demonstrations against avant-garde modernism by composers of late-romantic music. Joseph Marx's subsequent affiliation with the conservative Right makes sadly clearer the political impossibility of such gestures, which were almost doomed to be associated in the modernist press with regressive conservatism.

Creatively Korngold had always registered his position with a directness that could infuriate Schoenberg's pupils (Berg and Webern in particular) and would readily have been heard in the context of contemporary aesthetic disputes by audiences—not least those with a clearly defined attitude toward the often outspokenly conservative views of Korngold's father, Julius (who was Hanslick's successor as music critic for the Vienna *Neue freie Presse*). The younger Korngold's musical contribution to the early-twentieth-century "style wars" can readily be heard in the way he could mobilize and orchestrate dissonant vertical harmonies of the post-*Elektra* variety, only to resolve them tonally.

This he would do with a deliberate luxuriance that has been mistaken for betraying an investment in decadence, but might best be associated with Korngold's youthful and often quite deliberate conflation of Viennese *Heiterkeit* with an intended Nietzschean "Mediterraneanization" of post-Wagnerian musical heaviness and self-important modernist morbidity.

Perhaps this is what his 1920 opera *Die Tote Stadt* is really about: with Frank and Marietta trying to persuade Paul out of his necrophiliac obsession with his dead wife. *Das Wunder der Heliane* was an altogether more complex proposition. Its simultaneous 1927 premieres in Vienna and Hamburg fell unfortunately close to the arrival in Vienna of Krenek's up-to-the-minute *Jonny spielt auf*, became embroiled in a Nazi propaganda war (against Krenek), and was freighted by outmoded mysticism and post-Parsifallic hocus pocus (with multiple resurrections celebrated by vast orchestral forces). Rival cigarette novelties—budget-priced "Jonnys" and luxuriantly decadent "Helianes"—testified to the mass cultural reach of opera at this time.[18] *Das Wunder der Heliane* nevertheless has its own underlying symbolic message: the opera features a central character, "The Stranger," whose threat to the mysterious kingdom in which we find him imprisoned consists in his ability to bring joy and cheerfulness. He sees himself as openly importing youthfully erotic pleasure into an otherwise darkly serious and repressed realm, governed by an unloving Ruler with an inappropriately youthful wife (Heliane). The Porter who comes to the Stranger's cell in act 1 tells him this:

> Since you have entered this country
> all peace has gone!
> They run ahead of you like children . . .
> Are you a sorcerer
> that even the King has noticed you? . . .
> The King fears you.

As I have hinted, the libretto is, on the whole, a rather bizarre one (as indeed was that of *Die Tote Stadt* in certain respects). If Korngold had only learned from his hero Puccini the value of finding decent professional librettists his operas might have been as good as his best Hollywood films undoubtedly were. His prodigious musical imagination and facility perhaps needed the hard-nosed professional discipline that Hollywood imposed even on a "great" European composer who had more than usually generous treatment and deadlines (few in America really grasped that Korngold was seen in Europe as having retreated even further than Richard Strauss from the front line of modern musical relevance, having quite literally defected to the world of operetta arrangement before Hollywood revived his career).[19]

In what follows I will refer to some of the finest of Korngold's, as well as others', film scores, all of which might be understood as documenting the migration of his particular brand of aesthetically politicized late-romanticism into the world of the new mass culture form that Schoenberg had feared would "win" in the battle for opera's audiences. But lest it be thought that this entailed some root-and-branch abandonment of the older forms of romantic-classical music, I will approach these films through the intriguing refracting lens of his 1954 Symphony in F sharp. It is one of a group of late works with which Korngold seemed to be trying to reestablish a career as a "real" concert and opera composer and raises the specter of a conservative return to the form resolutely associated with Classical Music in its most culturally regressive manifestation. But we should note that most of his late works either quoted, or arose out of, film scores (like the Violin Concerto dedicated to Alma Mahler, or the one-movement Cello Concerto composed for *Deception*). The Symphony in F sharp, which Korngold intended publicly to dedicate to the memory of F. D. Roosevelt, in gratitude for America having saved him and his family in 1938, similarly alludes to recognizable film score material and presents a means of testing Korngold's attitude toward its original context and character. I say this because the symphony, and the things that Korngold said about it, mediated his ostensible ambivalence about Hollywood no less complicatedly than those humorous and yet also rather proudly excited score annotations of Steiner for the final moments of *Now, Voyager*.

KORNGOLD'S CINEMATIC SYMPHONY

The symphony *could* even be taken as Korngold's "response to just criticism"[20]—the work of a late-romantic admitting the folly of his ways and producing a stylistically mixed concert piece in which modernist and neoclassical traits seem to frame and even dominate the nostalgic references to late-romantic tonal practice (other works of this kind might include Rachmaninov's Third Symphony of 1936). Was Korngold even admitting defeat and bowing the knee to modernism? What we are and he was up against here is succinctly revealed in the following quotation from an unpublished program note that he wrote for a never-to-materialize American performance of the symphony in his lifetime (thanks to the critical failure of the Viennese premiere in 1954): "The composer characterizes his new symphony as a work of pure, absolute music with no program whatsoever, in spite of his experience that many people—after the first hearing—read into the first movement the terror and horrors of the years 1933–45 and into the Adagio the sorrows and sufferings of victims of that time."[21]

"It wasn't me, sir, it was *them*" is a standard enough line, of course, and neatly revives the old, pre–First World War public discourse about program music which Mahler had negotiated with no less ambivalent caution. Dare I suggest that the music tells us more; that it is full of the very hermeneutic windows that Helmut Pöllmann's introduction to the Schott score of 2000 seems intent on rushing about shutting in the best nineteenth-century romantic-idealist manner? Here he is:

> In the Symphony in F sharp the Adagio in particular, a large-scale slow movement reminiscent of Bruckner and Mahler, was suggested by a theme from *The Private Lives of Elizabeth and Essex* while in the fourth movement a theme from *Kings Row* can be heard.... This fact does not imply any reference to the films in question. Furthermore, it is in most cases merely a matter of the basic shape [Grundgestalt] of a theme, which is treated in a completely new way and in a completely different context.... It seems understandable that he did not want to leave these subjects to moulder in a film soundtrack.[22]

On the contrary, I think we can do better than that and follow Korngold's lead back to the intuition of the "ignorant audience," who probably understood him better than nervously tendentious critics or musicologists concerned for their job prospects. Apart from anything else, I can report that the Scherzo too includes a striking film quotation, and that, in all, five different film scores are clearly referenced: *Anthony Adverse* (1936), *The Private Lives of Elizabeth and Essex* (1939), *Kings Row* (1941), and *Deception* (1946), along with the 1935 *Captain Blood*—Korngold's first "real" Hollywood score. They are alluded to in ways that pose tantalizing hermeneutic challenges, precisely because they seem so deliberate and so nearly and strikingly coherent.

It would be as well to register first how relatively modern and removed from conventional late-romantic tonal practice the first movement does indeed sound, with its often angry, melodically, and metrically disjunct lines, as in the very opening bars. While specific film references are a matter of ongoing research in this movement, Korngold's own implicitly double elucidation of it as "pure, absolute music" into which, however, "many people" had nevertheless read "the terrors and horrors of the years 1933–45" will simply have to stand for the moment. The skittishly danceable Scherzo that follows seems given to passing moods and visions of its own, but its curious chromatic Trio motif, marked "molto meno (tranquillo)," for quiet tremolando strings and celesta, can be identified as an explicit quotation of music from Korngold's last original film score, for *Deception,* and is what he might have called a "psychological" motif, since it quietly underscores Bette Davis's agonized confession to her husband that she has murdered her former lover, the composer of the concerto he has just premiered.[23] It occurs specifically at the point in her revelation when she repeatedly recalls Hollenius's mocking challenge: "*If* he wanted to, he could break us." He could have revealed all and destroyed her marriage, "*if* he wanted to." But perhaps he didn't after all?

This incursion of a woman's tear-stained face and voice, the voice of a "fallen," indeed "undone" woman in the act of grasping and confessing her guilt in having murdered a composer, emerging mysteriously in a late, late-romantic symphony by that composer's living representative—this is a tantalizing moment. It is not just that it could be taken as a striking example of the kind of visualized, protocinematic interpretation that I have suggested characterizes the late-romantic experience of symphonic narrative, nor that it is specifically the face of a fallen woman played by Bette Davis that we are invited to contemplate in a kind of symphony that Korngold quickly discovered to be branded still by the frequently gendered discourse of modernism. It is what comes next that is fascinating, in the powerful extended Adagio in D minor. All of its significant material is derived from Korngold film scores. The sources are *Captain Blood, Anthony Adverse,* and most significantly of all, *The Private Lives of Elizabeth and Essex;* it is, however, the latter that is the dominant source.

With its rich repertoire of referential motifs, that film is in many respects a spoken historical grand opera, of the kind that Korngold often claimed to be writing in Hollywood. It is not, to my knowledge, a fashionable object of film-critical discussion, but it deserves to be for the power and urgency of its thematized gender politics. The relationship is, once again, between Bette Davis, playing Elizabeth I, and Errol Flynn—an actor she hated—playing Essex, the man she loves but will not give up her throne to. She too may be left a broken woman when Essex, now her prisoner, proudly marches away from their last confron-

FIGURE 6. Bette Davis in *The Private Lives of Elizabeth and Essex*. A characteristic evocation of the spectacular processional space required for the performance of power.

tation, to his death. She has reaffirmed her love for him, but she has also reaffirmed her belief that he would be a disastrous king of England; she lives and he loses his head. Her agonized and now lonely assumption of the duties of a monarch is made all the more dramatically powerful by our background knowledge of her in happier times, when Davis plays Elizabeth as a still flirtatious, coquettish Hollywood heroine, or, still more strikingly, when she later marches through the corridors of her power to confront the rebellious Essex, with an outfit to match and on a stage whose length and grandeur no opera house could possibly match (see figure 6).

What, then, should we make of the fact that the symphony's Adagio is wrought primarily out of Essex's motif, which always marks his role in the film as a public hero? Sometimes it takes the form of a grand fanfare; more often we hear it in the elegiac and latterly funereal version which dominates the closing scenes of the film. Is Korngold siding with the male hero and lamenting his fate? That a fragment of his first Hollywood hero theme is worked into the texture—that for Captain Blood (another Errol Flynn role, of course)—might reinforce that reading, were it not for the central episode, based on an expanding chromatic "wedge" motif like a fugal counter-subject. This proves to come from *Anthony Adverse*, for which Korngold won his first Oscar. Based on a popular historical novel set in the Napoleonic period, it told the story of the orphaned son of two proverbially star-crossed lovers. Anthony's adventures take him into a lucrative business career before he and his son, apparently abandoned by the boy's opera singer mother, set sail for America and a new beginning. But he is an ill-fated and decidedly tarnished hero, the climax of whose business career finds him turned into a slave trader in Africa. The chromatic motif referred to and cited in the symphony's Adagio features in a harrowing section of the film, in which Anthony only slowly grasps the full horror of what he is doing. Its gist is explained in an on-screen text card: "*Africa . . . Anthony sweated with fever and a new greed took hold of him. In three years his name became like a terrifying jungle sound to the harassed natives. He dealt in slaves . . . and became a slave to his own power*" (ellipses in original).

The provenance of all three thematic elements complicates this powerfully engaged elegy for the composite hero of many of the films Korngold had scored—a hero seen now as a decidedly flawed model of patriarchal power in a genre whose critical feminization Korngold seems tacitly to accept and celebrate. This movement revisits the disillusioned, funereal regret of Beethoven's *Eroica* no less movingly than Korngold's other musical hero, Richard Strauss, in the *Metamorphosen*. Far from being just "pure music" rescuing abstracted pieces of film score material, this movement, this symphony, seems equally to present itself as intertextually entwined with the films it alludes to, the modernist scorn of whose least sympathetic critics it seems to accept with a kind of tragic defiance. In response to a letter from an old European acquaintance, Korngold had written, while completing the symphony in 1952, in terms that echo some of Rachmaninov's statements of incomprehension at his own inability to embrace "the new way." "No," Korngold assured his friend: "I have *not* become atonal and I also think that my new symphony will prove to the world that monotony and 'modernism' at the cost of abandoning invention, form, expression, beauty, melody—in short, all things connected with the despised 'romanticism'—which, after all, has produced some not so negligible masterpieces!—will ultimately result in disaster for the art of music."[24]

That horse had long since bolted, but I would be prepared to number this symphony, along with *The Private Lives of Elizabeth and Essex* and the other films mentioned—among the not-so-negligible masterpieces of late romanticism. Its jaunty Finale, whose main theme some have heard as alluding to George M. Cohan's song "Over There," seems to avoid any cloying nostalgia of the more self-indulgent Hollywood variety, although its second theme nevertheless proves to be associated with another fictional cinematic orphan: the rather starchy Parris Mitchell of *Kings Row,* whose elegant European grandmother, Madame von Eln, it represents, along with the cultured home she makes for him in small-town America, where he even addresses her in French. That Korngold could rehabilitate that melody as one of the knowing markers of his acceptance both of who he was and that the world in which he found himself was quite different from that of his own happy European childhood in old Vienna—that is a testimony to how late-romanticism might have reconstructed itself without capitulating to "monotony and "modernism," might even, as Rachmaninov had put it, be popular and have something to say.

NARRATIVE, INTERTEXTUALITY, AND THE POPULAR NOVEL

It has become commonplace to diagnose a sad sort of cultural inevitability about the relationship between musical late-romanticism and the rapidly expanding world of mass entertainment cinema in the 1930s and 1940s. For conventional critics of mass culture, as for Adorno and Eisler in their book *Composing for the Films,* the links between "overblown" romantic music and the lucrative business of Hollywood film represented a conclusive final chapter of the debasement of bourgeois art music, indeed its effective demise as a tool of the capitalist manipulation of mass emotion.[25] From a less totalizing, less ideologically inflexible perspective, we might rather regard the complex, mutually supportive intertextual relationship between forms and media in this realm as opening up a range of new evidence relating to what in public discourse had hitherto been the "merely subjective" matter of the experience of musical meaning. In Korngold's case, the complex relationship between symphonic aspirations, the rejected and yet publicly acknowledged practice of associative, programmatic listening, and the operatically and symphonically inspired mass entertainment film is provocatively laid open to view. What we glimpse here is a broad intertextual field in which symphonic music, opera, and popular dramatic genres like melodrama form a constellation in which the mechanisms of late-romantic musical meaning seem not only displayed but also revealed as focusing and driving something of the whole character of the mass entertainment "art" experience of the early twentieth century and beyond. It is nevertheless important that the novel is brought more explicitly back into the picture—and future research will also need to address much more closely the musical character of "conventional" theater in the period, with its family ties to the world of melodrama; in both dramatic forms we must remember that music was long an integral part of the performance.

I refer to the novel here precisely because its own complicatedly mediated position between "art" and "entertainment" had been manifest throughout the nineteenth century, with critical (and often gendered) comments on its dangers for its popular readership (regularly construed as largely female) in tension with the cultural reality of some of the great educative nineteenth-century novels, like those of Dickens, which nevertheless first appeared as serialized magnets for magazine purchase. By the 1930s, the lucrative, high-selling market for novels—often associated with those female readers whom Holbrook Jackson accused of tending always to "think in pictures"—was already generating the now familiar commercial relationship between popular literary "hits," or "blockbusters," and the films derived from them, often at astonishing speed.[26] Margaret Mitchell's *Gone with the Wind,* which was first published in 1936 and filmed in 1939, is just one of many examples. All of them extend the possibility for comparative work that might illuminate issues of meaning and narrative in the kind of protocinematic subjective visualizations that I have explored in relation to the "romantic" experience of music. The topic is particularly interesting for the way in which film has generated a certain tension between opposing theoretical and analytical approaches to narrative that is directly relevant to the cultural uses of late-romantic music.

TWO OPENINGS AND A DEBATE

Rather than reflecting redundantly on larger-scale issues of narrative strategies concerning, for example, the use of spectacle or the teleology of the dramatic climax or the various "cliff-hanging" devices that were employed—all inherited from theatrical melodrama—it is relevant to my purpose here to look in more detail at the openings of two popularly successful 1941 novels—so successful, indeed, that they were both turned into no less successful films to which I have already had cause to refer. Given the date and the fact that their authors were American, it is not impossible that one or both novels were conceived with film adaptation in mind. Like much literary fiction, they both clearly seek to establish context by evoking things *seen,* or seeable; they call in other ways, too, upon standard modes of narrative that were common in the nineteenth-century novel and would subsequently be adopted by popular cinema. Each paints a scene (or scenes) which could be related to the cinematic "establishing shot" that gives us important information about the where and why of action about to unfold. Each also relies to some extent upon the age-old rhetorical manner of the storyteller who, having waited for us to settle into expectant attention, rewards us with "Once upon a time. . . ."

The first example is closest to that model, where we assume we are being addressed by what theorists sometimes call an "omniscient narrator." The text seems to be generated by a teller who may be improvising, recounting, or recalling (we can't be sure whether the specified date has autobiographical or merely narrative significance), cuing us in to the manner of a story that seems to be about something like "real life," albeit set in the past—the familiar sleight-of-hand of such narrators, who can start their story in any period or place they choose. This narrator is set on conjuring a landscape in detailed verisimilitude before our mind's eye, and we take it that characters will soon appear within it to act out their drama. In terms of the classical Greek theoretical labels that twentieth-century narrative theory has drawn upon, it is a form of "diegesis": a narrative told, related to us by a teller whose identity is unclear. Here we may simply call that person "the novelist":

> Spring came late in the year 1890, so it came more violently, and the fullness of its burgeoning heightened the seasonal disturbance that made unquiet in the blood.
> On this particular day, the twenty-eighth of April, the vast sky seemed vaster than ever—wider, bluer, higher. Continents of white clouds moved slowly from west to east, casting immense drifts of blue over the landscape which seemed alternately to expand and to shrink as sunlight and shadow followed in deliberate procession.

My second example is in some ways similar, but actually relies upon a different technique, closer to what is usually called "mimesis" (after Aristotle, who coined the term). The most obvious kind of "mimesis" is a conventional drama, where a story is performed by actors who assume the roles of characters within it. Here the tale is evidently told by, or at least the opening scene evoked on behalf of, one such a character:

> A blizzard was raging in New York, so she had read on the bulletin board before she left the ship. It was difficult to visualize sheets of fine snow driving

obliquely against facades, while sitting on an open terrace in the sun gazing at calla lilies in bloom bordered by freesia. It was difficult, too, to believe that the scene before her was reality. It was more like a drop curtain rolled down between herself and the dull drab facts of her life.

While an omniscient narrator clearly lurks in the background to tell us that the communicating individual is a "she" ("so she had read"), the text cues us to understand what we are reading at this point as arising from the interior experience of the novel's protagonist (to whom we are indeed being introduced), who has escaped from her usual world.[27] We presume she comes from New York and is on some sort of trip or vacation. We are invited to see through her eyes and to hear her (inner) "voice." At this stage our implied primary narrator might not prove omniscient, but be fixed somehow in the character's (fictional) body, knowing only what she is able to know. Oddly, interestingly, the passage concludes by establishing a kind of parallelism between her experience of "escape" (seeing exotic flowers rather than New York's "sheets of fine snow") and our experience as "escapist" consumers of the fiction in which she figures. The "drop curtain rolled down" might even evoke the film screen on which her story would indeed eventually unfold.

The first of these cited novels is *Kings Row;* the novel by Henry Bellamann became the 1941 film starring Ann Sheridan, Robert Cumming, Ronald Reagan, and Claude Rains). The second is *Now, Voyager* by Olive Higgins Prouty, which became the 1942 film starring Bette Davis, Claude Rains, and Paul Henreid.[28] Each was, as we know, decked out with a rich and complex orchestral score, respectively by Erich Wolfgang Korngold and Max Steiner—scores of a kind that would have been expected and unquestioningly enjoyed as a standard part of the entertainment by audiences who flocked to see such films, whether or not on the strength of the sensational and successful recent novels on which they were based. It was music to sweep one along and away, but also to draw one in and tug at the heartstrings. Where classical narrative theory relies on the distinction between "mimesis" and "diegesis," film theory, particularly as adapted for the use of film *music* study, has come to depend more on the distinction between diegetic and "nondiegetic." The actors' words in the various scenes of the film, along with the music implicitly or visually located as arising from within the diegetic world (a filmed opera scene, music played at a party or emanating from a radio or gramophone)—all would be reckoned to be realistically "diegetic," unlike the musical "underscore." There is no orchestra in the fields outside *Tara* when Scarlett O'Hara and her father gaze back at their family home in *Gone with the Wind*; its "nondiegetic" excess may be associated with the kind of speech heard in those moments of "voice-over" when a character in the drama, or an entirely unknown and presumably omniscient narrator, will speak to us about the film's events, perhaps reflecting back on them from some future vantage point. This distinction has been discussed and periodically challenged by film music theorists, but my concern here is to note that it arose precisely out of a concern to locate and critically theorize the "unrealistic" orchestral underscore and what its function might be. From a music-historical perspective, we can see that its ancestry is clearly related to Wagner and post-Wagnerian operatic practice—like that of Korngold, indeed, or Puccini (the concealed orchestra at Bayreuth has frequently inspired characterization as a technological forerunner of film's prerecorded "sound track" score, whose source and production are no less invisible to the audience). The underscore is, therefore, considered as part of the mechanism of what has been called "transparent narrative": meaning the technique whereby the illusion of narrative logic and continuity is created (particularly in film) by concealed processes of camera and microphone placement, of editing, cutting, and postproduction technical modification.

For the critical theorist of mass culture, all this may be taken to be part of the technology behind the "magic" of cinema, which may be equated with the ideological strategies that have governed the choices made by the editing and manipulating directors and their masters in the film studios for which they work. We are returned to the question of manipulation as a standard component of so-called classical film practice, relying as it appears to do on a spectator constructed as essentially passive (again we might recall Brecht's "wholly passive . . . helpless and involuntary victims"). Of particular interest here, then, and not least in respect of my earlier invocation of Stanley Cavell, is the intervention in the film-theoretical debate which was made in 1985 by the influential critic David Bordwell in his book called simply *Narration in the Fiction Film*.[29] Bordwell's suggestion was that narrative techniques in film might be more searchingly analyzed with the assistance of a kind of theorizing that could deal with both "high" and "low" forms in a less ethically driven and more objective comparison. His desire to reconstruct an *active* type of cinematic spectator was shaped by his reaction to others of the many theorists he cites. His goal, which might be described as one of democratizing and leveling the relationship between filmmakers and spectators, has relevance here in that it proposes a more objective analysis of classical Hollywood cinema, whose narrative effects of technical and technological "seamlessness" and "invisibility" may be construed as designed less to hoodwink than to cue the cinemagoer, as he puts it, "to execute a definable variety of operations"—mental operations, that is, in which a film "trains its spectators."[30] In a sense Bordwell's theoretical project is part of the larger one of removing the value-laden distinction between Hollywood and "art" cinema to the end of fully bringing to attention the aesthetic qualities and complexities of all kinds of film and thus problematizing the older, modernist distinction between the two categories as if it were one between nonart (that is "mere entertainment") and art.

While the leveling effect of Bordwell's project cannot in and of itself absolve us of the need to attend to *historical* debates and critical tensions about the distinctions between "high" art and mass culture, they remove from the making of value judgments some of the "objective" support they have often constructed for themselves in devising theoretical or analytical tools that were from their inception conditioned *by* those very value judgments—many methods of musical analysis have functioned in precisely this way. In the kind of theorizing that the study of film music has relied on, an example of such a value-judgment-driven approach might be that the underscore will be explained as facilitating or even "serving" the cinematic narrative in the way that led Adorno and Eisler to bemoan the "demotion" of music to such a role in film (a strategy that was itself, we know, a relic of Hanslick's approach to the idealizing aesthetic theorization of "absolute" music; for Adorno the key term would be *autonomy*). We might broadly accept that the Hollywood underscore will supply "atmosphere," may identify characters or significant locations with recurring motifs, or may somehow "tell us what the characters are feeling"—but that is deliberately to choose the language of facilitation. An alternative approach would be to suggest that music and narrative in film may at all times be participating in *constructing each other* in ways that suggest a shifting balance of power. As an extension and clarification of narrative processes across a range of media and forms, film may be as much about revealing the meaning of music as music being used to explain and provide continuity for cinematic narrative, as if in denial of its true nature.

This approach would complement or extend Claudia Gorbman's model in *Unheard Melodies,* where she indicated the ideological character of Hollywood's music when observing that even a listener outside the room where a film is showing on television might know when the tinction between a "story" and the way in which it is represented or "told" to accommodate the Formalist terms *fabula* and *syuzhet*.[36] The latter is taken to be the style and detailed structuring of the *way* the story is told; the *fabula* is understood to be the implied background story, the "real" story which the filmed or written narrative may reveal only piecemeal and in deliberately circuitous ways (as most obviously in a mystery or thriller).

The opening of Olive Higgins Prouty's novel *Now, Voyager* provides a useful literary example. In fact my initial descriptive interpretation of it as suggesting that its protagonist may have "escaped from her usual world . . . and is on some sort of trip or vacation" represented an example of simple *fabula* construction. The novel will of course go on to reveal more about the protagonist's history, having plunged into her story in medias res. If the *fabula* is her actual life history, the novelist's *syuzhet* strategy is to open with a nonchronological glimpse of her, midway through the relevant part of her life that in the film is presented in a more nearly conventional chronological fashion. The film's *syuzhet* is thus not really to be distinguished, in its organization of events, from the *fabula* (although Charlotte's first youthful experience of romance on a cruise liner is still presented as a "flashback"). In this theoretical model the music must evidently be associated with the presentational organization of the *syuzhet*, for all that it might evince an identificatory sympathy with the pathos of the *fabula* (in different kinds of film, "pathos" might rather have been "horror" or "triumphant good fortune"). It should be clarified that there is no deep structural correlation between Bordwell's formalist analysis of narrative and a Schenker-style analysis of the structure of "great" tonal music—largely because Schenker's theory was really a mode of critical validation.

It is highly relevant that my implicitly Bordwellian, "recuperative" approach to classical Hollywood music is associated in this key instance with a celebrated melodrama, a "woman's film" that has itself undergone a series of redemptive critical reinterpretations by writers like Jeanine Bassinger and Stanley Cavell.[37] Broadly speaking, the question has been, How do we interpret the therapeutic self-transformation of Charlotte Vale from repressed spinster-daughter into the liberated Beauty who finds love with a married man, only to reject its uncertain promise in favor of adopting his unwanted daughter? The double cigarette lighting and Charlotte's famous line about the moon and the stars takes place before an open window through which the night sky can indeed be seen. At the same time Steiner's celebrated theme, born in female star was on screen, thanks to the role of the euphonious string orchestra's tendency to "cue" the presence of Woman.[31] Laura Mulvey's ideas about classical narrative and the (male) gendered eye of the camera are implicated, in ways that are closely comparable to Catherine Clément's observations about operatic libretti and their concealed misogynist tendencies, and could prove useful here.[32] Mulvey's ideas were relevantly mobilized more recently by Rose Theresa in an interesting essay on what she describes as the "transitional" period in pre-sound cinema between spectacle and narrative: "From Mephistophélès to Méliès: Spectacle and Narrative in Opera and Early Film."[33] Tracing the implications of that transition in close study of both early stagings and early film versions of Gounod's *Faust,* Theresa highlights the implications of Mulvey's idea about the discursive and practical gendering of cinematic narrative as a masculine form of rationalizing control of mimetic "spectacle," conceived as correspondingly feminine. In spectacle an immediate form of pleasurable rapport is established between the viewer and the image's "otherness" (she quotes Mulvey's suggestion that this is aided by "a separation of the erotic identity of the subject from the object on screen").[34] Narrative, however, seems on this schematic to rely upon an assumed "identification of the spectator with a space constructed and shared within the fictional world of film."[35] If we accept the implicit gendering of these conflicting and interacting modes of mimesis and diegesis in the eventually established model of classical narrative cinema, the stakes of how we interpret the emotive tension between spectacle and narrative are raised. This is particularly so if we associate the ostensibly larger-scale structuring role of music with pivotal experiences of visualized spectacle—whose theoretical and ideological gendering brings us back full-circle to Claudia Gorbman's point about Music and Woman. We begin to see how interesting and how revealing it is that "classical" music's conventionally implicit association with structure and control is here performed precisely by its transgressive "late-romantic" descendant, whose character vis-à-vis the canonic norms of the classical style in European music has typically been framed as decadent, excessive, feminine.

The relationship between women and music across my period here has been understood as complicatedly one in which the equation is sometimes demeaning to one, sometimes to the other. Perhaps it might favor both, in ways that could be clarified by David Bordwell's invocation of Russian formalist theories of narrative. His approach in *Narration in the Fiction Film* was ultimately to extend the Aristotelian dis-

Charlotte's moment of self-deprecatingly grateful acknowledgment of a love she seems to accept as "impossible" from the start, almost loses itself on a chord of the flat submediant (D-flat), to which its C natural adds a languishingly Delian major seventh, before rising via a chromatically altered D-flat minor chord to an almost triumphant rhetorical close in F major—notated on the composer's short score with that urgently excited haste and accompanied by the exuberant annotations which I cited earlier. This is simultaneously both excessive and complex, manipulative and expressive in a way that indeed demands that we care to find words for it, to capture "its power of feeling and intelligence," as Cavell had put it.

CONTEMPLATING "UNHEARD" MUSIC

Many in the cinema audiences of the 1930s, 1940s, or 1950s might never have attended a conventional opera performance or symphony concert, yet the passions, pleasures, and responses associated with cinematic experiences were arguably not significantly different. Mahler's relatively "popular" pre–First World War symphonic audience was regarded by some contemporary critics as an audience of endangered bourgeois receivers of socially disruptive "dionysian" excitement, rather like that of the Puccinian operas derided by Brecht or Weissmann.[38] To suggest this is to open up a route by which some of the great classical-Hollywood Westerns or gangster movies, as much as productions like *The Adventures of Robin Hood* (1938), *Gone with the Wind* (1939), *Rebecca* (1940), *Citizen Kane* (1941), or *Casablanca* (1942), might take their part in a still unmapped history of popular music-dramatic forms. These films elaborately revealed, negotiated, and indeed perhaps manipulated the shared tensions, fears, and aspirations of the mass audience of the first half of the twentieth century as it suffered rapid and disturbing social and cultural change, driven of course by powerful political and economic forces and two apocalyptic world wars.

The odd-sounding proposal that cinematic narrative might even, in some sense, have been born *out of* late-romantic music finds support in the various ways in which classical cinematic narratives often specifically represented and even featured music, both literally and as a situated form of cultural practice—showing how "old" European musical sources were appropriated and used in the new cinematic construction of social and subjective experience. Nineteenth-century concert music, laden with the cultural-historical baggage of both its classical and romantic aspects and often crossing the boundary between "diegetic" and "nondiegetic" narrative levels, figures in provocatively interesting ways in both the novel and film versions of *Kings Row* and *Now, Voyager*.

Henry Bellamann, author of the *Kings Row* novel, was himself a musician and former music teacher and was therefore able to mobilize with some degree of authority the "extramusical" implications of Lutheran pastor Axel Berdorff's activities as a teacher, above all of German music.[39] He instructs both the novel's hero-protagonist Parris Mitchell (whose schoolteacher, at the start of the novel, associates his musical talent with the "foreignness" of his background and ability to speak French and German) and the unfortunate violinist Vera Lichinsky, whose Bach playing Berdorff criticizes for its overemotional "sloppy Polish temperament."[40] Berdorff is appropriately described by Bellamann as having picture-book "Beethovenian" characteristics and, of course, that authentic underlying intellectuality and spirituality that were key components of "classical music" in the popular imagination that was also Hollywood's: "Herr Berdorff was a giant of a man. His thick black hair shook in every direction and his eyes, magnified behind shining lenses, sparkled and burned with intensity.... His extreme sincerity and earnestness reminded Parris of the thunderous German sermons he had heard in the little Lutheran church."[41]

The film version of *Kings Row* in fact knowingly performs what Berdorff might have called a "Polish," and therefore implicitly "feminine," form of appropriation of Beethoven (whose "greatness" Berdorff considered as self-evident as Chopin's lack of it).[42] In the film's closing scenes Parris himself assumes the role of teacher for the attractive Austrian girl who has come to live with her father in what had once been Parris's old home with his grandmother. Torrid and murderous events have since unfolded and Parris has trained in Vienna to become a doctor appropriately specializing in mental illness. As a result, he is multiply well equipped to act as mentor to Elise when she plays for him the opening of the Beethoven *Pathétique* sonata. But Korngold knew as much as Parris about the cultural legacy of such music as the "underscore" to bourgeois experience, perhaps to the construction of bourgeois subjectivity in the nineteenth century. When the cinematic music lesson stops, he permits himself to appropriate the second, more passionately lyrical version (from bar 5) of the sonata's grandiose opening evocation of a Baroque French overture. He coaxes it beautifully into a "late-romantic" version of itself, scored and reharmonized in the style of his own early opera *Violanta,* to act as underscore to the implicitly erotic conversation that ensues between the player and her would-be teacher. Its transition from the diegetic world of polite domesticity into the less restrained nondiegetic subjectivity of the underscore seems to model the secret history of musical development in the period with which I have been concerned.

The role of authentically "late-romantic" music as the subjectivity-enhancing underscore to social life in the early twentieth century figures in no less interesting ways in *Now, Voyager.* In Olive Higgins Prouty's novel it plays a rather significant role in the finale, whose otherwise faithful cinematic realization we have already considered. A key moment, a little earlier in Prouty's narrative, had been reached when Charlotte, in a room removed from her partying friends, confronts Jerry (who has tried to kiss her).[43] She tells him of Dr. Jaquith's warning about how she must deal with their relationship, presumably desexualizing it, if she is to keep Jerry's daughter, Tina. "Don't you see?" she pleads, "—O Jerry, please help me":

> He didn't sit down or reply. She walked back to the fire and waited, gazing at his back. His shoulders were squared, his chin was up, and she knew he was getting his disrupted emotions into line and under control again. They did not speak for several minutes, but the protracted silence was veiled by music. Neither tango nor rumba now, nor the syncopated beat of jazz. June and her friends had stopped dancing. The pure, exalted strains of Wagner's Prelude to *Lohengrin,* flowed into the room now, calming and uplifting.[44]

Where the novel invokes Wagner's beatific musical depiction of the passage to earth of the angel-borne Holy Grail, reinscribing late-romanticism's "realization" of the Romantic construction of classical music as both revelation and commodified bringer of harmonious calm, the film features diegetic music in a still more complex, participatory relationship with Charlotte's inner narrative and negotiation of her subjective drama.[45] In the novel a crucial scene had found her sitting between her fiancé, Elliot, and Jerry at the theater after a pretheater social gathering at which she had reencountered Jerry in person, though he remained ignorant of her engagement. They whisper: he has to leave for New York the following morning; he wants to come to her house that night for a few minutes. "I must talk to you," he says.[46]

In the film the theater is replaced by a concert hall in which we see the three characters seated as in the novel, but now attending a performance of the first movement of Tchaikovsky's Sixth Symphony ("Pathétique"). It was a work that still occupied (with Tchaikovsky's

Fourth and Fifth Symphonies) a key place in the popular concert repertoire, its powerfully dramatized, yet publicly unspecified emotional content inviting sympathetic private interpretation that was critically "feminized" (as nostalgic, self-indulgent, over-demonstrative, etc.) even before Tchaikovsky's sexuality became a topic of overt public discussion. But there is little evidence, from what we see, that any of the film's three cast members are really "listening"—all being occupied with their own internal discourse or, in Elliott's case, simply "being at a symphony concert" as a social duty.

Yet we know that the music has singular designs upon Charlotte, and that her own particular internal discourse seems to demonstrate a close affinity with the externalized passion of Tchaikovsky's symphony. We know precisely because it continues to play, unbroken and in real time, in the underscore (is it therefore in her head, too?) after the film cuts to her return home and her anxious, anticipatory pacing across the darkened drawing room floor, waiting for Jerry's arrival. Which does not happen. We watch her, in a movie, as she seems to rehearse private cinematic scenarios in her mind, to the accompaniment of the Tchaikovsky symphony; but her anxious reverie is interrupted by the telephone ringing, which rudely ousts the Tchaikovsky from the underscore (and, we presume, her mind). It returns later on the radio, as she talks to Elliot, to signify the "uninhibited" passion that is significantly absent from *their* relationship—which they cordially agree to terminate; the Tchaikovsky accompanies her as subjective underscore as she goes to confront her mother with the news, again significantly crossing the diegetic/nondiegetic boundary, but as if to explain rather than to erase it.

We have seen that public betrayal of the transgressive, secretly internalized symphonic "program" was often viewed in high-status concert culture like a sexual misdemeanor: concerning something that was probably widespread but best not discussed or acknowledged in public. Music's "transcendence" of the worldly remained the official ideological-aesthetic legacy of Romanticism, as the mask of "good" (rather than merely popular) classical music. Perhaps such programs may have been one source of actual cinematic narratives as much as their second-hand decorative coating. The excessive, feminine "sugariness" of such decoration (like the icing on the proverbial cake) was often just a descriptive trope—part of the machinery of discursive public protection from (and potentially *of*) music like Tchaikovsky's Sixth Symphony. Its dramatically staged soliloquy is one in which tragic brooding, an eruptive rhetoric of protestation and the self-destructive, self-justifying pathos of escapist lyrical abandonment construct a complex subjective narrative, perhaps like that of Charlotte Vale as she waits anxiously, hopefully, passionately for Jerry's arrival. Tchaikovsky's music may even have become for her the subjective underscore of a narrative like that of Olive Higgins Prouty's *Now, Voyager,* like that of Irving Rapper's film with Max Steiner's score. Literary fiction, film and late-romantic music constantly overlapped, intermingled, and exchanged with each other in the popular imaginative economy of mid-twentieth-century Europe and America. The new and the old forms of narrated subjectivity were linked in ways that challenge received readings of the history of culture and taste in the period; here the medium of film might even appear to have triumphed over Modernism in the name of a more than usually sympathetic form of modernity.

CHAPTER 6

The Bitter Truth of Modernism

A Late-Romantic Story

> *Moses:* Shall Aron, my mouth, fashion this image?
> Then I have fashioned an image too, false
> as an image must be.
> Thus I am defeated!
> Thus all was but madness that I believed before,
> And can and must not be given voice.
> O word, thou word, that I lack!
>
> —Moses, speaking the final lines of Schoenberg's
> *Moses und Aron*, 1928–32

> *Starkman:* Rosita, look!
> I sense Romanticism—
> It isn't dead yet!
> Enthralling, gripping,
> I prophesy . . .
> *Rosita:* Oh shut up!
>
> —A critic in Schreker's *Christophorus*, 1925–29, act 2, scene 5[1]

Some scene setting is required for my final engagement with late-romanticism in one of its more reactive and perhaps terminal modes. Here a late-romanticism that has taken critical self-awareness to a point where, as in the first movement of Korngold's symphony, it seems almost to enact its own invalidation and submit to the linear "history of modern music" which it has been my aim to problematize. But the late-romantic crisis involved here, like the post–First World War "Opernkrise" that it shadowed, was located in the interwar years, its outcomes terminally threatened, unsupported by factions or followers. Given its often localized, specifically conditioned nature, and the enormity of contemporary world-historical events, this late-romantic crisis was less widely noticed than those mythologized musical-modernist ones supposedly marked by the 1913 premiere of Stravinsky's *Le Sacre du Printemps* and Schoenberg's Viennese "Skandalkonzert" in that same year.[2] In order to understand events nearly two decades later, as experienced by one composer of the period, it is worth invoking the undoubted richness and almost chaotic diversity of the culture of "Weimar" Germany between the wars, even as it headed toward disaster.

Here, after all, was where the purveyors of late-romanticism could expect to meet (and did meet) the harshest and most articulate of their public critics in a musical culture as replete with criticism, journalism, and opinions as it was with orchestras, concert halls, and opera houses, not to mention cinemas, nightclubs, operetta and vaudeville theaters. Audiences were inevitably multiplying and fragmenting. My final subject, Franz Schreker, had in fact taken early Weimar period operagoers by storm with his richly erotic, veristic demonstrations of creative and psychosexual boldness in works whose settings and music glowed with a kind of magic-realist color. This his orchestra famously produced in tones that ranged from the apocalyptically "expressionist" to the most subtle experiments in late-romantic timbral alchemy, creating sounds that glistened and luminesced in extraordinary ways. Schreker's investment in the trappings of what could easily be put down to late-romantic nostalgia and decadence was certainly beginning to inspire more or less fond lampoons by his own composition students in the mid-1920s—but their fashion-conscious levity was unwittingly aligned with more dangerous forms of critical denunciation in a world where even music criticism could slip with threatening ease into explicitly political gear.[3]

After dismissive reviews of his opera *Irrelohe* in 1924, Schreker, the composition teacher who could turn his hand to many styles, responded to what he clearly saw (earlier than Korngold in Vienna) to be a decisive change in the cultural-political climate and the potential reconstitution of his audience. New Music was in fashion; it was the era of the International Society for Contemporary Music and a host of festivals devoted to music variously new and old, sometimes both together. The grand Romantic style of "art"-earnestness was at the same time being challenged by a new metropolitan fashion- and style-conscious embrace of mass cultural manners and sounds, whether in Brecht's high-minded political *Lehrstücke* for the common man or in satirical cabaret songs that embraced both decadence and modernity with wry irony. And then there were the "Zeitopern" (literally, "contemporary operas") exemplified by Schreker's pupil Ernst Krenek's *Jonny spielt auf* of 1927. That opera's programmatic "replacement" of the old-style glacier- and Nature-inspired composer Max by the black jazz violinist Jonny, who would strike up the dance embarkation number as they all boarded the train to America at the end, thematized something of the later Weimar fantasy—be it ironic or genuine. It played to a desire for modern urban escapism into the world of wealth, fast cars, and popular chic to which Berlin aspired, wishing away the wounds (and the wounded) of the First World War and the economic and associated moral tribulations that now beset it and would hasten its demise.

Something of the Berlin of that period was caught not only in contemporary films like *The Blue Angel* (1930), but also in Schreker's posthumous *Christophorus* (completed in 1929); this "Vision of an Opera" evokes a seedy nightclub world of drink, drugs, psychic novelty acts, and functional cabaret dance music. Its stylistic turn toward some of the manners of modernism begs the question as to what relevance or function late-romantic luxuriance might still have in this world. Set against the fascism of the National Socialist Party, defining a new political agenda, even a new culture of action and "belonging," Schreker's creative journey and fate pose a special challenge to the critical concerns that have shadowed my quest after ways of reconceptualizing and rehearing late-romantic music. One of my aims throughout has been to problematize the direct equation of apparent stylistic conservatism with its more political or ideological counterpart. As conditioned by the history of the publicly embattled issue of musical expression and "programmatic" meaning, much of the evidence has been ambivalent and complicatedly mediated. It is something which is in no way easily or conclusively read in a period that would witness ever bolder and more naively fundamentalist expressions of political and ethical artistic idealism that were conditioned by, and also generated, increasingly tangible and physical levels of threat. With Schreker the urgent beauty and deliberate grotesqueries of his later music and the ambivalence of his conceptual and ideological stance were heightened in ways that raise the stakes of my critical enterprise.

HEDONISTIC POETRY

At the beginning of this study, I indicated that its subtitle alluded to two specific operas by Schreker—*Der ferne Klang* (the distant sound) and

Der singende Teufel (the singing devil). These seemed to offer convenient metaphors both for the historical and critical location of the broad repertoire of European late-romantic music, and the more partisan and even ethical issues raised by it. As post–First World War Modernism's historical goad and converse, it was something modernist criticism sought to historicize and therefore distance. "Modernist" music in its turn would come to seek the clarity of historically validated forms and an ascetically reformulated musical language. We have seen that late-romantic works, on the other hand, with their grandiose orchestral technology of sensuous and emotional involvement, also became readable in part through their discursive mobilization of space: the social and cultural as well as geographical space in which some of their sounds were presented as more or less "distant" than others, suggesting hierarchy and implying numinous promise, or portent, linked to degrees of presence or absence. The "politics" of late-romanticism's move into the popular traffic in passion, not least in film, entailed an often-foregrounded confrontation with its own negative critical image as projected by the opposing discourse of high modernism. This is where the "singing devil" comes in—an image that accommodates variously theorized critical constructions of late-romanticism's style and cultural use, its cultural *project* even (particularly when it reached Hollywood).

Often that project is seen, in the light of mass culture critique, as one of anaesthetizing, sensualizing, and affirming: generating forms of aesthetic pleasure of which the twentieth century became advisedly wary. Put more simply, the question might retrospectively be, *Was* it all just bourgeois decadence and evasively escapist self-indulgence? *Was that* the end point of the century-and-a-half long musical quest of the Romanticism with which I have consistently associated this repertoire? Musicology has, we know, often sided with its dismissive distancing. Joseph Kerman's introduction to his 1990 collection called *Music at the Turn of Century* noted that the period "was also the period of *Madam Butterfly*, *The Merry Widow*, *Pomp and Circumstance*, and *Maple-Leaf Rag*," adding (as if to comfort the reader), "though nothing about these works or their like appears in the present collection."[4] And nothing of romantic modernism, to judge by what he goes on to say: "What the project did achieve was . . . a cross-section of the best writing now being devoted to those aspects of turn-of-the-century music that particularly interest scholars of today. The music of modernism, rather than the more conservative music of the time, or popular music, remains the focus of this interest."[5]

Behind such a project lay the powerful, usually masculine voices of the modernists themselves, even Aaron Copland's, whose little volume *The New Music, 1900–1960* in its "revised and enlarged" 1968 edition ("one of the classics of the twentieth-century literature on music," its cover proclaimed) had included the assessment that Sibelius's music "does not grapple with the problems of our own world. It belongs rather in the post-Tchaikovskian world of the early 1900s"[6]—and that, while Copland was broadly sympathetic toward him: "Debussy was the hedonistic poet of a thoroughly bourgeois world. There is something cushioned and protected, something velvety soft and uncomfortable about his music. . . . A time may come when it will seem overrefined, decadent, effeminate."[7]

The arguments are on one level compelling and seem to make sense, until we ask ourselves what specific or additional cultural work they are doing as they shift deceptively from history to criticism of a particular ideological hue. Criticism is a part of history, of the history of modernism, particularly from the perspective of its victims. Which is to say that as historians we might wish to understand such arguments as much as simply believe them—something which could certainly apply to the 1920s disparagement of Schreker, oddly close as its language came to that of Copland's thoughts about Debussy. Its exemplification of late-romanticism's uneasy complimentary relationship with modernism appropriately takes us back to the Germanic world quitted by Korngold in 1938, four years after Schreker's untimely death. A piece of off-the-cuff local criticism will evoke the kind of thing Schreker was up against. Writing to his friend Alban Berg, in the period of *Wozzeck*'s early triumphs in 1929, about a Berlin production of *Der ferne Klang* conducted by Schreker himself, Theodor Adorno put his feelings about it rather directly and succinctly, describing it as "palatable only to maidservants; a series of kitsch postcards."[8]

If ever there was a period put-down of a period work, this must take the prize. In another piece from around the same time, Adorno would sum up Schreker's output as a stylistic product of *Jugendstil*, "whose intensities might now be encountered in faded miniature in postcards from that time."[9] But it is the specificity of the terms of that 1929 put-down of *Der ferne Klang* that is so striking: something for women, but not even bourgeois women: women of the petit bourgeoisie or worse, the *servant* class—a class that seems to overspill the bounds of Copland's specifically American image of a decadent European bourgeoisie, "cushioned" and soft, like that cited in Charles Ives's frequent diatribes.¹⁰ As is often the case, Adorno can be at his most interesting when being catty. He writes, in fact, particularly revealingly about Schreker in passages less self-consciously addressed to his Second Viennese School friends. A good example is the 1959 radio talk which formed the basis of the Schreker essay in his 1963 collection *Quasi una fantasia*.

For Adorno, Schreker purveyed critically confusing "mixed drinks" of artistic taste: they were intoxicating but still sought to avoid turning into merely easily purchasable commodities.¹¹ Almost in exasperation, Adorno formulated his accusation against Schreker's music (the emphasis is mine): "Pre-artistically it ignores the distinction between the culinary—music as literal physical appeal—and the thoroughly formed, *it pays no attention to constructive discipline.*"¹² Not only had Schreker persevered, in Adorno's view, in following the path of pre–First World War Viennese radicalism without any recourse to the self-limiting economies of neoclassicism or hermetic organizational principles, he had taken the rarefied and ravishing sound, the *Klang* of decadent esoteric modernism, back into the popular arena where it may have belonged. There, musical effect and musical experience mattered first above the arduously acquired knowledge and technique that might nevertheless be required to generate it. Thus Adorno's shocked picture of Schreker's music as containing an authentically radical element within a "Kitsch" exterior.¹³ In spite of his subsequent and satirically infantilizing (or feminizing) allusion to Schreker's "music of puberty" ("A fifteen-year-old indulges in this manner when improvising at the keyboard"),¹⁴ we might note Adorno's readiness to engage, with Paul Bekker and all the other Schrekerians, in a fascinated verbal evocation of the Schreker sound:

> In unconscious surrealism the aesthetic distance is withdrawn, the listener's body enveloped in pleasure. . . . The consciousness of its unattainability . . . brings into prominence, with malicious cunning (by its appearance of wanting the opposite), weakness and impotence. Yet from that ambivalence the Schrekerian 'Klang' gains its smoldering subliminality and, in its highest moments, that sweetness which thrives where weeping could be as little repressed as happiness.¹⁵

Adorno's adherence to a self-sacrificingly idealistic, nonconsumable "progressive" art entailed persistent suspicion of the consumable, intellectually anaesthetizing "popular" art of modern mass society. This suspicion was too strongly conditioned by the orthodox musician in him for him to be able readily admit into his pantheon the manifestly popular and yet manifestly self-critical and often *stylistically* "modern" Schreker. Adorno's ambivalence was nevertheless so eloquently expressed that we may learn much from what most deeply worried him about Schreker's work, when he observes, "in that it is led by a compulsion stronger than shame, to testify to what culture socially and aesthetically forbids, doubt in culture itself is voiced in it."[16]

Not even Adorno could avoid disparaging Schreker in a way that makes his music sound highly interesting—and somehow representative of late-romantic musical energies and obsessions. This attribution of a modernistically anarchic side to it, something threatening to "culture itself," might be linked back to my earlier observation that what concerned Adorno was that Schreker seemed to purvey a complex kind of musical-sensual experience whose urgency and significance was dissociated from the usual "difficulty" of Great Music in the idealized German Romantic manner—as something professional and deep, out of the reach of the "ignorant audience." By commodifying music's experience, Schreker might therefore seem to invite an ironic, Leverkühnian reading of the double image that advertised this study in its original form as a series of lectures: Friedrich's lonely Wanderer drawing from "Nature" the inspiration he might then bestow upon the eagerly waiting throng of an urban concert audience (see figure 1). Perhaps that image was itself a kind of deception: a piece of manipulative Romantic ideology, constructing the Artist as mysteriously inspired sage: as "vessel" rather than agent, rather than the professional note smith working within an established form of cultural practice and with an audience seeking escapist experience of a kind and for reasons that were perhaps both profound and shared.[17] Perhaps—no, *precisely* this is what Schreker's *Der ferne Klang* addressed in a way that was as threatening to the popular but incomplete cultural image of "romantic art" as had been Wackenroder's skeptical monk, who had suggested that Joseph Berglinger might have been born to "enjoy art rather than to practise it."

THE DISTANT SOUND

Thematizing its own critique in a remarkable way, *Der ferne Klang* is a late-romantic opera that provides all the scenic and musical thrills and melodramatic climaxes that a popular audience could wish for. Schreker's libretto was often criticized for rather transparently facilitating all those things; at the same time conservative court opera intendants—perhaps like that of the Imperial and Royal Court Opera in Vienna (the city where Schreker wrote *Der ferne Klang*)—affected unease at the opera's inclusion of low-life characters and prostitutes.[18] These things have confirmed its status as in fact no less modern than it was popular. The most obviously recognizable models are threefold. There is the German folk- or fairy-tale opera (like Humperdinck's *Hänsel und Gretel*); there is contemporary naturalism drawing on Italian verismo (the increasingly "modern" settings of acts 2 and 3 include not only the inevitable prostitutes, but also steam-train whistles and urban traffic noise heard from a street café). And then there is the genre of the venerable Romantic *Künstlerroman*—novels or stories about artists and their lives and problems, like Wackenroder's "Joseph Berglinger" story and, of course, Mann's *Doctor Faustus,* with many interim examples. Three moments from the opera will give some idea of how it works on the various levels that I have referred to and, of course, what it sounds like.

We might appropriately turn to the first scene from act 1, set in the fadedly elegant but sparsely furnished living room of the Graumann's house in a small German town that could have come out of any folktale. Only the nearby railway line, of which we become aware later in the act, pulls the setting into the turn-of-the-century present. Grete Graumann is talking to her boyfriend, Fritz, who is standing outside the living room window (already there is a symbolic barrier between them). He tells her that he is going to "escape" to find fame and fortune and apologizes for having to leave her. She is clearly more than ready to come with him, but he knows the patriarchal script too well. She must look after her mother while he goes off, "Far—far away," to find the freedom he needs to realize his ambitions and to capture the inspirational otherworldly sound, associated of course with "Nature," on which his artistic fame will rest:

> A great, exalted goal / hovers before my eyes
> but I must be free—free!; / For no peace will I find
> for joy or pleasure / no peace for love and happiness—
> [*mysteriously*]
> until I have it in my grasp / that enigmatic, other-worldly [*weltfernen*]
>   sound / that I get snatches of—so oddly—
> you know, Gretel, / like when the wind—with spirit hands
> plays across harp strings—far off—far off.
> And so I'll seek the Master / who plays that harp;
> I'll find the harp / that produces that sound;
> and with that sound [*Klang*] / I'll be rich and free—
> an artist—then I'll come back / a famous man—
> anxiously to approach my / sweet love!
> But I'll be welcomed / with a cheerful smile,
> proudly I'll court / the loveliest of brides
> and lay at her feet / riches and fame—
> all my love— / my self![19]

In spite of the hallucinatory grandeur of the processional theme which accompanies the words "And so I'll seek the Master" (it had appeared in the Prelude and here briefly mesmerizes Grete into singing in duet with Fritz's repeated "like when the wind"), she resists this premature relegation to her gender role. When Grete finally jumps out of a ground-floor window of the inn over the road (where she has been "won" in a skittles game) and runs after Fritz, the opera appears effectively to become hers. Its one piece of old-style scenic magic comes in some scrubby woodland within earshot of the railway (this is where the train whistle is heard). Here she briefly contemplates drowning herself in a pond, before it is transformed in her eyes into a naively utopian vision of natural beauty with animals coming to drink in the moonlight. In her ensuing sleep, she is found by an old procuress who might have been a fairy godmother, but who instead takes her off into a life of sin.

Fritz is still far away and "out there" searching for his sound when act 2 opens in the Venetian island bordello where Grete now reigns as its leading attraction. The pleasurable opera thus features a feminized site of sensual pleasure which is introduced by an extraordinary welter of acousmatic music—multiple women's voices, siren voices, calling to their clients who come across the lagoon in gondolas. The unsung music is no less multiple: what starts out as a light scherzando overture gives way to atmospheric effects overlaid with "Venetian" music and then a "gypsy" band, later featuring elaborately notated quasi-improvised cimbalom passages.[20] All of its unsynchronized voices are situated in a confusingly limitless space whose focus remains unclear for some time, and Schreker's stage direction stipulates that he wanted the listener to be enveloped, as if directly involved as a guest at the "Casa di maschere":

> *"La Casa delle Maschere." A "dance hall" on an island in the Gulf of Venice. A hall, on both sides of which marble stairs lead to an upper floor....*
>
> *The hall opens onto a small section of garden with southern flowers, palms, pines etc. Still further back is the sea. Hall & garden are lit, Chinese lanterns etc. Visible on the sea are separated points of lights from approaching small craft, barques, periodically music is carried across by the wind....*
>
> *The following scenes, whether more or less comprehensible is unimportant, should be played and delivered vividly, so that the various on-stage sounds (singing from above, gypsy music, music from gondolas, the Count's serenade) mix in such a way that the listener has as true an impression as possible that he find himself in the midst of it all, that it creates a mysterious and confused overture to the entertainment that follows.*
>
> *For the action itself, important events must be presented so that they clearly reach the listener and grab his attention.*

FIGURE 7. Schreker, *Der ferne Klang*, 1912. Act 3, scene 1, set design by Alfred Roller. Grete (Lisbeth Sellin) can be seen lying in the foreground, having been brought from the opera house that is visible in the background. (By permission of the Franz Schreker Foundation.)

In fact, Fritz does eventually appear in this act—passing through the bordello as romantic artists must—only to encounter Grete, to recognize her, but then to melodramatically reject her as a "whore." Her response is bitter: she angrily fights off her feelings by falling into in a wild Czardas with another admirer—this ends the act.

By act 3, however, she has fallen on harder times. Having lost her youthful luster, she is back in Vienna as a common streetwalker, seeking her clients where she can. She has indeed fallen more or less to the level of a maidservant and thematically offers herself to music history as a model female audience member for the very opera we are watching, which is what has moved her—ostensibly as Fritz's opera, of course: we hear distant but recognizable motifs and snatches of its music from the nearby opera house (played by an offstage orchestra) as they drift over to the street theater café where Grete has been brought (figure 7):

> *Act III/i: The fore-garden of a theater-café. A broad street runs diagonally in front of it. Not unduly busy, but occasional trams, buses, carriages etc. Clearly visible on the street is the Court Theatre. Brightly lit. Periodically can be heard coming from it, very mutedly, the sound of passionate music and applause. Many coaches wait nearby. It is late evening.*

She had been there in the theater, listening to his opera (or is it still hers?)—perhaps in the cheap *Stehplätze*. She had collapsed, partly from tiredness but implicitly from her emotional response to what she has been hearing and seeing. This is richly modeled at the end of the first scene that gives into the great *Nachtstück* interlude that will facilitate the final scene change but is in reality a focal point of the opera. When the curtain rises again, it will be on the ailing and older Fritz, "waiting for her," as she has been told by Dr. Vigelius (an old friend who has recognized her). As Vigelius supports her in the sidewalk cafe, she begins to revisit her youthful vision of long ago, thinking of Fritz, but hearing the music, with us. Swooning, like any opera-going "maidservant," she appropriates it as hers, whispering, "Ach, die wilde Musik!":

End of scene 1 *[The street has grown quiet, the lamps extinguished.]*

Grete: *[very faintly, dreaming]*
>The trees murmur / a wonderful song.
>Far away it sounds / from the tree tops.
>But it was so lovely— / and he—longs for me.
>Ah, the wild music!
>And he—longs for me.—[Interlude (*Nachtstück*)]

Here, for a few wonderful minutes, we are left alone in the theater with this music, the curtain having fallen on the stage picture.[21] Amid the recalled memories, fears, regathered hopes, and breaking waves of ecstatic affirmation, we are returned to the late-romantic symphonic experience. We become Grete, and we become the expectant, rueful Fritz in what must count as one of the great subjective musical monologues (in reality, a duologue?) of late-romantic music. Following his visionary aria in the scene that follows, celebrating the almost aleatory dawn chorus that he realizes he has never before truly "heard," Fritz too finds himself lost in music, in the "distant sound" that now surrounds him, and also Grete when she arrives. But *this* music is only atmospherics—an enigmatic series of arpeggiated chromatic chords for offstage piano and harp, its source and nature still obscure. He begins at last to realize that she, of course, is its true origin; all he can do is fully assume the role and gender behavior of Catherine Clément's Undone Woman and die in Grete's arms—leaving her, once again, to confront the reality that *he* has consistently evaded.

SINGING DEVILS

The opera was a runaway success and set Schreker on a path to early fame that led, via *Das Spielwerk und die Prinzessin* (1913) and *Die*

Gezeichneten (1918), to his being appointed to the directorship of the Berlin Musik-Hochschule in 1920, where his growing band of successful composition students included Ernst Krenek (of *Jonny spielt auf* fame) and Alois Haba. With his honorary membership of the Prussian Academy of Arts, as senator, his colleagues could eventually be taken to include Schoenberg, Hindemith, Busoni, Pfitzner, and other notable musicians of the day. But these were, to say the least, difficult times, politically and economically, and particularly so for a part-Jewish composer (for all that he had been brought up by his Catholic mother from the age of ten, when his Jewish father had died). First came runaway inflation, then widespread unemployment, and the ever more tense and factionalized politics for which Schreker had little taste, but could in no way avoid and felt increasingly oppressed by—particularly as reflected in the factionalism of the musical press. Criticism of his works increased after Adolf Weissmann (author of *Der klingende Garten* and other works on contemporary music and the most powerful Berlin critic of the day) had played his part in trashing *Irrelohe* in 1924. In a sense all Schreker's operas after that bore the marks of self-imposed compromise and realignment of the kind that we encountered to some degree in Korngold's Symphony in F sharp; but for Schreker the direct confrontation with German cultural as well as party politics in Berlin imposed an additional requirement somehow to accommodate conservative as well as modernist taste. The latter was probably his main concern. Even as his students were becoming prominent in European "new music" circles, Schreker, having produced the first new operatic success of the Weimar Republic in *Der Schatzgräber,* had found himself relegated to the modernists' scrap heap, The creative results, in *Christophorus* (an extraordinary "Zeitoper" never performed in his lifetime), in *Der singende Teufel,* and finally, *Der Schmied von Gent* are of extraordinary interest.

Much of what he achieved in these operas was presaged in *Der ferne Klang,* whose problematization of the male Romantic Artist might conceivably be read as opening the way for the factionalized defeat of late-romanticism by musical modernism, leaving "decadents," ladies of the night, and of course, maidservants, to entertain themselves with Puccini and performances of *Die tote Stadt* or *Der ferne Klang* (in a sense these might indeed be recategorized as "women's operas" just as we now talk about "women's films" as a historical category, without opprobrium). The ever more public and politicized tension between these two, now opposing poles of musical cultural practice became the dangerous territory in which Schreker's inspiration found the energy to extend further his series of sensational operas. These had consistently tended symbolically to allegorize Art, and specifically Music (even more specifically late-romantic music), in the form of instruments: most strikingly ambivalent, never-quite-under-control mechanical ones like the fantastically complex music machine of Meister Florian in *Das Spielwerk* that can inspire both beneficially sacred and destructively profane celebrations, or the great organ, the "singing devil" of the penultimate opera, that becomes the instrument not only of the local tribal people's pacification but also of their subsequent massacre.

That such things could be produced at all at that time tells us something about the diversity and richness of late Weimar culture which I sought earlier to evoke, but less about its dangers. Alexandra Ritchie, in her book *Faust's Metropolis,* has succinctly described the darkness of what was really happening in Berlin:

> The illusion of success was shattered by the devastating world economic crisis which reached Germany at the end of 1929, a crisis which destroyed the last vestiges of support for the republic and which pushed the moderate left towards the communists and the frightened middle classes into the waiting arms of the Nazis. The terrible images of Weimar Berlin in its death throes, with its extremism, its lines of starving unemployed workers, its increasingly brutal street violence and the scenes of Jews and other "enemies" of the community being harassed and beaten up foreshadowed that which was to come.[22]

Already in 1931, the venerable Jewish theater critic Alfred Kerr had, with crude gallows humor, put the number of theater closures down to "an overflowing of directors' pants."[23] It is little short of bizarre that Schreker's last opera, *Der Schmied von Gent,* could have been premiered in Berlin's Städtische Oper in late October 1932, just months before Hitler became chancellor and with the anti-Semite Wilhelm Rode taking the leading role (he would join the Nazi Party in the spring of 1933 and later took over the theater, as a favorite of the Führer).[24] Terrorist acts were so frequent in 1932 that martial law had been declared: street battles were commonplace. It was a year in which the "half-Jewish" Schreker had to deal professionally with a serious anti-Semitic dispute in the Hochschule, before himself bowing to pressure and stepping down as director; it was also a year in which organized groups of Brownshirts might be encountered at almost any event sponsored by, or foregrounding, Jews. *Der Schmied von Gent* had indeed just five performances before it disappeared from the stage, subsequently to be

FIGURE 8. Photograph, apparently taken on set during rehearsals for *Der Schmied von Gent*, Berlin 1932. Schreker is in the rear, with Charlotte Müller (Smee's wife) to his left. In front of them Wilhelm Rode (Smee) converses with stage director, Rudolf Zindler. Conductor Paul Breisach sits front right (Theatermuseum der Universität zu Köln).

"replaced" with a fully Aryan opera based on the same Flemish tale of *Smetse Smee* from Charles de Coster and called *Die Schmiede* (by the Dresden composer Kurt Striegler).[25] Was Schreker himself dicing with the Devil, supping with the Devil or mocking the Devil in this "grand magic opera" that marked the end of his career? It was also effectively the last big operatic premiere of the Weimar Republic. We know that it was well attended and warmly applauded, but also that Schreker himself was booed rowdily from the stage by a cohort (one assumes) of Brownshirts when *he* came on to take his bow.[26] Perhaps no late, late-romantic German work is quite so revealing of the complexity of what might be called the politics of late-romantic passion in this period. But what devils and what passions—political, cultural, or personal—are we confronting here? Much is revealed in the rather tense body language and expressions of Schreker, Wilhelm Rode, and Charlotte Müller (costumed for their roles of Smee and his wife), with stage director Rudolf Zindler and conductor Paul Breisach, in a photograph taken during the rehearsals for *Der Schmied von Gent* in 1932 (see figure 8).

Since my reading of the work was inspired by the fine production of it that I saw in Chemnitz early in 2010, I will permit myself a final, brief, but I hope relevant autobiographical interlude that bears upon the difficulty of reading texts that themselves might be responding to wider problems about grasping the true nature of, and the true threat posed by, chaotic and violent sociopolitical events of the kind Schreker would have been experiencing in the period of *Der Schmied von Gent*.[27] Devotees of so-called forgotten late-romantic operas are used to feeding their passion with air miles and railway tickets. As chance would have it, my journey to Chemnitz started with a flight into Dresden on the evening of Saturday, 13 February. The plan was to take the train from there to Chemnitz, formerly the GDR's Karl Marx Stadt. However, it soon became clear that something was wrong when I asked at the airport information desk how best to get to the *Hauptbahnhof*. With a guardedly worried expression, the woman behind the counter told me that she would normally have directed us to the "S-Bahn," but that it was not running. My ear for German was still not fully tuned, and I missed some of the details, but "protests" and "demonstrations" came through clearly enough, along with the advice that a taxi would be the only way to reach the station that evening.

It emerged that it was the sixty-fifth anniversary of the horrifying Allied destruction of Dresden by firebombing in 1945; the next day we learned that many hundreds of moderate Dresdeners, in what sounded in itself like a scene of Meyerbeerian operatic grandeur, had joined hands to encircle the impressively reconstructed *Altstadt* and prevent the threatened demonstration there by what the papers called "old and new Nazis" who wanted to turn the day into one of protest at the Allies' war crime.[28] Complex historical and political experiences determined the various opposed agendas, but by the time our taxi had set off into the night in the direction of Dresden's *Hauptbahnhof*, large numbers of young neo-Nazis, kept on the other side of the river by the police during the day, had now evidently spilled back into the town center, not least to make *their* way to the station for night trains home. The frozen, snow-banked streets were intermittently lit by flashing police car lights; many road bridges were blocked by the police; five or six large, heavy-duty armored cars were lined up at one point. Our young female taxi driver was evidently nervous but did a virtuosic job of avoiding rubbish bins that had been dragged into the center of some streets, where groups of youths on corners were eagerly communicating on mobile phones. Then, as we turned into another broad avenue, a phalanx of dark-clad youths were suddenly marching toward us across its full width, a large unadorned black flag (anarchist?) waving in their midst. It was the first of many hasty U-turns, but eventually we made it to the station, only to encounter the highly threatening presence of green-boiler-suited police, a number armed, both outside and inside the station—even lined up across our platform. They let us through to the far end but were apparently intent upon keeping the "trouble" at the station-end of the train—whose final destination was, of all places, Nuremberg.

We were not personally threatened in any way, but threat and tension and what I might venture to call hermeneutic confusion were somehow in the air. What signified here? Who had been trying to do what to whom? Even when we got out of the train at Chemnitz, more police were waiting on the platform. It is easy to overdramatize such experiences, but it was bizarrely relevant to the opera we had come to see: the last opera by the "halb-Jude" (half-Jew) Schreker, as he would have been documented and dealt with, had not a stroke, no doubt brought on by the shocks of 1932–33, killed him in 1934. For us it was all too easy; twenty-four hours later we were in the well-appointed Chemnitz Opera (its renovation a project from the GDR days), in a charming old-town ensemble of buildings surrounded by avenues of deserted and empty apartment blocks of a grandeur, now decidedly faded, that once might have looked appropriate in the vicinity of Vienna's *Ringstrasse*.

From the start there was a "buzz" about this piece, both in the audience and in the pit, when the Prelude struck up with its brassy, aggressive fanfares that seem aware of Puccini's *Turandot* (1926). We were soon enjoying the energetic smithying songs of Smee and his lads, wielding Soviet-style hammers of the kind that used to figure in the old East German flag. Here was a piece—and a production—crying out to be "read" on many levels, as I suspect was the case in 1932. Schreker's 1931 *Anbruch* article on the opera merits quotation for its suggestion of how his new style might be construed as marrying *neue Sachlichkeit* with social consciousness and the aim to achieve a kind of "escape" from present concerns, perhaps even as a decadent late-romantic's "response to just criticism."[29] Recalling a trip to Pallanza and his encounter with "a true folk art" of Italy, Schreker described the setting-up of a Punch-and-Judy show (*Kasperltheater*) in the market square:

> One becomes a different sort of being even than a German in these southern parts, and when the sun burns hot and the sky is deep blue the taste for serious creative problems wanes. . . . All Pallanza, rich and poor, young and old, was as enthusiastically involved in the performance as if it had been

Toscanini, Verdi or a famous singer. But these were only primitive puppets, the familiar characters from the old Punch-and-Judy shows: the handyman, Death and the Devil, Pierrot and Columbine—I think even Mussolini came into it (his name was for ever being enthusiastically applauded when it was mentioned), since the performance drew on contemporary political events, which were alluded to in the play. There, during this entertaining show, I got the idea of writing for once a completely primitive, naïve work for the theatre, an opera for Everyman.[30]

Der Schmied von Gent advertises its relation to contemporary events by appearing to avoid them entirely, with overcompensating brashness—although it is a decidedly "political" opera that deals subtly with power and its pretensions on many levels, temporal and metaphysical. The work might appear to want to be taken (as it was by many) as a German "Volksoper." But remember, this is a *Flemish* tale retold by De Coster: we are in the sixteenth century and Smee the Smith is a low-countries lad; he comes over admittedly as decidedly German, something of a "Hans Wurst" even, but his political affiliations (now more recalled than practiced) were with the "Geusen," the piratical rebels who had done their best to fight off and disrupt the colonizing efforts of the Spaniards, particularly when the infamous, "bloody" Duke Alba was sent to quell them with tangible threats of the Inquisition. It would be tempting to associate the evil Spaniards with the National Socialists, but it does not quite work—they are far too grand, too decadently "old world" in appearance. The uncomfortable truth is that the Geusen themselves might fit the role rather better—and may well have appeared to do so for those in the audience who were aware of the Schmied's (Wilhelm Rode's) real-life political tendencies.

But Smee does not prevail in his world, where he is the victim of a malicious trick that loses him his customers (many of whom are rich Spaniards). He sinks into suicidal despair and falls vulnerable to "magical" voices in a tree that entice him into a Faustian pact with the Devil—his soul (or rather his body, since he is going to be physically eaten by hungry devils) is given up in return for seven years of plenty and a thriving smithy. In act 2, seven years later, he manages to outwit the devils but still loses his smithy to a vengeful, naked Lucifer, who intervenes as a kind of *diabolus ex machina*. In act 3, Smee has survived the destruction of his smithy, but now tells his wife that he is tired and will die, which he does; we then see him following the long road to Heaven, but he is denied entry by St. Peter. So he sets up a stall outside the pearly gates to cater for the needs of travelers more blessed. In the end, thanks to his wife, he talks his way through a divine trial and is admitted into Heaven and C major with much ceremony and laughter, and a robust chorus of angels.

For two brief examples of how this piece works on the "pantomime" level, we might turn initially to the last of Smee's three confrontations in act 2 with the devils who come to claim him when the seven years are up. Just before that he and his wife had sheltered what proves, with suitably naïve anachronism, to be the Holy Family—Joseph, Mary, and the infant Jesus. Smee reshoes Joseph's donkey and his wife feeds and cares for Mary and the child in simple, homely fashion. In return, Joseph offers Smee three wishes. In each case the latter hits on a magical "holding" device that only he can release. The devils now duly arrive to claim him: Hessels the Hangman gets stuck in the plum tree into which Smee entices him to try the fruit (see figure 9). Hessels's historical master, the "bloody" Duke Alba, can't rise out of the armchair he is given to rest in. Astarte, the Devil's mistress, proves a little more complex: not least in that she, even more than the other devils, is characterized by music that is immediately identifiable as alluding to Schreker's "old" style of fantastically orchestrated, chromatic sound magic. She mobilizes this effectively in her attempt at a devilish seduction, appearing crowned, but naked, under a deep red robe that reveals unhealing wounds all over her body. These Smee concentrates on, sympathetically offering her his "magical healing-sack"; he carefully ties her into it and leaves just her head sticking out. She too cannot now escape, of course. Smee's wife duly puts paid to her by fetching holy water and sprinkling her all over with it, and with some down-to-earth, god-fearing diatonic chords of vengeful "benediction":

> *Astarte:* Help! Help! Lucifer, help!
> Save me from this dreadful woman.
> Smith, let me go! *He* can give you the pact—help Lucifer! Ah!
>
> *Smee:* *(laughing)*
> In spite of all my cunning and tricks—that I
> should have forgotten this one!
>
> *Wife:* *(returns with a big basin and a holy-water sprinkler and "anoints" Astarte)*
> In the name of the Father and the Son and the Holy Ghost,
> Disappear you evil temptress![31]

True to type and mindful of Brechtian theater (something noted in at least one of the 1932 reviews quoted in Hailey's biography),[32] Smee's wife

FIGURE 9. *Der Schmied von Gent*, Berlin 1932, act 2. Smee holds the devil Hessels (Wilhelm Gombert) captive in his plum tree (Theatermuseum der Universität zu Köln).

remains devotedly honest and direct throughout (something that allows *her* to fly straight up to Heaven when she dies). She conveys her puppet-show matter-of-factness in a particularly touching way when Smee dies at the start of act 3; she sings her little farewell blessing (marked "simply, without sentimentality, as one might sing a folksong") before laying a candle either side of his body (has she also been to see *Tosca* while Professor Kerman wasn't looking?); she also makes sure Smee stays in his "smithy" clothes, as he had asked, for his next and last journey. This we shortly see him setting out on, in the cheery, rather Mahlerian orchestral interlude whose purposeful contrapuntal lines see him on his way:

> *Wife:* He was as he was, Smee:
> someone who could laugh and be merry to the end,
> when weariness got the better of him.
> So now rise up, fasten your knapsack my Smee!
> Find your way on the final journey, the right one I expect.
> I'll get over the pain in the end and I'll find you again
> at the last.
>
> (*She gets up, lights 2 candles and puts one on each side of Smee. A black scrim descends and obscures the scene. The stage becomes completely dark, apart from the 2 candles, which burn ever more faintly. The candles go out completely.*
> *The scene is filled with an unearthly green light. Smee is seen to stand up, pack his provisions and valuables in the sack, and set off . . .*)

In the end, Smee, the celestial outsider (who has hardly played by the rules of the Good Book and has even been rejected by the now fearful devils he had vanquished in act 2) is interceded for by his wife. He receives the Judgment trial with St. Peter that he has requested, and his crimes are weighed in the balance. He just manages to succeed in proving his goodness and his final welcome into Heaven is marked by a *Meistersinger*-like festival march (recalling perhaps the march which had accompanied Fritz's first description of the "distant sound"). Only some elaborately chromatic angelic melismas in the background seem to recall Schreker's old style of late-romantic decadence, as if the devils too were now welcomed to the celestial party.

What seems clear is that Schreker's complex and rather dangerous negotiation of both contemporary politics and the critical stylistic requirements of what had become by the late 1920s a kind of "official" modernism rather poignantly reveals the latter's now deceptively safe and oddly conventional affiliations for him—we might think of the opera's prevailing sound world as a sort of dissonant neoclassicism,

Stravinsky via Hindemith and Kurt Weill. In *Der Schmied von Gent*, that new "normative" style is, however, triangulated on the one hand with the conventional, almost naïve folklike tonality of diatonic triads and clear cadences (there lay the road to Heaven), and on the other with the feminized "self-indulgence" (as it was thought to be) of his late-romantic style. *That* is apparently now distanced as an attribute of troublesome singing devils.[33] The pragmatically modernist "normality" of *Der Schmied* is mostly dominated by good-humored, masculine men (the evil ones get their comeuppance) and women who keep in their place as wives, angels, or passing devilish femmes fatales. The opera is thus marked by irony, repressions, and self-censorship, for reasons that seem to position the modernist fragmentation that those characteristics define closer to worldly fashions and fads than a conventional romantic-idealist account might suggest. From this perspective, *Der Schmied von Gent* gloriously problematizes any conventional binarism of late-romantic versus modernist that would mockingly demonize the one in favor of what, in that period, was the historically rather precarious advantage of the other.

A BURNING ORGAN, A DISAPPEARING HERO, AND A STRING QUARTET

When, in the spring of 1932, his last opera, *Der Schmied von Gent*, was premiered at the Berlin City Opera, he hoped to have found a new path with it. But whatever our world could do to make that path difficult it did, with steady application. Whether Schreker was far from having any partisan political convictions, and inwardly inclined more to the right than the left, he was stamped as a moderate. He may have been a product of the prevailing "system," but he was first recognized by the left-leaning press.

He thus became in himself a sort of "marked one" [*Gezeichneter*] and was to be one of the first victims of the "national revolution," just a few months after its official inauguration.

—From Paul Bekker's obituary essay for Schreker in the *Pariser Tagblatt*, 25 March 1934[34]

Bekker's obituary of Schreker, written from Paris, is a document both moving and complex. As Schreker's first significant critical supporter, Bekker clearly felt obliged now to question the "failing" works (*Irrelohe* and *Der singende Teufel*). These he cites as the cause of the deep bitterness which he suggests may have brought about the later decline of Schreker's productivity, when he felt himself suddenly rejected, like "scrap metal," as less talented younger composers started to overtake him and find success. In fact, the obituary ends with a warm recommendation that Schreker should be considered "one of those to whom the world owes justice."[35] But the note of ambivalence, even of personal blame, reads a little painfully, coming as it did from the relative security of an exile that Schreker himself had failed to secure, finding himself hedged by tendentious misunderstanding. His old Viennese friend Joseph Marx (to whom he had ventured the suggestion that he might help him return to Vienna) wrote in July 1933 expressing his sympathy for the National Socialist "revolution" in Germany and assuring Schreker that every cloud has a silver lining and that the regime's initial harshness would surely soften. It can hardly have helped that he went on to blame the Jews for anti-Semitism and, with crushing insensitivity, remind Schreker of his own past expressions of exasperation with "them."[36]

Against the contemporary background of external threat and privately increasing despair, one can well see why Schreker might have tried to write an outwardly "conservative" German folk opera, incorporating elements of an apologetic demonization of his own former musical style (whose diaphanous textures first reappear precisely to accompany the deluding, devilish voices that call from the glittering tree, to offer the Faustian pact of seven years of plenty in return for his soul, as Smee prepares to kill himself). The 2010 Chemnitz production, perhaps drawing upon old East German sympathy with the victims of fascist oppression, dramatized the dark tragedy lurking behind the opera's creation by making explicit the possible identificatory association of Smee with Schreker—as whom the singer playing Smee was seen at the beginning of the opera, sitting surrounded by music manuscript paper in his study on the right forestage and significantly, if awkwardly, escaping back therefrom Heaven at the end (dodging under the falling curtain). During one of the later orchestral interludes the stage was touchingly filled with a projected photograph of Schreker and his wife, scrawled over as if with anti-Semitic graffiti.

This production has given rise to the only commercially available recording of the opera, but it may still be too early in the development of our critical understanding of it for a clear reading of its concealments, allusions, and ambivalences (as much as of its rude energy and fun) to be fully decipherable.[37] That it must surely be seen as one of the key operatic texts of the period grows clear. It is with the aim of locating it more clearly within his output that I conclude here with some brief observations about Schreker's two other late operas. *Der singende Teufel* and *Christophorus* have a significant bearing both on Bekker's charge of a productive "block" affecting Schreker after *Irrelohe,* and on the vexed question of the apparent retreat from his former late-romantic style and capitulation (unlike the more resistant attitude of Rachmaninov or Korngold) to the modernism of his pupils and even of Schoenberg (to whom *Christophorus* was dedicated).[38] Both of these works support a critical analysis of their underlying thematics as referring to and possibly seeking to negotiate broadly "political," or at least newly politic*ized,* issues of the period. It will be helpful to deal with them chronologically, starting with *Der singende Teufel* (premiered in 1928) and concluding with *Christophorus,* completed in 1929 and published by Adler in Berlin in 1931, although plans for its staging were almost inevitably abandoned.

I have of course already ventured some comments about these operas. What is important here is to point out that both are in the strictest sense late Romantic musical dramas which thematize the quest to present or call forth a form of musical "essence"—its perfection and purity reproducing all the conventional values of the Romantic construction of "classical" music as possessing spiritual, even divine or "angelic" qualities that had always been implicitly utopian, transformative, and redemptive. Both operas nevertheless problematize that very construction in different ways within their dramatic unfolding, and strikingly reflect contemporary themes and preoccupations. Both are couched in that more dissonant, more contrapuntal and timbrally "spare" musical language that Schreker seems to have picked up from his pupils and from composers with whom he had direct dealings, like Schoenberg, Busoni, and Hindemith. So too did that new and fundamentally more linear style echo the sound-world of Hans Pfitzner (cited by Bekker in his Schreker obituary as a kind of angrily polemical polar *opposite* to Schreker; *his* sense of having been abandoned by his audience was more internalized than Pfitzner's and was managed in more creative ways).

Der singende Teufel could even be seen as a kind of critical response to Pfitzner's *Palestrina,* in that its central character's musical and spiritual quest is presented not as heroic, so much as self-deceivingly idealistic. The bloodbath that occurs at *its* climax is the direct responsibility of Amandus Herz, the young organ builder whose goal is to complete the great instrument that his father had failed to perfect. The setting is an early medieval monastic community whose Christian idealism is deliberately set against the contrasting vitality and nature worship of the pagan tribespeople of the forest, outside the monastery gates. As the spring solstice approaches, Amandus's love for the pagan Lilian encourages her to seek to enlist him as their "leader" (*Führer*), who might help channel their unruly energies in more productive ways: specifically toward their goal of crushing the Christian monastery and renewing their life-affirming commitment to the old German gods of nature and the forest.

It is relevant here to note that the historian the late Nicholas Goodrick Clark was one of those who ventured to study what a recent obituary article on him, referring to his 1985 book *The Occult Roots of Nazism*, described succinctly as treating the interplay between the modern occult revival and "ideologies and nationalism, racism and revolution" and emphasizing "the hostility of Nazism to Christianity as well as its approach to Judaism."[39] We may not be able to reconstruct the precise route that Schreker took to this extraordinary operatic subject in the mid-1920s, but its outcome is certainly more darkly critical than supportive of any National Socialist fantasy of regressive Germanic renewal. Amandus eventually resists Lilian's nearly successful ideological as well as physical seduction, but his recommitment to his Christian faith and the organ he appears finally to complete leads to the opera's climax, when the warlike Christian monks crush the pagans' attempted invasion and destruction of their monastery. This is done with a show of ecclesiastical force, in the great nave of their church: through ritual, ceremonial Latin and vestments, and including, of course, a terrifying outburst from Amandus's great organ (the "singing devil" of the tribespeople's imagination), at which point the cowering and kneeling would-be invaders are slaughtered by the knights of Christ (see figure 10).

Up to this point, the ideological ambivalence of this tragedy seems emphasized, but the opera is not over. Amandus's devastation at this outcome (he, after all, had been playing the organ) is attended by an obsessive conviction that somehow his "fault" lies in not having mastered and perfected the more complex mixtures and registers of the organ, whose intended "angelic" voices are, he believes, tainted by devilish imperfections (shades here of Meister Florian's *Spielwerk* in the earlier opera). When we encounter Amandus in the fourth and final act, he is sheltering with Lilian in the forest, in the cave of the priestess Alardis. He becomes locked in conversation with a strange Moorish pilgrim who pulls behind him a miniature organ that needs mending. The pilgrim wildly asserts a nihilistic philosophy (against the protestations of the priestess Alardis), responding in the negative to Amandus's tormented question "Is there a god?" ("I am god," the pilgrim replies exasperatedly, "and he is a god and this and that is god / All that lives is god!").[40] At this

FIGURE 10. *Der singende Teufel,* act 3, scene 8 (Wiesbaden premiere). (By permission of the Franz Schreker Foundation.)

very moment news arrives that the monastery is ablaze. The final scene presents a melodramatic catastrophic tableau, with Lilian, having herself set fire to the monastery, now dying on the chancel steps as the tormenting organ's white-hot pipes above her emit the angelic sounds that Amandus had hitherto failed to perfect. The chorus finally murmurs a response to Amandus's deranged cry of "Why?" ("It remains an eternal riddle"), and the stage direction reads: "Everything sinks into darkness, only the organ pipes remain visible to the last in a pale, fading glow."

Der singende Teufel seems to have invoked anti-Christian Nazi occultism without reinforcing its ideological aspirations, and in a newly archaic-modernist contrapuntal language that offered so little of Schreker's usual late-romantic sensuality that Weissmann hailed it cruelly as a creative act of self-castration.[41] *Christophorus,* on the other hand, treats the quest for musical "essence" in the more immediate manner of a *Zeitoper.* In fact it takes the form of a true melodrama, whose mixture of spoken dialogue and music seems to invoke the world of "talking" film just as it had become a technical possibility (it was completed just two years after *The Jazz Singer* [1927], in which Al Jolson had famously first sung on screen). In what might equally be regarded as a prototypical "chamber opera" (although the orchestra is still of classical proportions, with added percussion and a musical saw), the setting is that of a composition teacher's studio (he is Meister Johann), whose students include the apparently rather effete and meditative Anselm, who is in love with Meister Johann's daughter Lisa. At the start the students are trying to work on their latest, enigmatic exercise: a programmatic string quartet on the subject of the legend of St. Christopher.

The students joke about their respective musical styles ("I write linearly," says Frederick, who accuses Heinrich of being "uncultured and conservative"),[42] but they are united in their scorn of the string quartet exercise, until Meister Johann appears and encourages them to think about the legend. "Christophorus" was the man who acquired his name by having once borne Christ. At first he had sought to serve "only the strongest" and thus joined the forces of the Emperor—until he realized that the Emperor's fear of the Devil suggested an even stronger Master, to whom Christopher had then turned (Meister Johann suggests they might try a "Scherzo di Diavolo"). However, a roadside crucifix, from which the Devil shrinks, indicates a more powerful force still. But the crucified figure eludes Christopher until, in old age, he carries a child across a river. The child grows progressively heavier, and Christopher sinks under the weight, whereupon the child names him "Christ-Bearer" (Christophorus). The work's subtitle, "Vision of an Opera," is explained in what follows. Anselm remains unconvinced after Meister Johann has left, and he falls into a reverie in which he imagines the subject matter as essentially dramatic, *operatic*. A black scrim curtain descends and the set is suffused with "an unreal, mysterious light." What follows is Anselm's imagined opera—a kind of *Zeitoper,* indeed, that finds a significant role for the figure of his beloved Lisa alongside the fictional Christoph, who shortly arrives in search of composition lessons. As Anselm's alter ego, he becomes the forceful composition student, a symphonist, who marries Lisa. She bears him a child but rejects the role of bourgeois wife and mother and admits this in an intimate conversation with Anselm (he has already manipulated her in his opera into performing for him the role of a dionysian 'artistic dancer'). Christoph enters as they talk and, in a jealous rage, shoots and kills Lisa.

Anselm's creative game has got out of hand, his hero out of control—this is not what he had intended. In the second act he accordingly becomes Christoph's friend and protector. We find them now as very modern seekers after experience in a seedy hotel (Christoph, running from the police, is in disguise). The stage is divided into two: the hotel cabaret-bar on one side and a backroom gambling and opium den on the other. Anselm follows Christoph between the two. The climax comes with a psychic cabaret act in which the medium Florence tries to contact the dead with the aid of her onstage audience members. Christoph is drawn in, seeking communion with Lisa, but finds himself revealing his crime—at which point a kind of Adornian "Durchbruch" occurs, and a door at the back of the stage opens to reveal Meister Johann with Christoph's child. They are dressed as street musicians, "beggar musicians" [*Bettelmusikanten*]; Johann has a guitar, the child a tambourine, and they are bathed in early morning light from outside. The child now sings an affectingly simple song, pleading destitution and begging for money. Christoph, deeply moved, runs to help his son—and here the curtain slowly falls and the lights fade to complete darkness.

In one of the strangest moments in twentieth-century opera, a voice is heard in the darkness (is it Meister Johann's?), from "a far distance, coming out of nothingness" ("Sehr entfernt, aus dem Nichts"): it intones verses from Lao Tzu's sixth-century B.C. *Tao Te Ching:*

> He who recognizes his masculine strength
> and yet abides in female frailty,
> he is the riverbed of the world,
> and eternal life will not desert him,
> he can turn again,
> and become like a little child.
>
> . . . .
>
> He who knows his worth
> and yet accepts disgrace,
> he is the valley of the world.
> As the valley of the world
> he has enough of eternal life
> and can turn again
> to simplicity.[43]

Anticipating by half a century the culturally oriented feminist criticism of European "great music," Schreker's *Christophorus* nevertheless remained an unheard, unstaged opera by a composer who felt abandoned by the audience for which he had so successfully written until that point (*too* successfully, for some of course). It remains a startling late, late-romantic critique not least of the very thing that its strong male "hero" has produced: "real" music, a virtual symphony—as projected that is, in Anselm's own would-be but now nightmarish opera. We have seen that he had earlier manipulated its primary female character (Lisa) into an erotic bodily performance that had prompted her fantasy hero husband unexpectedly to shoot her in an ill-considered act of domestic violence. Was all the "art" really about power and gender after all? About the fascination with *strength*? It seems to have been Schreker's purpose to suggest this. Bring on a veristic medium accompanied by a musical saw and the tear-jerking appearance on stage of a child and suddenly the conceptual and expressive range grows to embrace not only Puccini but also Mahler—with his distant visions of childlike humor and naïveté shimmering at the vanishing point of a grand symphonic landscape. And the way forward is suggested by a disembodied voice from the darkened orchestra pit intoning ancient Chinese wisdom in almost liturgical fashion—as if counseling all those young male modernists who were overtaking Schreker to get in touch with their feminine side and realize that their art had too often invoked dominance and power and forgetfulness of the childlike (Schreker's 1932 "Foreword to *Christophorus*" explicitly associated his vision with "true theatre in the sense of the spectaccolo of the Italians," evidently referring to *Der Schmied von Gent*).[44]

But *Christophorus* is not yet over. As light returns to the stage we find ourselves returned to Meister Johann's studio, as at the beginning. The operatic "vision" nevertheless continues to occupy Anselm, who gazes at Christoph, still visible at the bedside of his dying child in the corner of the room. Expressing a kind of Faustian regret, Christoph realizes that his self-indulgence and his power-fascination with both Emperor and Devil had been false paths. Meister Johann, as if seeing Anselm's vision and sensing his disquiet, encourages him to let his character conclude the drama as he will. Together, they watch Christoph bid farewell to his dying son, hailing his vulnerably innocent simplicity as the embodiment of all he would now wish to serve. In his own feverish dream the child seems actually to "see" the theater auditorium in which "we" might sit. His last little song includes these words:

> There, there— / a large house—
> many lights, / a thousand people.
> Father, turn out the lights!
> On your back, / through the water,
> through the black, / wild water
> you'll carry me.

Finally Christoph flicks a switch, and once again all is indeed darkness, "even in the orchestra pit" (as the stage direction reads). Just enough onstage light remains for us to see Christoph walking away with the child, exiting through the door he had first entered. Only now was the black scrim curtain to be raised as the child begs for a last time, "Father, put out the lights!" and Master Johann pronounces from the darkness: "Die Welt des Theaters endet, versinkt" (The world of the theater ends and sinks away). The voices, whose singing is heard faintly by Lisa as well as Anselm are themselves now "far away" in the distance. Meister Johann observes that Anselm's characters nevertheless live "in" him and that the legend of St. Christopher "becomes for you: music and nothing more—a quartet movement my son." Pronouncing the tempo imagined long ago, Anselm murmurs, "Andante con rigore" and "mechanically" goes to the blackboard to write—perhaps what we now hear: a beautifully unfolding passage from a string quartet, whose oddly delicate voice leading prepares an angelic cadence in an unclouded C major, quietly accompanied at the last by the full string orchestra. Hardly "nothing more" than music, this fragment of a string quartet is thus embedded in a complex musico-dramatic text that represents one of late-romantic music's most complicatedly touching closing gestures, emerging from the ruins of a self-critical, self-destructive drama, without which this fragmented and pared-down "music" would, however, be all but meaningless.

. . .

In evoking the fear and chaos of the late Weimar years in Berlin, I cited Alexandra Ritchie's description of the fatal polarization toward left and right extremes that the Nazis visited upon German society. Those political camps were and are, perhaps, too easily equated with modernist and conservative tendencies in terms of both taste and ideology. For good or ill, the equation clearly emerged in the period, as a result of the polemics of both camps (one thinks of Pfitzner's assertion of music's guiltless transcendence of the political, while blaming Bolsheviks and Jews for all the art that failed to achieve such transcendence).[45] The political polarization of the times was complicatedly linked to the fragmentation of Schreker's audience, for all that his precariously liberal, precariously humane late-romantic path led him to attempt, all too idealistically, to reconstruct that audience in *Der Schmied von Gent* on the model of those "ordinary" spectators of the Italian puppet show that had so impressed him—their historically specific character and ideological persuasion nevertheless accommodating a warm response to references to Mussolini, we recall. That model might well have been inspired not only by Schreker's love of Italy but also by his reading of

Franz Werfel's novel *Verdi*—an example of a late romantic text "about" music, in the Wackenroder tradition, of which so many of his own operas had been examples:

> The youthful Verdi, a composer of operas, obliged to write with an eye upon opera seasons and opera singers, had hated, all his life, the canting intonations of the word "Art." He did not give to the art of music the romantic title of a vocation, or a mission in life; it did not connote for him the ideal of super-manliness that flourishes in the lofty air of the garret, or any of the flimsy formulas that have so deteriorated in value since then.
>
> Art was a thing that had its place in the life of men because from it they derived the highest forms of pleasure.[46]

In the event Schreker's idealism was destroyed, as he himself was, by catastrophic circumstances and events that were quite beyond his grasp or control—his death in 1934 after a form of stroke seems, as I have suggested, to have had its origins in the traumatic events of 1932–33. Perhaps his first piece of posthumous good fortune was to have been caustically memorialized in *Die Musik* as a cultural Bolshevik and tarred with the leftist brush of being "part of the November system" (referring to the left-wing *Novembergruppe* that had been involved in the revolutionary activism after the First World War).[47] Bekker, for all *his* uncertainty about his old friend's allegiances, was surely right in looking for historical justice for Schreker in the future. Perhaps we are approaching a point where we can imagine what that justice might look like, and imagine the broader historical picture within which he might take his place as a far from inconspicuous colleague of Schoenberg's whose precisely contemporary *Moses und Aron* owed not a little to Schreker's earlier type of operatic dramaturgy. Alongside that unfinished work's tortured journey into silence, Schreker's last three operas emerge as complex and provocatively moving products of the period: a period in which a major part of the late romantic tradition advisedly relocated to Hollywood, and a wider audience than Schreker had ever commanded, even at the height of his fame. In other circumstances, he might have found himself joining the company there of composers like Korngold, Steiner, and Waxman (who had studied at the Hochschule); he might even have completed the once planned film of *Der ferne Klang*, revealing late romanticism's long developed affinity with the form in which it found, perhaps, its final and (if we are honest) by no means unworthy home. There, in movie houses often aspiring in their way to the grandeur of old-European opera houses, it also found an audience that welcomed it with eager emotional intelligence—and perhaps understood it better than émigré European composers and even some of its own members may have realized. Within that "ignorant audience" (as Stravinsky would presumably have it) we might expect, and indeed hope, to have found not a few discriminatingly appreciative maidservants. Who now were the Philistines?

Notes

INTRODUCTION

1. See Christopher Small, *Musicking: The Meanings of Performing and Listening* (Hanover, NH: Wesleyan University Press, 1998). My epigraph comes from his opening section: "Prelude. Music and Musicking," 1.

2. Carl Dahlhaus, trans. J. Bradford Robinson, *Nineteenth-Century Music* (Berkeley and Los Angeles: University of California Press, 1989), 334.

3. Jim Samson, ed., *The Late Romantic Era: From the mid-19th Century to World War I,* Man and Music Series (London: Macmillan, 1991).

4. Stephen Downes, *Music and Decadence in European Modernism: The Case of Central and Eastern Europe* (Cambridge: Cambridge University Press, 2010).

5. Lawrence Kramer, "Music, Historical Knowledge, and Critical Inquiry: Three Variations on *The Ruins of Athens*," *Critical Inquiry* 32, no. 1 (Autumn 2005): 65.

6. Laurence Dreyfus, *Wagner and the Erotic Impulse* (Cambridge, MA: Harvard University Press, 2010); and J. P. E. Harper-Scott, "Wagner, Sex and Capitalism," *Wagner Journal* 5, no. 2 (June 2011): 46–62.

CHAPTER 1

1. See Richard Taruskin, *Music in the Early Twentieth Century,* vol. 4 of *The Oxford History of Western Music* (Oxford and New York: Oxford University Press, 2010 [originally 2005]), 5–6ff. My epigraph is from the opening of the relevant section on p. 5.

2. See Thomas Mann, *Doctor Faustus: The Life of the German Composer Adrian Leverkühn as Told by a Friend,* trans. H. T. Lowe-Porter [misprinted as "Parker"] (London: Penguin/Secker, 1968), "Author's Note," 491.

3. Taruskin, *Music in the Early Twentieth Century,* xiv (the introduction is repeated at the start of each volume of his *Oxford History of Western Music*).

4. Ibid., xvii.

5. Ibid., xiii.

6. Richard Leppert, *The Sight of Sound: Music, Representation and the History of the Body* (Berkeley and Los Angeles, London: University of California Press, 1993).

7. Ibid., 16.

8. Ibid.

9. I refer to Lawrence Kramer, *Classical Music and Postmodern Knowledge* (Berkeley, Los Angeles, and London: University of California Press, 1995), chap. 2, "From the Other to the Abject: Music as Cultural Trope," 33–66.

10. Leppert, *Sight of Sound,* 24.

11. Ibid., 25.

12. Ibid., 215, 221.

13. Ibid., 233.

14. John Carey, *The Intellectuals and the Masses: Pride and Prejudice among the Literary Intelligentsia, 1880–1939* (London and Boston: Faber & Faber, 1992), 8.

15. Ibid., 21.

16. Ibid., 140.

17. Ibid., 139.

18. Ibid., 152.

19. Ibid., 8.

20. Richard Taruskin, *Music in the Seventeenth and Eighteenth Centuries,* vol. 2 of *The Oxford History of Western Music* (Oxford and New York: Oxford University Press 2010 [originally 2005]), 643–45.

21. Ibid., 651

22. *Richard Wagner to Mathilde Wesendonck,* trans. William Ashton Ellis (London: H. Grevel and Co., 1905), 185.

23. Carl Dahlhaus, trans. J. Bradford Robinson, *Nineteenth-Century Music* (Berkeley and Los Angeles: University of California Press, 1989), 15. As my argument develops here, I will adopt a capital R for Romanticism as a self-conscious historical movement, particularly in German ideas and the arts in the early nineteenth century, lower case for the more colloquial and generalized use of the term.

24. Cambridge University Press, http://www.cambridge.org/gb/knowledge/isbn/item1168947/The%20Persistence%20of%20Romanticism/?site_locale = en_GB (accessed 10 September 2012).

25. Margarete Kohlenbach, "Transformations of German Romanticism, 1830–2000," in *The Cambridge Companion to German Romanticism,* ed. Nicholas Saul (Cambridge: Cambridge University Press, 2009), 257.

26. See Julian Johnson, *Mahler's Voices: Expression and Irony in the Songs and Symphonies* (Oxford and New York: Oxford University Press, 2009), 270, for example.

27. Oliver Strunk, ed., *Source Readings in Music History,* rev. ed., vol. 6, *The Nineteenth Century,* ed. Ruth Solie (New York and London: Norton,

1998), 19–30. Subsequent quotations are taken from Wilhelm Heinrich Wackenroder and Ludwig Tieck, *Outpourings of an Art-Loving Friar*, trans. Edward Mornin (New York: Frederick Ungar, 1975). Where Mornin updated his translation for a modern American audience (e.g., "conductor" for *Kapellmeister*), I have reverted to Strunk's translation, first published in 1950.

28. Wackenroder and Tieck, *Outpourings*, 103.
29. Ibid., 105.
30. Ibid., 105–6
31. Ibid., 106
32. Theodor Adorno, *In Search of Wagner*, trans. Rodney Livingstone ([no place]: NLB, 1981), 30–31.
33. Wackenroder and Tieck, *Outpourings*, 119.
34. Ibid., 118.
35. Ibid., 123.
36. Alma Mahler, *Gustav Mahler: Memories and Letters*, trans. Basil Creighton [first published 1946], ed. Donald Mitchell and Knud Martner, 4th ed. (London: Cardinal [Sphere Books Ltd.], 1990), 213.
37. Ibid., 213–14.
38. Knud Martner, ed., *Selected Letters of Gustav Mahler*, trans. Eithne Wilkins and Ernst Kaiser (London: Faber, 1979), 329.
39. Ibid., 346.
40. Robert Musil, *The Man without Qualities*, trans. Eithne Wilkins and Ernst Kaiser (London: Pan Books, 1979), 2:25.
41. Ibid., 2:32.
42. See Peter Franklin, *Mahler Symphony no. 3*, Cambridge Music Handbook (Cambridge: Cambridge University Press, 1991), 31–32 (and 109, note 44). The original source was the *Wiener Abendpost*, 5 November 1909 (no. 254), 1–3.
43. Knud Martner, ed., *Selected Letters of Gustav Mahler*, 148–49. Martner identifies Tolney-Witt as the subsequent Gisela Selden-Gotha (1884–1975).
44. Taruskin, *Music in the Early Twentieth Century*, 14.
45. Ibid., 16.
46. Herta Blaukopf, ed., *Gustav Mahler, Richard Strauss; Correspondence, 1888–1911*, trans. Edmund Jephcott (London: Faber, 1984), 119.
47. Theodor Adorno, *Mahler, A Musical Physiognomy*, trans. Edmund Jephcott (Chicago and London: University of Chicago Press, 1992), 6, 30.
48. Taruskin, *Music in the Early Twentieth Century*, 22.
49. Conclusive critiques of this notion have been mounted by both Lawrence Kramer, in *Classical Music and Postmodern Knowledge*, and Richard Taruskin, in, for example, his essay "Stravinsky and the Subhuman"; see Richard Taruskin, *Defining Russia Musically: Historical and Hermeneutical Essays* (Princeton, NJ: Princeton University Press, 1997), 168.
50. Adorno, *Mahler*, 41.
51. Alma Mahler, *Memories and Letters*, 212.
52. *Gustav Mahler: Letters to His Wife*, ed. Henry-Louis de La Grange and Günther Weiss, in collaboration with Knud Martner (London: Faber, 2004), 62. A fuller and differently translated text of this letter to Justine is printed in

174 | Notes to Chapters 1 and 2

Stephen McClatchie, ed. and trans., *The Mahler Family Letters* (New York: Oxford University Press, 2006), 363–64. The original German texts of these letters appear respectively in Henry-Louis de La Grange and Günther Weiss, eds., *Ein Glück ohne Ruh'. Die Briefe Gustav Mahlers an Alma* (Berlin: Siedler Verlag, 1995); and *Gustav Mahler, Liebe Justi! Briefe an die Familie*, ed. Stephen McClatchie, German edn. Helmut Brenner (Bonn: Weidle, 2006).

53. Alma Mahler, *Memories and Letters*, 212.

54. See Ludwig Schiedermair, *Gustav Mahler. Eine biographisch-kritische Würdigung* (Leipzig, 1901), 13; also Herbert Killian, *Gustav Mahler in die Erinnerungen von Natalie Bauer-Lechner* (Hamburg, 1984), 170–71.

55. Alma Mahler, *Memories and Letters*, 213–14.

56. Ibid., 214.

57. Natalie Bauer Lechner, *Recollections of Gustav Mahler*, trans. Dika Newlin, ed. Peter Franklin (London: Faber, 1980), 44.

CHAPTER 2

1. Henry Pleasants, trans. and ed., *The Musical World of Robert Schumann: A Selection from His Own Writings* (London: Gollancz, 1965), 32.

2. For a fascinating example (concerning an 1829 ballet-version of Beethoven's Sixth Symphony), see J.Q. Davies, "Dancing the Symphonic Beethoven-Bochsa's *Symphonie Pastorale*, 1829," *19th-Century Music* 27, no. 1 (2003): 25–47.

3. More on Richard Strauss's position on this matter later in the chapter and in note 27 below.

4. This was the stated aim of the short-lived (1904–5) Viennese *Vereinigung Schaffender Tonkünstler;* for a short account, see Peter Franklin: *The Life of Mahler* (Cambridge: Cambridge University Press, 1997), 150–54.

5. Arnold Schoenberg, *Letters*, ed. Erwin Stein, trans. Eithne Wilkins and Ernst Kaiser (London, Faber & Faber, 1964), 243 (in a 1947 letter to Hans Rosbaud).

6. Leonid Sabaneyeff, *Modern Russian Composers* (London: Martin Lawrence, n.d. [1927?]), 18.

7. Christopher Redwood, ed., *A Delius Companion*, rev. ed. (London: Calder, 1980), 37 (from Delius's 1920 article in *The Sackbut*, "The Present Cult—Charlatanism and Humbug in Music").

8. Paul Bekker, *Beethoven* (Berlin and Leipzig: Schuster & Loeffler, 1911).

9. The best source of information on this is perhaps the catalog of the 1988 reconstruction in Düsseldorff of the 1938 exhibition: Albrecht Dümling and Peter Girth, *Entartete Musik. Eine kommentierte Rekonstruktion zur Düsseldorfer Ausstellung von 1938* (Düsseldorf: Landeshauptstadt Düsseldorf & Düsseldorfer Symphoniker, 1988)

10. See Hans Pfitzner, *Futuristengefahr. Bei Gelegenheit von Busoni's Ästhetik* (Leipzig-Munich: Süddeutsche Monatshefte, 1917); and *Die neue Aesthetik der musikalischen Impotenz. Ein Verwesungssymptom?* (Munich: Verlag der Süddeutsche Monatshefte, 1920; Alban Berg's response to the latter, originally published in *Musikblätter des Anbruch* (Vienna, second year, no. 11–12, June

1920, was translated as "The Musical Impotence of Hans Pfitner's 'New Aesthetic'" in Willi Reich, *Alban Berg*, trans. Cornelius Cardew (New York: Vienna House, 1974 [orig. London, 1965]), 205–18.

11. Thomas Mann, *Betrachtungen eines Unpolitischen* (Berlin: S. Fischer, 1918), English translation as *Reflections of a Nonpolitical Man*, trans. Walter D. Morris (New York: Frederick Ungar Publishing, 1983.

12. See Christopher Small, "Performance as Ritual: Sketch for an Enquiry into the True Nature of a Symphony Concert," in *Lost in Music: Culture, Style and the Musical Event*, ed. Avron Levine White (London and New York: Routledge & Kegan Paul, 1987), 6–32, subsequently elaborated as Christopher Small, *Musicking: The Meanings of Performing and Listening* (Hanover and London: Wesleyan University Press, 1998); and William Weber, *Music and the Middle Class: The Social Structure of Concert Life in London, Paris and Vienna* (London: Croom Helm, 1975; 2nd ed., Ashgate, 2003).

13. Eduard Hanslick, *On the Musically Beautiful*, trans. Geoffrey Payzant (Indianapolis: Hackett, 1986), 29.

14. Simon Frith, *Performing Rites: On the Value of Popular Music* (Cambridge, MA: Harvard University Press, 1998), 141.

15. See Theodor Adorno, *In Search of Wagner*, trans. Rodney Livingstone (London: NLB, 1981), 46.

16. E. T. A. Hoffmann, *Tales of Hoffmann*, selected and ed. R. J. Hollingdale (London: Penguin Books, 1982), 135

17. Ibid., 136.

18. J.-K. Huysmans, *À Rebours* [*Against Nature*], trans. Robert Baldick (London: Penguin Books, 1979), 39.

19. Oscar Wilde, "The Picture of Dorian Gray," in *Stories* (London: Collins, 1952), 22.

20. See Friedrich Nietzsche, *The Birth of Tragedy* and *The Case of Wagner*, trans. Walter Kaufmann (New York: Vintage, 1967)—*The Birth of Tragedy*, 166.

21. See Max Graf, *Modern Music* (New York: Philosophical Library, 1946), 21; and Max Nordau, *Degeneration*, trans. from the 2nd ed. of the German work [*Entartung*] (New York: D. Appleton, 1895).

22. See Arthur Seidl, *Moderner Geist in der deutschen Tonkunst. Gedanken eines Kulturpsychologen zur Wende des Jahrhunderts* (Regensburg: Gustav Bosse, n.d. [1913?]), 15–16. The lecture titles translate as "What Is Modern?" "The Modern Spirit in Dramatic and Instrumental Composition," "Thus Sang Zarathustra," and "The Modern Musical Lyric."

23. Ibid., 38–39.

24. Ibid., 64 (Seidl's discussion of the distinction between *Lied* and *Gesang* appears on 146ff).

25. Ibid., 63–64.

26. See Ibid., 69–72, 152.

27. See Richard Strauss, *Recollections and Reflections*, ed. Willi Schuh, trans. L. J. Lawrence (London: Boosey & Hawkes, 1953), 67–68.

28. Ibid., 16 (from Strauss's essay "Is There an Avant-Garde in Music?").

29. Sergei Bertensson and Jay Leyda, *Sergei Rachmaninoff: A Lifetime in Music* (London: George Allen and Unwin, 1965), 20.

30. Ibid., 88.

31. Theodor Adorno, *Introduction to the Sociology of Music* (New York: Seabury Press, 1976), 166–67.

32. *Stravinsky in Conversation with Robert Craft* (London: Penguin Books, 1962), 56.

33. I have proposed an alternative view at greater length in Peter Franklin, *Seeing Through Music: Gender and Modernism in Classic Hollywood Film Scores* (New York: Oxford University Press, 2010), chap. 1, 32–35.

34. Sabaneyeff, *Modern Russian Composers,* 104–5.

35. Rachmaninov heard *Salome* in Dresden in 1906, and was considerably impressed, but had felt a sense of inferiority and lack of sophistication by comparison. See Bertensson and Leyda, *Sergei Rachmaninoff,* 130.

36. Ibid., 109.

37. It was in an interview published in 1939 in *The Musical Courier* that Rachmaninov spoke of feeling "like a ghost in a world grown alien" and on the "new kind of music" whose composers "think rather than feel. They have not the capacity to make their works 'exult,' as Hans von Bülow called it . . . and do not concern themselves with soul states." See Bertensson and Leyda, *Sergei Rachmaninoff,* 351–52; for the comment to Olin Downes, see p. 220.

38. Eric Fenby, *Delius as I Knew Him* (London: G. Bell & Sons Ltd., 1936), 4.

39. This passage from Nietzsche's *Also sprach Zarathustra,* as set in Delius's *A Mass of Life,* is quoted in Fenby, *Delius as I Knew Him,* 6–7.

40. I rely here on Geoff Brown's article "Delius on the Golden Road" in *The Times,* Wednesday, 27 June 2012, *artsmusic* section, 11, where he notes that "Tyne and Wear Metro's crime prevention officer in 1998 . . . chose a recording of [Delius's] *Hassan* to pipe through one of the area's stations to see if the music deterred youths from hanging around, vandalizing ticket machines. *Hassan* did the trick."

41. It was this book that inspired Ken Russell's celebrated 1968 television film *Delius. Song of Summer* (on which Fenby collaborated); it also, more distantly, provides material for one of the episodes in David Mitchell's 2004 novel *Cloud Atlas.*

42. Percy Grainger, "The Personality of Frederick Delius," in *A Delius Companion,* rev. ed., ed. Christopher Redwood (London: Calder, 1980), 127.

43. See Frederick Delius, *Koanga,* vocal score by Eric Fenby, revised libretto by Douglas Craig and Andrew Page (London: Boosey and Hawkes, 1974).

44. A version of the rather complex history of the various revisions of *Koanga* is provided in the preface to the revised libretto by Craig and Page in the 1974 vocal score (see above, n. 42), iii-viii. See also the helpfully researched and critically alert account of *Koanga* by Eric Saylor: "Race, 'Realism,' and Fate in Frederick Delius's *Koanga,*" in *Blackness in Opera,* ed. Naomi André, Karen M. Bryan and Eric Saylor (Urbana, Chicago, and Springfield: University of Illinois Press, 2012), 78–100.

45. Ibid., vi.

46. This is taken from the second revised libretto, published as KOANGA/ Opera/ IN THREE ACTS/ With Prologue and Epilogue/ by/ FREDERICK

DELIUS/ Text by/ C. F. KEARY/ Revised by/ SIR THOMAS BEECHAM, Bart./ and EDWARD AGATE (London, Winthrop Rogers Edition, Boosey and Hawkes, n.d [1935]), 5. See also Sayler, "Race, 'Realism,' and Fate," 82–83.

47. Saylor, "Race, 'Realism,' and Fate," 94.

48. Christopher Small, *Musicking: The Meaning of Performing and Listening* (Hanover and London: Wesleyan University Press, 1998), 7.

49. Ibid., 220.

50. Peter Warlock [Philip Heseltine], *Frederick Delius*, reprinted with additions, annotations, and comments by Hubert Foss (London: The Bodley Head, 1952 [first published 1923]), 113.

51. My translation is of the text that appears at the foot of the page bearing the orchestral requirements, on the reverse of the title page of the 1906 score published by Harmonie, Berlin.

52. See Boosey and Hawkes Pocket Score, p. 106. Christopher Palmer makes the significant observation that Paul Robeson might have been a "wonderfully idiomatic" and revelatory soloist here, in Christopher Palmer, *Delius: Portrait of a Cosmopolitan* (London: Duckworth, 1976), 39.

53. I refer to Abbate's essay "Opera; or, the Envoicing of Women" in *Musicology and Difference. Gender and Sexuality in Music Scholarship*, ed. Ruth Solie (Berkeley, Los Angeles, and London: University of California Press, 1993), 225–58.

54. From Delius, "The Present Cult. . .," in Redwood, *Delius Companion*, 38.

55. See Fenby, *Delius as I Knew Him*, 122–25.

CHAPTER 3

1. The Tchaikovsky essay forms the final section of the chapter "Sexual Politics in Classical Music," in Susan McClary, *Feminine Endings: Music, Gender and Sexuality* (Minnesota and Oxford: University of Minnesota Press, 1991), 68–79; McClary's reading of Brahms's Third Symphony appears in her essay "Narrative Agendas in 'Absolute' Music: Identity and Difference in Brahms's Third Symphony," in *Musicology and Difference: Gender and Sexuality in Music Scholarship*, ed. Ruth Solie (Berkeley, Los Angeles, and London: University of California Press, 1993), 326–44.

2. William Weber, *The Great Transformation of Musical Taste: Concert Programming from Haydn to Brahms* (Cambridge: Cambridge University Press, 2008), 38.

3. Ibid.

4. Ibid.

5. William Weber, "Mass Culture and the Reshaping of European Musical Taste, 1770–1870," *International Review of the Aesthetics and Sociology of Music* 8, no. 1 (June 1977): 21.

6. Carl Dahlhaus, *Esthetics of Music,* trans. William Austin (Cambridge: Cambridge University Press, 1982), 90.

7. See Zoltan Roman, *Gustav Mahler and Hungary*, Studies in Central and Eastern European Music 5 (Budapest: Akadémiai Kiadó, 1991), 78–81.

8. See Weber, *Great Transformation of Musical Taste,* 34

9. Richard Taruskin, *Music in the Nineteenth Century*, vol. 3 of *The Oxford History of Western Music* (Oxford and New York: Oxford University Press, 2010), 426.

10. Lawrence Kramer, "Music, Historical Knowledge and Critical Inquiry: Three Variations on *The Ruins of Athens*," *Critical Inquiry* 32, no. 1 (Autumn 2005): 76.

11. See Matthew Pritchard, "'A heap of broken images'? Reviving Austro-German Debates Over Musical Meaning, 1900–36," *Journal of the Royal Musical Association* 138, no. 1 (2013): 129–74.

12. Ibid., 170; translation by Drabkin, cited in *Heinrich Schenker, Der Tonwille: Pamphlets in Witness of the Immutable Laws of Music, Offered to a New Generation of Youth*, ed. William Drabkin, 2 vols. (Oxford: Oxford University Press, 2004–5), ii, 162.

13. Pritchard, "'A heap of broken images'? 170. (This is cited from the same English edition of Schenker's *Der Tonwille* as detailed in n. 12 above, here 165).

14. Richard Taruskin, *Defining Russia Musically: Historical and Hermeneutical Essays* (Princeton, NJ: Princeton University Press, 1997), chap. 14, "Shostakovich and the Inhuman," 480.

15. James H. Johnson, *Listening in Paris: A Cultural History* (Berkeley, Los Angeles, and London: University of California Press, 1995), 276; I would not wish to oversimplify Johnson's fascinating study, but his afterword returns (285) to the implicit suggestion that musical experience may be reducible to outward modes of behavior and comportment at public concerts.

16. See Richard Taruskin, *Music in the Early Twentieth Century*, vol. 4 of *The Oxford History of Western Music* (Oxford and New York: Oxford University Press, 2010 [originally 2005]), 351–53.

17. All extracts from Hugo's 1829 poem (from the *Feuilles d'Automne*) are quoted in the translation by Humphrey Searle printed in Eulenburg miniature score No. 447, Liszt, *Ce qu'on entend sur la Montagne* (London, Zürich, Mainz, New York: Ernst Eulenburg Ltd., 1976)—revised with corrections, x–vii.

18. The quoted phrases appear in *The Song of the High Hills* over the horn part on p. 23 of the UE miniature score 13875, six bars before cue 18, where the voices enter, marked "(In the far distance)."

19. Theodor Adorno, *Introduction to the Sociology of Music*, trans E.B. Ashton (New York: Seabury Press, 1976), 61–62.

20. Stanislaus Przybyszewski, *Zur Psychologie des Individuums. 1. Chopin und Nietzsche* (Berlin: Fontane, 1892), 47.

21. Laurence Dreyfus, *Wagner and the Erotic Impulse* (Cambridge, MA: Harvard University Press, 2010), 37.

22. Ibid., 35.

23. From *The Case of Wagner* in Friedrich Nietzsche, *The Birth of Tragedy and The Case of Wagner*, trans. Walter Kaufmann (New York: Vintage Books, 1967), 159.

24. See E. Lockspeiser: *Debussy: His Life and Mind*, vol. 1 (London: Cassell, 1962), 8.

25. Ibid., 59.

26. Claude Debussy, "Monsieur Croche the Dillettante Hater," trans. B. N. Langdon Davies, in *Three Classics in the Aesthetics of Music* (New York: Dover, 1962), 19.

27. Ibid., 7.

28. See Thomas Mann, *Buddenbrooks,* trans. H. T. Lowe-Porter, Penguin Modern Classics, part 10, chap. 6, 518. Concerning mountains, see Christopher Morris, *Modernism and the Cult of Mountains: Music, Opera, Cinema* (Farnham, UK: Ashgate, 2012).

29. J.-K. Huysmans, *À Rebours* [*Against Nature*], trans. Robert Baldick (London: Penguin Books, 1979), 192.

30. Ibid.

31. Theodor Adorno and Max Horkheimer, *Dialectic of Enlightenment,* trans. John Cumming (London: Verso, 1979), 32.

32. Ibid., 34.

33. Ibid.

34. Homer, *The Odyssey,* trans. E. V. Rieu (London: Penguin Books, 1964), 190 (from book 12).

35. I am grateful to my colleague Richard Parish for assisting with the translation of this passage, the French text of which I take from the Peters Edition score [Nr. 9156a, 1977] of Debussy *Nocturnes. Triptyque Symphonique,* Ausgabe nach der Quellen (ed. Pommer), Postface, 122.

36. Roger Nichols, *Debussy Remembered* (London: Faber & Faber, 1992), 218.

37. Roger Nichols, *The Life of Debussy* (Cambridge: Cambridge University Press, 1998), 109.

38. Jacques Rivière, 1902, cited in Nichols, *Life of Debussy,* 107.

39. Ibid.

40. Ibid., 118.

41. Ibid.

42. Debussy, "Monsieur Croche," 18.

43. I refer specifically to Chowrimootoo's use of this phrase with reference to an "aria under erasure" in a paper on *Peter Grimes* delivered in Oxford on 8 May 2012.

44. See Peter Franklin, "Underscoring Drama—Picturing Music," in *Wagner and Cinema,* ed. Jeongwon Joe and Sander L. Gilman (Bloomington and Indianapolis: Indiana University Press, 2010), 52–55.

45. James H. Johnson, *Listening in Paris: A Cultural History* (Berkeley, Los Angeles, and London: University of California Press, 1995), 263. (The watercolor sketch by Eugène Lami is captioned "La Première audition de la Septième Symphonie de Beethoven.")

46. Quoted in Karl Eckman, *Jean Sibelius, His Life and Personality,* trans. Edward Birse (New York: Tudor, 1946), 233.

47. Gustav Mahler, *Letters to His Wife,* ed. Henri-Louis de La Grange and Günther Weiss, trans. Antony Beaumont (London, Faber, 2004), 240.

48. The phrase "the profound logic" comes from Eckman's report of Sibelius's famous conversation with Mahler, in which Sibelius had expressed his

admiration for the "severity and style and the profound logic" of the symphony; see Eckman, *Jean Sibelius*, 32.

49. The comment on the Fourth Symphony as "pure cold water" is reported (after Furuhjelm) in Cecil Gray. *Sibelius: The Symphonies* (London: Oxford University Press, 1935), 56. It was to Rosa Newmarch in 1911 that he made the comment about there being "nothing of the circus" about the Fourth (see Erik Tawaststjerna, *Sibelius*, vol. 2, 1904–1914, trans. Robert Layton (London: Faber, 1986), 172.

50. The primary adumbration of "rotational form" is in James Hepokoski, *Sibelius: Symphony no. 5* (Cambridge: Cambridge University Press, 1993), 23–27; on the swans, see 36–38.

51. This appears in English translation, by Susan H. Gillespie, in Daniel M. Grimley, ed., *Jean Sibelius and His World* (Princeton, NJ, and Oxford: Princeton University Press, 2011), 333–37.

52. Ibid., 331.

53. Translation of Adorno's "Glosse über Sibelius," by Susan H. Gillespie, in *Jean Sibelius and His World*, 334.

54. Ibid., 333.

55. Glenda Dawn Goss, *Jean Sibelius and Olin Downes: Music, Friendship, Criticism* (Boston: Northeastern University Press, 1995), 62.

56. Hepokoski, *Sibelius: Symphony no. 5*, 2.

57. Cecil Gray, *Sibelius*, 2nd ed. (Oxford: Oxford University Press, 1943; 1st ed., 1931), 146–47.

58. See Donald Francis Tovey, *Essays in Musical Analysis,* vol. 2, *Symphonies (II), Variations and Orchestral Polyphony* (London: Oxford University Press, second impression 1936 [originally 1935]), 128–29.

59. To my knowledge, this version is accessible only in the recording made by Osmo Vänskä with the Lahti Symphony Orchestra: Jean Sibelius, Symphony no. 5 in E flat major, op. 82 (Original 1915 Version), BIS CD-800 (no. 38 of their Complete Sibelius series).

CHAPTER 4

1. Thomas Mann, *Pro and Contra Wagner,* trans. Allan Blunden (London: Faber and Faber, 1985), 30.

2. Norman Lebrecht, "The Long Shadow Over Bayreuth," *Standpoint*, September 2012, www.standpointmag.co.uk/node/4574/full, accessed on 13 September 2012. I am grateful to Philip White for drawing my attention to this article—no less for facilitating my trips to Bayreuth.

3. Lebrecht, "Long Shadow Over Bayreuth."

4. Ibid.

5. "Coming to Terms with Richard Wagner," as translated in Mann, *Pro and Contra Wagner,* 46.

6. Ibid., 31.

7. Ibid., 34.

8. See Thomas Mann, *Reflections of a Nonpolitical Man,* trans. and with an introduction by Walter D. Morris (New York: Frederick Ungar, 1983). The

introduction summarizes the history of the book, responses to it, and Mann's subsequent change of intellectual direction.

9. Thomas Mann, *Death in Venice*—in *Death in Venice, Tristan, Tonio Kröger*, trans. H.T. Lowe-Porter (Harmondsworth, UK: Penguin, 1955), 13.

10. See Gilbert Adair, *The Real Tadzio: Thomas Mann's "Death in Venice" and the Boy Who Inspired It* (London: Short, 2001).

11. Mann, *Death in Venice*, 53.

12. Mann, *Pro and Contra Wagner*, 46.

13. Ibid., 47.

14. Ibid., 48.

15. Lebrecht, "Long Shadow Over Bayreuth."

16. A commercial DVD of the production has been planned; meanwhile fuller documentation, description, and illustrations of the production may be found in two published books already devoted to it: Susanne Vill, *Parsifal: Richard Wagners Bühnenweihfestspiel in Stefan Herheims Inszenierung Bayreuther Festspiele. Eine Inszenierungsanalyse mit Kommentaren* (Bayreuth, Germany: [no publisher], 2009); and Antonia Goldhammer, *Weisst du, was du sahst? Stefan Herheim's Bayreuther Parsifal* (Berlin and Munich: Deutscher Kunstverlag, 2011).

17. Theodor Adorno, *In Search of Wagner*, trans. Rodney Livingstone ([no place]: NLB, 1981), 46.

18. I am thinking, for example, of his description of the G major episode in the first movement of the Fourth Symphony in Theodor W. Adorno, *Mahler: A Musical Physiognomy*, trans. Edmund Jephcott (Chicago and London: University of Chicago Press, 1992), 44 ("a blissful passage, lies before the listener like a village before which he is seized by the feeling that this might be what he seeks").

19. Here I cite the Wagner's stage direction as translated in *Parsifal: A Festival Drama by Richard Wagner*, trans. H.L. Corder and F. Corder (New York: Fred Rullman Inc., [n.d.]), 15 ("Endlich sind sie in einem mächtigen Saale angekommen, welcher nach oben in einer hochgewölbte Kuppel, durch die einzig das Licht hereindringt, sich verliert").

20. Piotr Ilyich Tchaikovsky, *Letters to His Family: An Autobiography*, trans. Galina von Meck (New York: Stein and Day, 1982 [1981]), 109.

21. See Adorno, *In Search of Wagner*, 30–31.

22. Ellen Lockhart, "Photo-Opera: *La Fanciulla del West* and the staging souvenir," *Cambridge Opera Journal* 23, no. 3 (November 2011): 145.

23. Alain Badiou, *Five Lessons on Wagner*, with an afterword by Slavoj Žižek, trans. Susan Spitzer (London and New York, Verso, 2010).

24. Lockhart, "Photo-Opera," 147.

25. See Lockhart, "Photo-Opera," 146, citing David Levin, *Unsettling Opera: Staging Mozart, Verdi, Wagner and Zemlinsky* (Chicago: University of Chicago Press, 2007).

26. Lockhart, "Photo-Opera," 145.

27. Ibid., 146.

28. Ibid., and Lockhart's n. 6 there (where she cites Badiou, *Five Lessons*, 81–82: "we are on the cusp of a revival of high art and it is here that Wagner should be invoked").

29. I am grateful to my former colleague Emanuele Senici, author of *Landscape and Gender in Italian Opera: The Alpine Virgin from Bellini to Puccini* (Cambridge: Cambridge University Press, 2005), whose advice about the following sections of this chapter was invaluable.

30. See Tash Siddiqui, "Flying the Republican Colours: The 1929 Krolloper Production of *Der fliegende Holländer*," *Wagner Journal* 6, no. 1 (March 2012): 15–34.

31. Richard Taruskin, *Music in the Early Twentieth Century*, vol. 4 of *The Oxford History of Western Music* (Oxford and New York: Oxford University Press, 2010); his discussion of *Wozzeck* ranges across pp. 506–26. The crux of his argument referred to here occupies pp. 520–26.

32. Alban Berg, *Wozzeck,* Evelyn Lear, Dietrich Fiescher-Dieskau etc., Conductor Karl Böhm, Deutsche Grammophon [n.d. (1965)—138 991, 138 992], liner notes 11–13. The source of the diagrammatic table was that initially prepared by Berg's pupil Fritz Mahler and cited by Willi Reich as "suggested by Berg himself." Willi Reich, *Alban Berg,* trans Cornelius Cardew (New York: Vienna House 1974), 120.

33. Taruskin, *Music in the Early Twentieth Century*, 526.

34. Ibid.

35. Ibid. The reference here is to Joseph Kerman, *Opera as Drama*, rev. ed. (London: Faber, 1989 [1956], 188. (In fact Kerman has more to say about this interlude later, but the passage referred to suggests that "once you have heard the interlude as a slow waltz in the lachrymose tradition of Mahler, you can no longer surrender, and everything is lost.")

36. See Anthony Pople, "The Musical Language of *Wozzeck*" in *The Cambridge Companion to Berg,* ed. Anthony Pople (Cambridge: Cambridge University Press, 1997), 152; citing Theodor W. Adorno, *Alban Berg: Master of the Smallest Link,* trans. J. Brand and C. Hailey (Cambridge: Cambridge University Press, 1991), 10.

37. Taruskin, *Music in the Early Twentieth Century*, 522.

38. Mosco Carner, *Puccini: A Critical Biography* (London: Duckworth, 1958), ix.

39. Richard Specht, *Giacomo Puccini: The Man, His Life, His Work,* trans. Catherine Alison Phillips (London: Dent, 1933), ix (German original published Berlin: Max Hesser, 1932).

40. Ibid., 3.

41. Ibid., 5.

42. Ibid., 122

43. Adolf Weissmann, *Der klingende Garten—Impressionen über das Erotische in der Musik* (Berlin: Verlag Neue Kunsthandlung, 1920).

44. I refer of course to Susan McClary, *Feminine Endings: Music, Gender and Sexuality* (Minneapolis: University of Minnesota Press, 1991).

45. Weissmann, *Der klingende Garten,* 53.

46. Ibid., 55–56.

47. Bertolt Brecht, "On the Use of Music on an Epic Theatre" (1935), in *Brecht on Theatre: The Development of an Aesthetic,* 2nd ed., ed. John Willett (London: Methuen, 1974), 89.

48. Relevant here is an 1826 account of Weber conducting his own music in London, facing the audience and startling it by offering "listener-viewers a visual analogue of what his music signified." See J. Q. Davies, "Dancing the Symphonic Beethoven-Bochsa's *Symphonie Pastorale*, 1829," *19th-Century Music* 27, no. 1 (2003): 35.

49. Peter Brooks, *The Melodramatic Imagination: Balzac, Henry James, Melodrama, and the Mode of Excess* (New Haven, CT: Yale University Press, 1976; reprint 1995 with a new preface), xii.

50. Katherine Astbury makes the point in her essay "Music in Pixérécourt's Early Melodramas" that popular novels were themselves often the sources of successful melodramas; see Sarah Hibberd, ed., *Melodramatic Voices: Understanding Music Drama* (Farnham, UK: Ashgate, 2011), 16.

51. Andrew Davis, *"Il Trittico," "Turandot," and Puccini's Late Style* (Bloomington and Indianapolis: Indiana University Press, 2010); James Hepokoski, "Structure, Implication, and the End of *Suor Angelica*," in *Studi Pucciniani 3, "L'insolita forma"—Strutture e processi analitici per l'opera italiana nell'epoca di Puccini*, ed. Virgilio Bernardoni, Michele Girardi, and Arthur Groos (Lucca: Centro studi Giacomo Puccini, 2004), 241–64; Arman Schwartz, "Puccini, in the Distance," *Cambridge Opera Journal*, 23, no. 3 (November 2011): 167–89.

52. Carner, *Puccini*, 424.

53. Arman Schwartz notes that this had in fact been prefigured earlier, following Cue 36; see Schwartz, "Puccini in the Distance," 183.

54. Schwartz, "Puccini in the Distance," 188.

55. Hepokoski, "Structure, Implication," 257.

56. I nevertheless remain skeptical about Arman Schwartz's comments on *verismo* and the protofascist implications of *Tosca* in his essay "Rough Music: *Tosca* and *Verismo* Reconsidered," *19th-Century Music* 31, no. 3 (Spring 2008): 228–44 (see below, and my alternative reading of *Tosca*, act 1, in Peter Franklin, *Seeing Through Music: Gender and Modernism in Classic Hollywood Film Scores* (New York: Oxford University Press, 2011), 42–47.

57. See Senici, *Landscape and Gender*, 229 (the whole of the final chapter is dedicated to *Fanciulla*).

58. See Richard Sennett, *The Fall of Public Man* (New York: Knopf 1977 [1974]).

59. Kerman, *Opera as Drama*, 205.

60. See Roger Parker, *Remaking the Song: Operatic Visions and Revisions from Handel to Berio* (Berkeley and Los Angeles: University of California Press, 2006), 90–120.

61. Ibid., 96. The reference is to Barbara Spackman, *Fascist Virilities: Rhetoric, Ideology and Social Fantasy in Italy* (Minneapolis: University of Minnesota Press, 1996). See also Alexandra Wilson, *The Puccini Problem: Opera, Nationalism and Modernity* (Cambridge: Cambridge University Press, 2007), 215, where Lualdi is quoted as suggesting of Calaf's relationship with Turandot that he "should have slapped her, beaten her. Some women enjoy this means of gentle persuasion." The complexity of how we might read the political implications of *Turandot*, given Puccini's apparent late inclination toward Mussolini,

are subtly dealt with in Arman Schwartz, "Mechanism and Tradition in Puccini's *Turandot*," *Opera Quarterly* 25, no. 1–2 (Winter–Spring 2009): 28–50.

62. Dante del Fiorentino, *Immortal Bohemian: An intimate Memoir of Giacomo Puccini* (London: Gollancx, 1952), 212.

63. Ibid., 144.

64. *Letters of Giacomo Puccini,* ed. Giuseppe Adami, rev. ed., trans. Ena Makin, ed. Mosco Carner (London: Harrap, 1974), 321.

65. Wilson, *Puccini Problem,* 215.

66. Ibid., 268.

67. It is intriguing, in this respect, to note that not only his father, Timur, but also the influential courtiers Ping, Pang, and Pong consistently mock Calaf's aspirations in ways that could accommodate this reading, as when they advise him to "Go, this is the gate to the great butcher's shop! / Madman. Go away!" subsequently adding, "There exists only the Nothingness in which you annihilate yourself!" (see *Turandot,* trans. William Weaver, Opera Guide 27 (London: John Calder in association with the English National Opera, 1984), 75–79.

68. Arnold Schoenberg, *Style and Idea* (London: Williams & Norgate, 1951), 51 (the final page of the essay "New Music, Outmoded Music, Style and Idea").

CHAPTER 5

1. Susan McClary, *Feminine Endings: Music, Gender and Sexuality* (Minneapolis: University of Minnesota Press, 1991), 21.

2. I am thinking of the statement "We cannot help admitting that the term 'music,' in its true meaning, must exclude compositions in which words are set to music." See Eduard Hanslick, *The Beautiful in Music,* trans. Gustav Cohen (Indianapolis: Bobbs Merrill, 1957), 30.

3. Abbate cites a 1989 *New York Times* review by Paul Robinson which does precisely this; see Carolyn Abbate, "Opera: or, the Envoicing of Women," in *Musicology and Difference: Gender and Sexuality in Music Scholarship,* ed. Ruth A. Solie (Berkeley, Los Angeles, and London: University of California Press, 1993), 254.

4. Catherine Clément, *Opera, or the Undoing of Women,* trans. Betsy Wing (London: Virago, 1989), 21 (originally *L'Opéra ou la Défaite des femmes* [1979]).

5. Abbate, "Opera: or, the Envoicing of Women," 254.

6. Thomas Mann, *Doctor Faustus: The Life of the German Composer Adrian Leverkühn as Told by a Friend,* trans. H.T. Lowe-Porter (Harmondsworth, UK: Penguin Books, 1968), 132. The Wackenroder allusion is to the passage quoted in chapter 1 of this volume.

7. Mann, *Doctor Faustus,* 211.

8. Mann's wife records that her husband "was more or less under the influence of Richard Wagner his whole life long, especially as a young man, and he never missed a *Tristan* performance." See Katia Mann, *Unwritten Memories,* trans. Hunter (Hildegarde Hannum) (London: Andre Deutsch, 1975), 90.

9. Claudia Gorbman, *Unheard Melodies: Narrative Film Music* (London; Bloomington and Indianapolis: BFI Publishing and Indiana University Press, 1987).

10. On Cavell, see the following note. For a study of the score with music examples, see Kate Daubney, *Max Steiner's "Now, Voyager": A Film Score Guide* (Westport, CT, and London: Greenwood Press, 2000).

11. Stanley Cavell, *Contesting Tears: The Hollywood Melodrama of the Unknown Woman* (Chicago and London: University of Chicago Press, 1996), 117–18.

12. Ibid., 118.

13. This issue is explored further in chapter 4 of my book *Seeing Through Music: Gender and Modernism in Classic Hollywood Film Scores* (New York and London: Oxford University Press, 2011), 85–114.

14. See Andrew Davis, *"Il Trittico," "Turandot," and Puccini's Late Style* (Bloomington and Indianapolis: Indiana University Press, 2010); the issue of strategic stylistic plurality in Puccini is addressed on page 2 and further theorized in the first chapter, "Stylistic Plurality, Narrative, Levels of Discourse, and Voice," 8–27.

15. Leonard Stein, ed., *Style and Idea: Selected Writings of Arnold Schoenberg*, with translations by Leo Black (London: Faber, 1975), 336–37.

16. See Rudy Behlmer, *Inside Warner Bros. (1935–1951)* (London: Weidenfeld & Nicolson, 1986), 52–53.

17. His teacher Alexander Zemlinsky published a short memoir of Korngold in the January 1921 edition of *Auftakt* in Prague, in which he observed somewhat nervously of the young Korngold that when he started teaching him, at the age of eleven, "he had a great passion for Puccini—a passion which I believe has since changed very much" (there is no evidence that it did). See Brendan G. Carroll, *The Last Prodigy: A Biography of Erich Wolfgang Korngold* (Portland, OR: Amadeus Press, 1997), 39; also 158 on Salzburg in 1923.

18. On the premieres of *Das Wunder der Heliane*, see Carroll, *Last Prodigy*, 197–200.

19. The issue is addressed in Jessica Duchen, *Eric Wolfgang Korngold* (London: Phaidon, 1996), chap. 5, "Opera and Operetta, 1927–34," 128–48.

20. I refer to the tendentious public designation as "a Soviet artist's creative response to just criticism" of Shostakovich's Fifth Symphony (1937) in the wake of the official denunciation of his opera *Lady Macbeth of the Mtsensk District* and retraction of his Fourth Symphony. See Taruskin, *Defining Russia Musically*, 516.

21. Carroll, *Last Prodigy*, 348.

22. Helmut Pöllmann, "Preface/Vorwort" to the score of *Korngold, Symphony in F#, Op. 40* (London, Mainz etc.: Eulenburg, 1977), iv–vii.

23. See Peter Franklin, "Modernism, Deception and Musical Others: Los Angeles circa 1940," *Western Music and Its Others: Difference, Representation, and Appropriation in Music,* ed. Georgina Born and David Hesmondhalgh (Berkeley, Los Angeles, and London: University of California Press, 2000), 143–162; also "Deception's Great Music: A Cultural Analysis," in *Film Music 2: History, Theory, Practice,* ed. Claudia Gorbman and Warren B. Sherk (Sherman Oaks, CA, Film Music Society, 2004), 27–41.

24. Carroll, *Last Prodigy*, 348.

25. Published as Hanns Eisler, *Composing for the Films* (New York: Oxford University Press, 1947). The new edition presented it as Theodor Adorno and Hanns Eisler, *Composing for the Films*, with new introduction by Graham McCann (London and Atlantic Highlands, NJ: Athlone Press, 1994), same pagination as the 1947 edition from 3 onward.

26. See chapter 1. "Sonoric surveillance and the masses," where Holbrook Jackson is cited by John Carey.

27. Subsequently the narrator here becomes more obviously and conventionally "omniscient."

28. Henry Bellamann, *Kings Row* (1941) and Olive Higgins Prouty, *Now, Voyager* (1941); the editions consulted were Henry Bellamann, *Kings Row* (London: Panther, 1959); and Olive Higgins Prouty, *Now, Voyager*, afterword by Judith Mayne, "Femmes Fatales: Women Write Pulp" (New York: The Feminist Press at the City University of New York, 2004).

29. David Bordwell, *Narration in the Fiction Film* (London: Routledge, 1988 [originally Methuen, 1985]).

30. Ibid., 29, 45.

31. Gorbman, *Unheard Melodies*, 80.

32. The reference is to Laura Mulvey, "Visual Pleasure in Narrative Cinema," first published in *Screen* 16, no. 3 (Autumn 1975): 6–18.

33. Rose Theresa, "From Méphistophélès to Méliès: Spectacle and Narrative in Opera and Early Film" in *Between Opera and Cinema*, ed. Jeongwon Joe and Rose Theresa (New York and London: Routledge, 2002), 1–18.

34. Ibid., 3.

35. Ibid.

36. See Bordwell, *Narration in the Fiction Film*, 49–51.

37. See Jeanine Bassinger, *A Woman's View: How Hollywood Spoke to Women, 1930–1960* (Hanover, NH, and London: Wesleyan University Press, 1993), 438–44; and Cavell, *Contesting Tears*, chaps. 3 and 4.

38. Particularly articulate on this topic was the Viennese critic Robert Hirschfeld; see Peter Franklin, *Mahler Symphony No. 3*, Cambridge Music Handbooks (Cambridge: Cambridge University Press, 1991), 31–33.

39. See Behlmer, *Inside Warner Bros.*, 141–42. The material reproduced here indicates that a story had been put around that Bellamann was intending to assist Korngold with the scoring of the film of his novel, something Korngold commented wryly upon.

40. Bellamann, *Kings Row*, 12, 112.

41. Ibid., 113.

42. Ibid.

43. Prouty, *Now, Voyager*, 261.

44. Ibid., 262.

45. For more on Wagner's detailed and visualized description of the *Lohengrin* Prelude, see Peter Franklin, "Underscoring Drama—Picturing Music," in *Wagner and Cinema*, ed. Jeongwon Joe and Sander L. Gilman (Bloomington and Indianapolis: Indiana University Press, 2010), 54–55.

46. Prouty, *Now, Voyager*, 187.

CHAPTER 6

1. Schoenberg translation by Allan Forte, from the booklet accompanying the Boulez recording of *Moses und Aron* (CBS 79201, n.d.); Schreker translation by Susan Marie Praeder (amended), liner notes libretto accompanying the CPO, DDD recording of *Christophorus oder "Die Vision einer Oper"* (CPO 999 903–2, 2005).

2. This concert was to have included the premiere of Webern's *Six Orchestral Pieces* op. 6, followed by four of Zemlinsky's Maeterlinck songs with orchestra, Schoenberg's op. 9 *Chamber Symphony*, the premieres of songs number 2 and 3 from Berg's *Altenberg Lieder*, and Mahler's *Kindertotenlieder*. Noisy responses in the *Grosser Musikvereinssaal* increased after the Berg songs to the point where chaos broke out and the police had to be called; the Mahler songs were not performed. See Juliane Brand, Christopher Hailey, and Donald Harris, eds., *The Berg-Schoenberg Correspondence: Selected Letters* (London: Macmillan, 1987), 166–72.

3. The most detailed source of information on this late phase of Schreker's life is Christopher Hailey, *Franz Schreker, 1878–1934* (Cambridge: Cambridge University Press, 1993), chaps. 10–12.

4. Joseph Kerman, ed., *Music at the Turn of Century* (Berkeley, Los Angeles, and Oxford: University of California Press, 1990), preface, viii.

5. Ibid.

6. Aaron Copland, *The New Music, 1900–1960*, revised and enlarged edition (New York and London: W.W. Norton, 1968), 40.

7. Ibid., 31.

8. Henri Lonitz, ed., *Theodor Adorno and Alban Berg: Correspondence, 1925–1935*, trans. Wieland Hoban (Cambridge: Polity, 2005), 150.

9. Theodor Adorno, "Berliner Opernmemorial," in *Gesammelte Schriften Band 19, Musikalische Schriften VI*, ed. Rolf Tiedemann and Klaus Schultz (Frankfurt am Main: Suhrkamp, 1984), 272.

10. On Ives's gendered put-downs of most European music (of which his renaming of Rachmaninov as "Rachnotmanenough" is the most succinct), see Judith Tick, "Charles Ives and Gender Ideology," in *Musicology and Difference: Gender and Sexuality in Music Scholarship*, ed. Ruth Solie (Berkeley, Los Angeles, and London: University of California Press, 1993), 83–106 (here 99). Richard Leppert authoritatively explains how "music under the conditions of modernity was concatenated with woman (especially with her dangerous sexuality) and sometimes with the body of the prostitute" in *The Sight of Sound: Music, Representation, and the Body* (Berkeley, Los Angeles, London: University of California Press, 1993), 207 and passim.

11. Theodor Adorno, *Quasi una Fantasia: Essays on Modern Music*, trans. Rodney Livingstone (London and New York: Verso, 1992), 130–44. The reference to Schreker's textures as, figuratively, a "mixed drink" (in English in the original) appears on p. 136. In what follows I rely on the original German text, cited in the following note. For an extended critical discussion of Adorno's Schreker essay, see also Sherry D. Lee, "A Minstrel in a World without Minstrels: Adorno and the Case of Schreker," *Journal of the American Musicological Society* 58, no. 3 (Fall 2005): 639–96.

12. My own translation, here and in what follows, of the original German in Theodor W. Adorno, *Gesmmelte Schriften,* Band 16 (Musikalische Schriften I-III), ed. Rolf Tiedemann (Frankfurt am Main: Suhrkamp, 1978), 375 (see Livingstone trans., 137–38).

13. Adorno, *Gesammelte Schriften,* Band 16, 371–72.

14. Ibid., 379 (Livingstone trans., 142).

15. Ibid., 375–76 (Livingstone trans., 138–39).

16. Ibid., 380 (Livingstone trans., 143).

17. I am thinking here of Stravinsky's famous statement (as reported by Robert Craft), "I am the vessel through which *Le Sacre* passed." Igor Stravinsky and Robert Craft, *Expositions and Developments* (London: Faber, 1981), 148.

18. In this the Catholic establishment, represented by the court-appointed Intendant, might have over-ruled both Bruno Walter, to whom the opera was dedicated, and Mahler's successor as director, Felix Weingartner, both of whom seem to have spoken out in favor of the work. See Hailey, *Franz Schreker,* 32.

19. Translation by Richard Arsenty, accompanying MRF records recording of *Der ferne Klang* (1984), amended by the author.

20. For a fuller picture of what happens here, see the 1912 full orchestral score, which was published as a companion volume to Ulrike Kienzle, *Das Trauma hinter dem Traum. Franz Schrekers Oper 'Der ferne Klang' und die Wiener Moderne* (Schliengen, Germany: Edition Argus, 1998). The score appears as Franz Schreker, *Der ferne Klang. Oper in drei Aufzugen. Studienpartitur* (Schliengen, Germany: Edition Argus, 1998), II Aufzug (the pages of each act are numbered from 1).

21. On the late-romantic orchestral interlude, see Christopher Morris, *Reading Opera Between the Lines: Orchestral Interludes and Cultural Meaning from Wagner to Berg* (Cambridge: Cambridge University Press, 2002). His chapter 5, "A Torrent of Unsettling Sounds," deals specifically with Schreker but concentrates on the famous love scene from *Der Schatzgräber.*

22. See Alexandra Ritchie, *Faust's Metropolis: A History of Berlin* (London: HarperCollins, 1999), 389–90.

23. See Michael H. Kater, *Composers of the Nazi Era: Eight Portraits* (New York and Oxford: Oxford University Press, 2000), 59.

24. Nazi-period articles and correspondence of Wilhelm Rode are included in Joseph Wulf, *Musik im Dritten Reich. Eine Dokumentation.* Zeitgeschichte. Ullstein Buch Nr33032 (Verlag Ullstein GmbH, Frankfurt-Berlin-Wien 1983—[Ungekürzte Ausgabe 1966]).

25. See Hailey, *Franz Schreker,* 282.

26. Ibid., 278.

27. The production of *Der Schmied von Gent* at Die Theater Chemnitz was directed by Ansgar Weigner. Oliver Zwarg was Smee, Undine Dreissig his wife. The conductor (of the Robert-Schumann Philharmonie) was Frank Beerman.

28. The *Frankfurter Allgemeine Zeitung* of Monday, 15 February 2010, had a picture of the "Menschenkette" demonstration with a caption explaining that disruption of Dresden's commemoration by "Fremde, Rechtsextremisten" was rejected by the line of silent demonstrators. The accompanying article (on page 3) quoted the Oberburgmeisterin Helma Orosz's speech vowing that efforts by

the "Jung- und Altnazis," who sought to hijack the event, would not be tolerated. "Before Dresden burned, the Semper Synagogue burned, Warsaw burned, and Rotterdam and Coventry."

29. See above, chapter 5, note 20. Schreker's article on *Der Schmied* appeared as "Smee und die sieben Jahren," *Anbruch* 13, nos. 6–7 (August–September 1931): 150–52.

30. Ibid. This and some other passages from the article were also reproduced in the Chemnitz 2010 program book for *Der Schmied von Gent*.

31. Author's translation (and following extracts).

32. See Hailey, *Franz Schreker,* 279

33. The 2010 Chemnitz program quoted a significant ironic comment from Schreker's essay on *Der Schmied* (see notes 29 and 30 above), which translates as follows: "In accordance with my wicked musical past, the sections involving temptation, sinfulness and Hell glitter with my own (god-given) colors—which those who despise this manner claimed so sorely to have missed in *Singende Teufel.*"

34. Christopher Hailey, ed., *Paul Bekker/Franz Schreker Briefwechsel, mit sämtlichen Kritiken Bekkers über Schreker* (Aachen, Germany: Rimbaud, 1994), 410–11.

35. Ibid., 411

36. See Hailey, *Franz Schreker,* 289–90. I am grateful to Timothy Jackson for drawing my attention to the complete text of this letter, which is deposited in the Österreichischer National Bibliothek, Schreker-Fonds, 414/7.

37. See Franz Schreker, *Der Schmied von Gent,* CD recording of the Chemnitz production, conducted by Frank Beerman, issued by CPO in 2012 (777 672-2).

38. Schoenberg responded warmly to Schreker for the dedication of *Christophorus*. See Friedrich C. Heller, *Arnold Schoenberg—Franz Schreker Briefwechsel. Mit unveröffentlichen Texten von Arnold Schoenberg* (Tutzing, Germany: Hans Schneider, 1974), 80.

39. *The Times* (unsigned), 11 October 2012, 54.

40. Author's translation from the published libretto: Fran Schreker, *Der singende Teufel* (Vienna and Leipzig: Universal Edition, 1928), 59, 61.

41. Hailey, *Franz Schreker,* 223.

42. *Christophorus, oder "Die Vision einer Oper,"* act 1, scene 1, libretto translated by Susan Marie Praeder in the liner notes to the CPO recording (see note 1 above), 72.

43. Susan Marie Praeder translation (see note 1; amended). The text recited in the opera is a version of chapter 28 of the *Tao Te Ching* by "Lao Tzo." There exist many quite widely differing translations of this influential collection of ancient Chinese spiritual teachings.

44. The "Vorwort zu *Christophorus*," written in 1932, appears in both German and English in the liner notes to the CPO recording, 66–68; see also Christopher Hailey, "Zur Erstehungsgeschichte der Oper *Christophorus,*" in Franz-Schreker-Symposion, ed. Elmar Budde and Rudolph Stefan (Berlin: Colloquium Verlag, 1980), 136–37.

45. See Peter Franklin, "Audiences, Critics and the Depurification of Music: Reflections on a 1920s Controversy," *Journal of the Royal Musical Association*

14, part 1 (1989): 82–85; the Schopenhauer epigraph to *Palestrina* that is alluded to here is quoted on p. 84; the other reference is specifically to Hans Pfitzner, *Die Neue Ästhetik der musikalischen Impotenz. Ein Verwesungssymptom?* (Munich: Verlag der Süddeutsche Monatshefte, 1920).

46. Franz Werfel, *Verdi* (1923), trans. Helen Jessiman (London: Jarrolds, n.d.), 44 (from chapter 3). Schreker refers to his reading of the novel in a letter to Emil Hertzka of 1924, see Hailey, *Franz Schreker*, 197.

47. See Hailey, *Franz Schreker*, 296.

Index

Abbate, Carolyn, 111
Adami, Giuseppe, 109
Adler, Guido, 18, 96
Adorno, Theodor, 2, 4, 12, 16, 19, 20, 24, 28, 29, 34, 36, 43, 60–61, 66, 68–70, 78–79, 84, 87, 89, 95, 127, 132, 144–46, 166; *Composing for the Films* (with Hanns Eisler), 127, 132; "Durchbruch" [breakthrough], 28, 166; *Quasi una Fantasia,* 144–46
Adventures of Robin Hood, The, 120, 135
Alfano, Franco, 108
Amsterdam, 55
analysis (musical), xiii, 28, 29, 37, 60, 73, 77, 78, 102, 112, 132, 134
Anthony Adverse, 123, 124, 126
anti-Semitism, 83, 89, 152–53, 161
Aristotle, 120, 133–34

Bach, J. S., 49, 97, 104, 136
Badiou, Alain, 90–91
Bartók, Béla, 93
Bassinger, Jeanine, 134
Baudelaire, Charles, 68
Bauer-Lechner, Natalie, 21
Bayreuth, 11, 67, 83, 85–88, 89, 97, 131; *Festspielhaus,* 67, 83, 85–88, 89, 97, 131; *Wahnfried,* 86–88, 91
Beatles, The, 61
Beecham, Sir Thomas, 46, 48

Beethoven, Ludwig van, 9, 17, 18, 24, 25, 27, 29, 33, 37, 58, 59–60, 61, 67, 74, 75, 83, 92, 126, 136–37; "Pathétique" Sonata, 136–7; *The Ruins of Athens,* 59–60; Symphony no. 3, 37, 126; Symphony no. 6, 67; Symphony no. 7, 75; Symphony no. 9, 23, 25, 29, 60, 83
Bekker, Paul, 27, 59–60, 77, 145, 160, 161–62, 169
Belasco, David, 90
Bellamann, Henry, *Kings Row,* 130, 136
Bennett, Arnold, 8–9
Berg, Alban, 26, 28, 93–95, 101, 102, 103, 112, 120, 144, 174n10; *Lulu,* 94; *Wozzeck,* 93–95, 101, 103, 112, 117, 144
Berglinger, Joseph (character in Wackenroder), 11–13, 15, 20, 24, 28, 36, 44, 62, 63, 75, 83, 85, 109, 112–13, 147
Berio, Luciano, 108
Berkeley, xvi-xvii, 4
Berlin, 93, 100, 142, 144, 151, 152, 160, 162, 168; Musik-Hochschule, 151, 152, 169; Städtische Oper, 152, 160
Berlioz, Hector, 57–8; *Symphonie fantastique,* 57
Bernstein, Leonard, 50
Blacking, John, 29
Bloomsbury (literary group), 8
Blue Angel, The [Der blaue Engel], 142
Böcklin, Arnold, 35

bodily experience of music, 29, 36–37, 54, 63, 71–72, 98–100, 144–45, 165–67
Boethius, 6
Böhm, Carl, 94
Bolshevism, 168, 169
Bonn, 86
Bordwell, David, 131–32, 133–34; *Narration in the Fiction Film*, 131, 133
Boulez, Pierre, 16
Bradford, 47
Brahms, Johannes, 54
Brecher, Gustav, 32
Brecht, Bertolt, 97, 100, 111, 131, 135, 141, 157; *Lehrstücke*, 141
Breisach, Paul, 153
Brief Encounter, 35
Brooks, Peter, 101, 106, 114; *The Melodramatic Imagination*, 101
Bruckner, Anton, 116, 123
Büchner, Georg, 94
Budapest, 55, 57
Busoni, Ferruccio, 27, 151, 162

cabaret, 141–42
Cable, George, 47; *The Grandissimes*, 47
Calvocoressi, M.D., 71
Cambridge University Press, 10–11
Cannes, 117
Captain Blood, 123, 124, 125
Carey, John, 7–9, 10, 15, 84, 95; *The Intellectuals and the Masses*, 7–9
Carner, Mosco, 96, 104, 106, 107
Casablanca, 135
Cavell, Stanley, 114–15, 118–19, 131, 134–35; *Contesting Tears*, 114
Chaliapin, Fyodor, 33
Chemnitz (formerly Karl Marx Stadt), 154–55, 161
Chéreau, Patrice, 90
Chopin, Fryderyk, 66, 97, 99*fig.*, 115, 136; *Revolutionary Étude*, 115
Chowrimootoo, Christopher, 74
cinema, "the cinematic" (as critical/technical category), 36, 37, 63, 75, 78, 89, 93, 103–4, 109, 116–19, 122, 123–24, 127–27, 128–29, 130–32, 135, 164, 169–70
Citizen Kane, 135
class, social (and taste), 6–9, 11–13, 15–16, 20, 24–25, 30, 32–33, 56–57, 62, 66, 70–71, 83–84, 103–4, 108–9, 114, 144
classical music, 4, 16, 29, 54–59, 63, 65, 133, 136, 137, 145–46, 162
Clément, Catherine, 111, 133, 150

Cohan, George M., 127; "Over There," 127
Common, Thomas, 45
Conan Doyle, Sir Arthur, 9, 96; "Sherlock Holmes" stories, 9
concert hall, its culture and the symphony concert, xi, xvi, 2–4, 7, 9, 19–20, 23, 24–25, 28, 29, 31, 34, 35–36, 37–44, 53, 55, 61–63, 69, 135, 137–39, 141
conductor, role of, xi, 12, 15, 89, 100, 183n48
Copland, Aaron, 50, 144; *The New Music, 1900–1960*, 144
Craig, Douglas, 46, 47
Creighton, Basil, 14,
Cumming, Robert, 130

Dahl, Dr. Nicolai, 34
Dahlhaus, Carl, xii, xiii, 4–5, 9, 10, 56–57, 60; *Esthetics of Music*, 56–57
D'Albert, Eugen, 92; *Tiefland*, 92
Darwin, Charles, 35
Davidsbund (Band of David), 25, 30, 62
Davies, James Q., 174n2, 183n48
Davis, Andrew, 102, 116
Davis, Bette, 114–15, 116*fig.*, 124–26, 125*fig.*
Debussy, Claude Achille, 13, 59, 61, 66, 67–75, 76, 78, 79, 93, 100, 112, 144; as "Monsieur Croche," 67; *Fêtes*, 70; *Jeux*, 73; *La Mer*, 71–75, 112; *Nocturnes*, 68; *Pelléas et Mélisande*, 68, 71, 74, 93; *Sirènes*, 67–70, 71–2, 74, 75
decadence, decadents, xiii–xiv, 23–24, 28, 30–32, 35, 39, 43, 45, 54, 62, 66–67, 68, 71, 76, 84–85, 133, 141, 143–44, 145
Deception, 122, 133–24
De Coster, Charles, 153, 156
Deleuze, Gilles, xiv
Del Fiorentino, Dante, 108
Delius, Frederick, 27, 44–52, 54, 57, 61, 62, 65, 70, 76, 112, 135; *American Rhapsody*, 49; *Appalachia*, 49–52, 57, 112; *Hassan*, 176n40; *Koanga*, 46–50, 51; *The Magic Fountain*, 46; *Mass of Life, A*, 44–45, 46, 52, 65; *Sea Drift*, 46; *The Song of the High Hills*, 46, 65
Derrida, Jacques, 74
Des Esseintes (character in Huysmans), 30, 45, 62, 68
Dickens, Charles, 128
Dietrich, Marlene, 86
dionysian, the, xiii, xv, 16, 72, 97, 135, 165

Downes, Olin, 44, 79
Downes, Stephen, xiii, xv, 31
Dresden, 14, 153, 154–55, 188n28
Dreyfus, Laurence, xv, 66
Düsseldorff, 28
Dvořák, Antonín, 34, 57

Eichendorff, Joseph von, 8
Eigner, Pauline, 91
Eisler, Hanns, 127, 132; *Composing for the Films* (with Adorno), 127, 132
Eldridge, Richard, 10
Elgar, Sir Edward, 44, 52, 57
Eliot, T. S., 8, 94
Enlightenment, 24, 68
Entartete Kunst Exhibition (Munich, 1937), 28
Entartete Musik Exhibition (Düsseldorff, 1938), 28
eroticism, xv, 31, 65–66, 97–99, 121, 133, 137, 141, 166
exoticism, 47, 50–52, 102, 130
Expressionism, 16, 93, 94, 103, 141
"extra-musical," 19, 29,

fascism, 2, 142, 161, 163–64, 168–69
femininity, xiv, 7–8, 15–16, 19, 53, 66–68, 69, 71, 95, 97–100, 106–7, 108, 111, 128, 132–34, 136, 144–45, 148–49
Fenby, Eric, 44–45, 52, 61–62; *Delius as I Knew Him*, 44–45
film music, 29, 110, 113–20, 122–128, 130–31, 138–39, 143
fin de siècle, 1, 31
Fingesten, Michael, 97, 98–99*figs.*
Fischer-Dieskau, Dietrich, 94
Flaubert, Gustave, 68
Flynn, Errol, 124, 125
"folk" music, 33–34, 36, 43, 47, 155, 156, 161
Forster, E. M., 8
Forzano, Giovacchino, 120
Franck, César, 74
Franta, Andrew, 10
Freud, Sigmund, 97
Friedhofer, Hugo, 115
Friedrich, Caspar David, *The Wanderer above the Mist*, 3*fig.*, 4, 63, 146
Frith, Simon, 29, 72, 100

Gál, Hans, 120
Gallen-Kallela, Axeli, 76; *Symposion*, 76, 77*fig.*

Gautier, Théophile, 68
gender (and musical practice), 7, 53, 67, 71, 105–6, 111, 128, 133–34, 136, 157, 160
Gershwin, George, 34
Gissing, George, 8
Gone with the Wind (film), 128, 130–31, 135
Goodrich Clark, Nicholas, *The Occult Roots of Nazism*, 163
Gorbman, Claudia, *Unheard Melodies*, 113, 117, 132–33
Goss, Glenda Dawn, 78
Gounod, Charles, 133
Graf, Max, 31
Grainger, Percy, 46
Gramsci, Antoni, 6
Gray, Cecil, 80
Grimley, Daniel, 78
Grimmer, Abel, 6, 35
Guattari, Félix, xiv

Hailey, Christopher, 157
Hamburg, 21, 121
Hanslick, Eduard, 25, 29, 32, 58, 120, 132; *On the Musically Beautiful*, 25, 29
Hardy, Thomas, 8
Harper-Scott, J. P. E, xv
Haydn, Joseph, 9
Hegel, Georg Wilhelm Friedrich, 79
Henreid, Paul, 116*fig.*, 130
Hepokoski, James, 77–78, 80, 102, 104, 105
Herheim, Stefan, 85–88, 89, 181n16
hermeneutics, 4, 53–54, 58, 90–91, 109, 110, 112, 117–20, 123, 155
Heseltine, Philip, 49
Hindemith, Paul, 151, 162
Hirschfeld, Robert, 16–17
Hitchcock, Alfred, *Psycho*, 105
Hitler, Adolf, 8, 89, 120, 152
Hoffmann, E. T. A., 9, 11, 24, 30, 115; *The Artushof*, 30
Hollywood, "classical," xii, 113, 117–20, 121–22, 123–24, 127, 131–32, 134, 135, 143, 169
Homer, 68–69
Horkheimer, Max, *Dialectic of Enlightenment* (with Theodor Adorno), 68–70
Howat, Roy, 71, 74
Hugo, Victor, 53, 63–65
Humperdinck, Engelbert, 32, 92, 147; *Hänsel und Gretel*, 92, 147
Huysmans, J.-K., *À Rebours*, 30, 60, 68

Ibsen, Henrik, *A Doll's House*, 115
International Society For Contemporary Music, 141
Ives, Charles, 144–45, 187n10

Jackson, Holbrook, 7–8, 10, 128
Jackson, Timothy L., 189n36
Jazz, 142
Jazz-Singer, The, 164
"Jean Paul" (Jean Paul Richter), 11
Jews, Jewishness, 15–16, 151, 152–53, 155, 161, 163, 168
Johnson, Celia, 35
Johnson, James H., *Listening in Paris*, 62, 75, 100, 178n15
Johnson, Julian, 11
Jolson, Al, 164
Joukovsky, Paul von, 88
Jugendstil, 144

Kajanus, Robert, 76, 77fig.
Keary, Charles, 47
Kerman, Joseph, 95, 107, 143, 159; *Music at the Turn of Century*, 143
Kerr, Alfred, 152
Khnopff, Fernand, *Listening to Schumann*, 7, 54
Kienzl, Wilhelm, 18
Kienzle, Ulrike, 188n20
King of Saxony, 20, 21, 22
Kings Row (film), 123, 127, 130, 136–37
Klopstock, Friedrich Gottlieb, 21
Knepler, Georg, 4–5
Kohlenbach, Margarete, 11, 13
Korngold, Erich Wolfgang, 92–93, 119–27, 130, 136–37, 140, 141, 144, 151, 169; *Cello Concerto*, 122; *Symphony in F sharp*, 122–27, 140, 151; *Die Tote Stadt*, 93, 121; *Violanta*, 137; *Violin Concerto*, 122; *Das Wunder der Heliane*, 121
Korngold, Julius, 120
Kramer, Lawrence, xiv, 6, 54, 59
Krenek, Ernst, *Jonny spielt auf*, 93, 121, 142

Lacoue-Labarthe, Philippe, 91
Lamartine, Alphonse Marie Louis de, 59
Lambert, Constant, 78
Lao Tzu, *Tao Te Ching*, 166
Larrissy, Edward, 11
Lawrence, D.H., 8
Lear, Evelyn, 94

Leavis, F.R., 8
Lebrecht, Norman, 83, 85
Lee, Sherry D., 187n11
Lehàr, Franz, *The Merry Widow*, 143
Leipzig, 45
Leoncavallo, Ruggero, 92
Leppert, Richard, *The Sight of Sound*, 6–7, 9, 10, 35, 53–54, 100
Lermontov, Mikhail, 33
Leverkühn, Adrian (character in Mann's *Dr Faustus*), 2, 24, 112–13, 114, 146
Levin, David, 91
Lewis, Wyndham, 8
Lindenberger, Herbert, 94
Liszt, Franz, 3fig., 4, 25, 33, 57–59, 60, 63–65, 66, 81; *Ce qu'on entend sur la montagne (Bergsymphonie)*, 63–65; *Hamlet*, 58; *Die Legende von der heiligen Elisabeth*, 3fig., 4; *Les Préludes*, 59; *Orpheus, Prometheus*, and *Tasso*, 58
Lockhart, Ellen, 89–91, 95, 109, 110
London, 55
Lortzing, Albert, 92
Los Angeles, 113

Mahler, Gustav, 5, 11, 12, 13–15, 16–22, 25–26, 28, 31, 32, 36–37, 54–55, 56, 57–58, 63–64, 65, 74, 76, 78, 92, 96, 104, 112, 123, 135, 159, 167; *Symphony no. 1*, 14, 15, 57–58, 63; *Symphony no. 2*, 5, 12, 13–15, 17–22, 25–26, 36–37; *Symphony no. 3*, 64–65
Mahler-Rosé, Justine, 14, 20
Mahler-Werfel, Alma Maria, 13–14, 20, 76, 96, 122; *Memories and Letters of Gustav Mahler*, 13–14
Mallarmé, Stéphane, 68
Mann, Thomas, 2, 11, 24, 28, 54, 68, 82, 83–85, 87, 89, 112–13, 147; *Buddenbrooks*, 68, 84; *Death in Venice*, 24, 84–85; *Doctor Faustus*, 2, 11, 83–84, 68, 112–13, 147; *The Magic Mountain*, 84; *Reflections of a Nonpolitical Man*, 84
Maple Leaf Rag, 143
Marschner, Heinrich August, 92
Marx, Joseph, 120, 161
Mascagni, Pietro, 92
mass culture, mass-entertainment, xiv, xvi, 7–9, 10, 12, 15, 16, 17–18, 22, 24–25, 26, 29, 31, 32–33, 56–57, 60–61, 66, 69–70, 71, 78, 83–84, 89–90, 93, 96,

99–100, 104, 106–7, 108–9, 114, 117, 121–22, 127–28, 131–32, 135, 141–21, 145–46, 169–70
"maximalism," 1, 13, 15, 16, 17, 20, 22, 23, 28, 76
McCarthy, Senator Joseph, 127
McClary, Susan, 6, 54, 97, 110; *Feminine Endings,* 97
meaning, musical, 4, 36–37, 53–54, 59, 110–11, 122–24, 127–28, 142
Méliès, Georges, 133
melodrama, 101–2, 104, 109, 114, 115, 127–28, 146, 149, 164
Mendelssohn, Felix, incidental music to *A Midsummer Night's Dream,* 120
Merikanto, Oskar, 76, 77*fig.*
Meyerbeer, Giacomo, 154
Mitchell, Margaret, *Gone with the Wind,* 128
modernism, xiii-xiv, 1, 2–4, 6, 8, 16–17, 23–24, 25–26, 27, 31–32, 34, 52, 54, 57, 60–61, 62, 65, 67, 70, 71, 78–80, 84–85, 92, 93–94, 100, 101, 112–13, 120–21, 122–23, 126, 139, 140–41, 142–44, 145–46, 151, 159–60, 161–62, 167, 168
"modern musical lyric" (Seidl), 32, 35, 37, 45, 50, 66
Morris, Christopher, *Modernism and the Cult of Mountains,* 179n28; *Reading Opera Between the Lines,* 188n21
Moscow, 35, 55
Mozart, Wolfgang Amadeus, 9, 45, 49, 92, 97
Muck, Karl, 18
Müller, Charlotte, 153*fig.*
Mulvey, Laura, 133
Munch, Edvard, 45
Munich, 28, 31
Musil, Robert, *The Man without Qualities,* 15–16
Mussolini, Benito, 156, 168, 183n61

narrative, 128–35, 137–38; diegesis, 129, 130–31, 133, 136, 137; fabula, 134; mimesis, 129–30, 133; syuzhet, 134
national identity, nationalism, 26, 28, 32, 45, 54, 61, 65, 67, 76, 89, 99–100, 106, 161, 163
nature, xv, 21, 49–50, 64–65, 67–68, 69, 70–72, 73–74, 79, 80–81, 142, 146, 148, 162
Nazis, 83, 93, 120–21, 142, 152–53, 154, 156, 161–63, 164

neoclassicism, 122, 145
neo-Platonism, 64
Neuenfels, Hans, 85
neue Sachlichkeit, 155
New German School, 25, 57–58
Newman, Ernest, 78
new musicology, 4, 6, 19, 54
New York, 55, 100, 129–30, 137
Nietzsche, Friedrich, xiii, 30–32, 45–46, 65–66, 84, 89, 97, 113, 121; *Also sprach Zarathustra,* 65, 82–83
Nordau, Max, *Entartung,* 31
novels, 128–30, 136–37, 139
Now, Voyager (film), 114–15, 116*fig.,* 118*fig.,* 122, 137–39
Nuremberg, 155

Offenbach, Jacques, 11
opera, as cultural medium and institution, 82–84, 85–97, 100–109, 110–12, 116–17, 121, 125, 135, 140–41, 146–47, 169–70
operetta, 93, 122, 141
Ortega y Gasset, José, 8

Page, Andrew, 46–47
Palestrina, Giovanno Pierluigi da, 97, 104
Pallanza (Italy), 155–56
Paris, 27, 45, 55, 72, 100, 160
Parker, Roger, 108
Pfitzner, Hans, 27–28, 59, 92, 151, 162, 168; *Futuristengefahr,* 28; *The New Aesthetic of Musical Impotence,* 28; *Palestrina,* 28, 162; *Die Rose vom Liebesgarten,* 92; *Von deutscher Seele,* 28
"Philistines," 25, 30, 117, 170
piano music, 65–66, 71
Plato, 4
Poe, Edgar Allan, *The Fall of the House of Usher,* 68
Pöllmann, Helmut, 123
Pritchard, Matthew, 60
Private Lives of Elizabeth and Essex, The, 123–25*fig.*
program, programmaticism (and musical meaning), 13–15, 19–22, 23, 25, 28, 36, 57–59, 63–65, 75, 101, 122–24, 127–28, 138, 142
Proust, Marcel, 54
Prouty, Olive Higgins, *Now, Voyager* (novel), 130, 134, 137, 139
Przybyszewski, Stanislaus, *Chopin und Nietzsche,* 66, 97

Puccini, Giacomo, 89–91, 95–100, 101–9, 110, 112, 113, 114, 116, 120, 131, 135, 155, 159, 167; *La Bohème*, 103; *La Fanciulla del West*, 90, 106, 114, 116; *Madama Butterfly*, 99, 106, 143; *Manon Lescaut*, 96–97; *Suor Angelica*, 101–6, 109, 112, 116; *Tosca*, 107, 159; *Il Trittico*, 102; *Turandot*, 103, 107–9, 155
Pushkin, Alexander, 33

Rachmaninov, Sergei, 27, 33–44, 54, 56, 60, 61, 62, 63, 66, 70–71, 72, 74, 75, 100, 103, 112, 122, 126, 127, 176n37; *The Isle of the Dead*, 35; *Piano Concerto no. 2*, 34–35; *Prelude in C sharp minor*, 34; *Song Op. 21, 1, "Fate,"* 33; *Symphony no. 1*, 33; *Symphony no. 2*, 35–43, 72; *Symphony no. 3*, 122
Rains, Claude, 130
Rapper, Irving, 114, 139
Reagan, Ronald, 130
Rebecca (film), 135
Redlich, Hans, 14
Regietheater ("director's opera"), 83, 85–86, 91–92, 93, 110–11
Reinhardt, Max, 120
Ritchie, Alexandra, *Faust's Metropolis*, 152, 168
Rivière, Jacques, 71
Rode, Wilhelm, 152, 153fig., 156, 158fig.
Romanticism, late-romanticism (definitions), xii-xvi, 2–4, 5, 9–13, 15, 16, 19, 23–24, 25, 26–27, 28–32, 34, 45, 47, 54–55, 56–57, 58–59, 60–61, 63, 67, 72–72, 74–75, 82, 86, 89, 91, 101, 111–13, 115–17, 120, 122–24, 126–28, 135–36, 137–39, 140–41, 142–44, 146, 150, 153, 160, 162, 169–70, 172n23
Roosevelt, F.D., 122
Rosen, Jelka, 45
Rousseau, Jean-Jacques, 9
Royal Festival Hall, London, 13

Sabaneyeff, Leonid, 27, 33, 35, 39
Sackbut, The (journal), 46, 52, 174n7
Salzburg, 120
Samson, Jim, xii
Saul, Nicholas, 11
Saylor, Eric, 49, 176n44
Scarborough, 44, 61
Scheele, Heike, 86
Schenker, Heinrich, 59–60, 77, 134

Schillings, Max von, 32, 92; *Mona Lisa*, 92
Schoenberg, Arnold, 2, 25–26, 28, 62, 65, 79, 93, 117, 119, 120, 122, 140–41, 151, 162, 169; *Erwartung*, 93; *Die Glückliche Hand*, 93; *Moses und Aron*, 140, 169
Schreker, Franz, xv, 92, 120, 140–43, 144–69; *Christophorus*, 140, 142, 151, 161–62, 164–68; *Der ferne Klang*, xv, 92, 142, 144, 146–50, 151, 169; *Die Gezeichneten*, 150–51; *Irrelohe*, 141, 151, 160, 162; *Der Schatzgräber*, 151; *Der Schmied von Gent*, 151, 152–54, 155–61, 167, 168; *Der Singende Teufel*, xv, 142, 151, 152, 160–64; *Das Spielwerk und die Prinzessin*, 150, 163
Schumann, Clara, 66
Schumann, Robert, 7, 23, 25, 29, 30, 54, 57–58, 60, 62, 83
Schwartz, Arman, 102, 104, 105, 183–84n61
Scriabin, Alexander, 66, 72, 78; *The Poem of Ecstasy*, 66
Second Viennese School, 16, 25–26, 60, 145
Seidl, Arthur, 31–32, 35, 37, 45, 50, 66
Senici, Emanuele, 106
Sennett, Richard, *The Fall of Public Man*, 106
Shakespeare, William, *Titus Andronicus*, 115; *A Midsummer Night's Dream*, 120
Shaw, Bernard, 56, 62
Sheridan, Ann, 130
Shostakovich, Dmitri, 60
Sibelius, Jean, 38, 52, 59, 61, 75–81, 144; *Finlandia*, 76; *The Oceanides*, 76; *Symphony no. 4*, 76, 79; *Symphony no. 5*, 75, 76–81; *Symphony no. 8*, 80; *Tapiola*, 65, 80; *Valse Triste*, 76
Simoni, Renato, 109
Small, Christopher, xi, xv, 28, 49, 51, 53, 61; *Musicking*, xi, 49
Solti, Sir Georg, 13
song composition, 32, 63
Spackman, Barbara, 108
Specht, Richard, 96–97, 100–101
Steiner, Max, 115–16, 118fig., 119fig., 122, 134–35, 139, 169
Strauss, Richard, xii, xiii, 18, 25, 31–32, 35, 43, 65, 68, 92–93, 96, 120, 122, 126; *Alpine Symphony*, 68; *Also sprach Zarathustra*, 65; *Elektra*, 93, 120; *Metamorphosen*, 126; *Der Rosenkavalier*, 80, 92

Stravinsky, Igor, 2, 34, 72–72, 79, 95, 117, 141, 170; *Le Sacre du Printemps,* 70, 72–73, 141
Striegler, Kurt, *Die Schmiede,* 153
Strunk, Oliver, 11
Subotnik, Rose Rosengard, 6
Sue, Eugène, 96
Syberberg, H. J., 86
symphonic poems, 25, 57–59, 101
symphony, 5, 13–15, 16–17, 18–22, 23, 25, 25, 28–30, 32, 34, 35–44, 54–61, 63, 72, 74, 75–81, 94–95, 100–101, 103, 122–27, 166–67
symphony concert. *See* concert hall

Tappert, William, 66–67
Taruskin, Richard, 1, 4–5, 9–10, 16, 18, 19, 59, 60, 62, 94–95, 112; *The Oxford History of Western Music,* 1, 4, 59, 94–95
Tchaikovsky, Piotr Ilyich, 26, 34, 37, 40, 54, 57, 61, 73, 89, 116, 137–39, 144; "Manfred" *Symphony,* 73; *Symphony no. 4,* 54, 137–38; *Symphony no. 5,* 137–38; *Symphony no. 6,* 115, 137–39
Theresa, Rose, 133
Tieck, Ludwig, *Herzensergiessungen eines Kunstliebenden Klosterbruders* (with Wackenroder), 11
Tolney-Witt (also Tolnay-Witt), Gisela, 17, 32
Tolstoy, Count Leo, 33–34, 36, 43, 47, 54
Törne, Bengt de, 78
Torre del Lago, 108
Toscanini, Arturo, 156
Tovey, Donald Francis, 80
Turin, 96

vaudeville, 141
Venice, 84–85, 148
Verdi, Giuseppe, xiii, 90, 95, 103, 156, 169; *Falstaff,* xiii; *La Traviata,* 115; *Otello,* xiii
verismo, 103, 106, 147
Verlaine, Paul, 68
Vienna, 15–16, 62, 92, 120–21, 123, 127, 141, 145, 146, 149, 155, 161; Hofoper, 15, 146; Musikvereinsaal, 16; *Neue freie Presse,* 120

Volksoper ("folk" or "people's" opera), 156, 161
Von Bülow, Hans, 21
Von Schuch, Ernst, 20

Wackenroder, W. H., 11–13, 15, 24, 28, 62, 85, 147, 169; *Herzensergiessungen eines Kunstliebenden Klosterbruders* (with Tieck), 11; "The Remarkable Musical Life of the Musican Joseph Berglinger," 11–13
Wagner, Katharina, 90
Wagner, Richard, xii, xv-xvi, 2, 10, 11, 12, 16, 17, 18, 29, 30–33, 43, 61, 66–67, 75, 82–94, 96–97, 99, 101–2, 104, 109, 121, 131, 137, 159; *Der Fliegender Holländer,* 93; *Lohengrin,* 137; *Die Meistersinger,* 113, 159; *Parsifal,* xvi, 32, 85–88, 102, 104, 109, 121; *Der Ring des Nibelungen,* xvi, 83–84, 89, 109; *Siegfried,* 91; *Die Walküre,* 83
Wagner, Winifred, 89
Walter, Bruno, 15
Waxman, Franz, 169
Weber, Carl Maria von, 92, 183n48
Weber, William, 28–29, 55–56; *Music and the Middle Class,* 28–29
Webern, Anton, 120
Weimar, 58; "Weimar Republic," 141, 151–53, 168
Weissmann, Adolf, 97–100, 108, 113, 135, 151; *Der klingende Garten,* 97–100, 98fig., 99fig., 151
Wells, H. G., 8
Werfel, Franz, 168–69; *Verdi,* 169
Wilde, Oscar, *The Picture of Dorian Gray,* 30
Williams, John, film scores for *E.T.* and *Star Wars,* 110
Wilson, Alexandra, 108–9
Woolf, Virginia, 8
"Wurst, Hans," 156

Zeitoper ("contemporary opera"), 93, 142, 151, 164–65
Zemlinsky, Alexander, 29, 93, 120
Ziegler, Hans Severus, 27
Zindler, Rudolf, 153fig.